Praise for *Dream Driven*

"Jason's journey from small-town Vermont to America's storied golf clubs shows that humble beginnings are not limitations, but fertile soil in which big accomplishments can grow. In *Dream Driven*, Jason shares powerful insights about navigating life's highs and lows. His story is an inspiration that so many of us can use in our own pursuits of greatness."

—John Eliot, PhD, author of *Overachievement*

"Drawing on the wisdom gained from navigating his own psychological struggles, Jason shares reflections that are clear, honest, and compassionately flexible. His work invites readers to journey inward and discover the clarity and confidence needed to forge a more purposeful path through life."

—Eric Welsh, PhD, Clinical Psychologist

"In *Dream Driven*, Jason Prendergast does something rare: he tells a story that is at once compelling and highly personal, but does it without the slightest hint of posturing or artifice. There is no glossing over his disappointments, nor any effort to burnish the rough edges of his experience. Jason's failures and triumphs are treated with the same candor. That, in itself, is startling. It simply isn't what we are used to anymore, and his unselfconscious honesty makes this memoir intensely timely and poignant. It is a tale that will restore your faith in dreams and perhaps make you remember how to conjure them up for yourself."

—W. Lawrence Deas, Attorney

DREAM DRIVEN

DREAM DRIVEN

TOWARD THE SELF NOT YET MET

A Memoir

JASON PRENDERGAST

Quadrifolium Press

Copyright © 2026 by Jason Prendergast. All rights reserved.

Library of Congress Control Number: 2025924767

Hardcover ISBN: 979-8-9939938-1-2

Paperback ISBN: 979-8-9939938-0-5

eBook ISBN: 979-8-9939939-2-9

All rights reserved. No part of this publication may be reproduced, stored in a retrieval system, or transmitted in any form or by any means (electronic, mechanical, photocopying, recording, or otherwise) without the written permission of the author and publisher.

Book cover design by Faceout Studio, Kate Gendruschke

Interior design by theBookDesigners

Editorial production by KN Literary Arts

For those I have lost,
whose presence is still felt and guides me every day.

For those who walk beside me:
family, mentors, and friends who remind me that
relationships matter most.

For Kathleen,
whose unwavering love and belief
steady me through every climb.

For Peanut,
whose heart and spirit remind me
how powerful we all are.

For my past self,
who dared to dream big, to take the first step,
and to keep climbing toward an intangible dream,
especially in the darkest moments.

For my future self,
whose vision keeps pulling me toward
the summit still unseen.

And for you:
I believe in you and your dreams.
The journey is worth the climb.

CONTENTS

Foreword ix
Introduction 1

Chapter 1: The List 7
Chapter 2: The Secret 13
Chapter 3: Walk the Track 25
Chapter 4: Hills 34
Chapter 5: Dirt Roads 48
Chapter 6: The Call 56
Chapter 7: The Graft 65
Chapter 8: A Snake's New Skin 76
Chapter 9: The Envelope 85
Chapter 10: A Clover Patch 94
Chapter 11: Heads or Tails 104
Chapter 12: The Airstream 118
Chapter 13: Five Dollars of Gas 124
Chapter 14: A Neck-Down 138
Chapter 15: Two Ducks 147

Chapter 16: The Web 158
Chapter 17: Cold Coffee 169
Chapter 18: The Question 174
Chapter 19: The Maze 182
Chapter 20: Lucky #7 194
Chapter 21: Moss in the Courtyard 206
Chapter 22: A New Table 212
Chapter 23: Who's the Best? 219
Chapter 24: A White Lie 227
Chapter 25: The Turnpike 237
Chapter 26: Life on the Porch 247
Chapter 27: A New Bridge 258
Chapter 28: Trash Gods 267
Chapter 29: Life's Canvas 275
Chapter 30: Eye on the Prize 282
Chapter 31: Don't We All? 292
Chapter 32: A Sleepy Clubhouse 303
Chapter 33: Homework 310
Chapter 34: Anchors Aweigh 318
Chapter 35: Crayola and Elmer's Glue 325
Chapter 36: A Secret Code 335
Chapter 37: The Ring Pop 348
Chapter 38: Peanut 352
Chapter 39: The Foothills of Greatness 365

Acknowledgments 375

FOREWORD

Life has a way of surprising us. One of its greatest gifts, through golf or otherwise, is watching someone discover who they are meant to be. In my years as a PGA professional, with 37 at Oakmont and 22 at Seminole, I've had the privilege of mentoring many young professionals with big dreams. Jason's unlikely journey from milking cows and pumping gas to Oakmont and a long, impactful career at the Country Club of Jackson is remarkable in its own merit, and it shows that dreams can come true through the power of belief.

Like many aspiring professionals, Jason was full of energy and hope when I met him for the first time, and like all of us, he was looking for someone to believe in him. What he proved to me early on was his unwavering work ethic, passion, and drive. Years later, he thanked me for giving him a chance and believing in him. I told him, "You're welcome, but I didn't take a chance on you; it was an educated guess." Looking back, I'm glad I trusted that instinct. Not long after, Jason shared that he was chasing the intangible dream of greatness, something he said had been pulling him since his earliest days at Oakmont. A dream like that takes humility and belief to keep climbing, and I'm glad to see him on this mountain. Those qualities—humility, belief, and a drive to impact others—are the same traditions the PGA of America has stood on for over a century. Jason's story is one more example of that proud legacy carried forward.

Dream Driven is not a book about golf. Like Jason himself, it goes deeper into life, belief, and the courage to keep climbing. Yes, golf is a backdrop, a vehicle for his life, but the story is about what is possible when you believe in yourself and your dream.

Jason doesn't share his story to celebrate his accomplishments. He invites you into his scenes to give you a front-row seat to what it is like to keep going when things look dark and the mountain appears too steep to climb. But along with the struggles, he lets you experience the victories, the small steps forward, the moments of connection that shaped his life, and the triumphs that remind us the steps are worth it. His honesty will nudge you to see your path more clearly. The hurdles in his life may look similar to yours, and his journey toward the self not yet met will inspire you to keep moving forward.

At the heart of Jason's story is a philosophy he calls the Clover: hope, belief, connection, and impact, all rooted in resilience. You don't need to be a golfer to understand those words. They are the language of anyone chasing a dream, anyone striving to become more than they are today.

That is why this book matters. It's about possibility. It's about remembering the dreams you once held, believing in

Foreword

the future self waiting for you at the summit, and finding the courage to keep going.

I've always admired Jason's passion. His writing, like his life, is honest and full of heart. Through this book, Jason answers another calling: as a storyteller. Don't just look for his story as you turn these pages. Look for your own; it will likely be hiding between the lines.

Jason's story will encourage you to chase your dream, and I am honored to introduce this book to you.

—Bob Ford, PGA

INTRODUCTION

I thought I had reached the summit. Two decades of hard work, long hours, and relentless drive had carried me higher than I ever imagined as I chased the intangible dream of greatness. Yet when I finally mustered the courage to ask my mentor (and golf legend), Bob Ford, if I had made it, what he told me changed my life again. I realized two things: a direct correlation between deep questions and how my life seemed to change when I had the answer. Additionally, I realized the most incredible journey of my life was about to begin.

That moment forced me to look backward at the steps I had taken and the dreams that first set me in motion. I remembered a boy in Vermont learning how to face his fears, a teenager milking cows long before the rooster crowed and standing in hayfields, covered in sweat and cow shit. I was happy but never satisfied, and I believed life had more to offer, but I didn't know what.

VERMONT ROOTS AND THE FIRST DREAM

I grew up in northern Vermont, where hayfields stretched wide, the Caledonia County Fair marked late summer, and motocross tracks carved the landscape. Lyndonville was a small town where dreams often stayed close to home.

Yet even as a boy, I carried something bigger. I dreamed beyond the fields and the town line. I didn't always know what the dream was—only that something tugged at me, asking me to keep climbing.

Those early years built resilience. Throwing hay, milking cows, pumping gas, crawling under a trailer at twenty below zero to fix a heating system—those jobs taught me a work ethic. Losing things I thought would always be there taught me to start again. I didn't know it then, but those lessons would prepare me for the golf operations at some of the best golf clubs in the country and shape the following chapters of my life.

THE CLOVER LENS

My Aunt Deb taught me to look for four-leaf clovers. What began as a childhood pastime became a way of seeing life. Over time, each leaf revealed itself as a force in my journey: Traditionally, the leaves represent hope, faith, love, and luck. But for me, they represent:

- **Hope**: the seed of every dream.
- **Belief**: courage to believe in yourself and others.
- **Connection**: the relationships that pull us forward.
- **Impact**: greatness measured by our impact, not accolades.

The stem holding it all together is **Resilience**: bending without breaking, remaining rooted through storms.

The Clover became my lens. On days I carried all four leaves, life felt full. On days I held only the stem, it was still enough. The four-leaf clover frames this book, symbolizing what carries us when dreams feel both fragile and possible.

REVERSE GOAL SETTING

For years, I chased goals the traditional way: by looking forward and setting benchmarks, climbing ladders, and checking boxes. But goals can be dangerous, leading you astray. You can achieve every benchmark and still miss the dream. This forward-planning philosophy is the reason we so often feel lost.

As a teenager, my grandfather taught me to plan backward. Instead of starting with the next step, I started at the summit. I imagined standing at the top of my dream and walking backward, identifying mile markers and decisions that would lead me there. Once I reached my current self, I simply turned around and followed my footsteps back up the mountain.

It's how a climber prepares for Everest: The path is mapped from the summit down, so every step aligns with the larger vision. Goals become mile markers, not destinations. That shift kept me from chasing short-term wins at the expense of long-term purpose. It enabled me to say no to job offers that were shiny but not on the path and reminded me that every choice should connect to something greater.

MENTORSHIP, LOSS, AND LEGACY

No journey is taken alone.

In 1997, I walked into Larry Kelley's office at St. Johnsbury Country Club and said, "Larry, I want to be you. How do I be you?" His answer led me to the Professional Golf Management Program at Mississippi State and opened a door to a life of service and leadership in golf.

Later, while working at Oakmont Country Club in Pennsylvania, I learned under the legendary Bob Ford, who is regarded as the greatest PGA professional of all time. I learned from Bob that greatness isn't measured by what you achieve but rather your impact on others.

I also lost people, such as family, mentors, and friends, whose presence still guides me. Their absence reminds me that the climb is fragile and that the summit is never promised. What lasts is the impact we leave behind.

This book is my way of honoring those influences, the colleagues who climbed alongside me, those who will join my journey in the future, the family who steadied me, and the reader who may be searching for their own path upward.

WHY THIS BOOK, WHY NOW

Dream Driven wasn't written to celebrate my story but to invite you into yours.

For years, it lived inside me through late-night reflections, hours spent battling self-doubt and fear, and long drives where I asked what really mattered. I realized my climb wasn't just about golf or career. It was about hope, belief, connection, impact, and resilience—the same forces that shape all of us.

I wrote this book because dreams matter, even the ones that feel intangible, even the ones we may never fully reach. Just like dreams matter, so do you, even if you feel insignificant in the world around you. Greatness is not about standing alone at the top but helping others climb.

Now feels like the right time because the world is hungry for hope, belief, connection, impact, and resilience. If my story helps you search for your Clover or pick up the one you see and keep climbing, it will have been worth writing.

AN INVITATION TO YOU

This book isn't just about me. It's about you.

As you read, I hope you'll see yourself in these pages, in the doubts and the small victories, in the moments when you carried all four leaves and the times when you held only the stem. You are not alone, and whatever you carry, it still matters.

What follows isn't a straight line but a series of climbs, falls, and recoveries. It's a journey through hayfields and fairways, through loss and resilience, through dreams both reached and still unseen. It is the story of what it means to be dream driven, not because I have all the answers, but because I have lived the questions.

So lean in. Carry what you can. Share what you have. And never forget: Even the stem alone is enough to keep you rooted when the wind begins to howl.

This is my story. More importantly, it is an invitation to reflect on yours. Together, we climb, we dream, and we are dream driven.

1
THE LIST

"Make a list of everything I would change about my life if I could. That's what you want me to do?" My eyes leapt from the carpet.

"Yes, Jason. Make a list," Zoe said. "That's what I want you to do."

Honestly, had she even been listening to me? Wasn't the point of therapy to be heard?

Air rushed through my nose like a hose yanked from an air compressor. I shook my head in disgust.

It wasn't like I'd held back. I'd hemorrhaged nearly every secret, every terrible thing that happened to me. I'd spent dozens of hours explaining all the good and the bad that had shaped the man sitting before her. I'd even justified most of it. Her office might as well have looked like a crime scene, with fragments of my life splattered on the walls and soaked into the carpet between our feet.

This would have been a whole hell of a lot faster had she simply thrown me into gear with this question in the beginning. But ohhhh, no. Nope. We took a lovely scenic tour, cruising slow past the same tired pain and stopping at every mountainous overlook. We looked at the same shit for more than a damn year, and only then, after we had traveled countless miles, would she ask me the most important question of all: "What would you change if you could?"

All of it, I thought, *that's what*. Well, not the good stuff. I wouldn't change that. But the bad stuff? Yup.

As frustrated as I was with the question and at her for having the gall to ask it, I had this strange, hard to describe surge of emotion that ran through me every time Zoe asked a question that forced me to dig deeper, to push past the surface of emotion I was feeling. Those questions and my shovel were at the heart of my growth. The simple fact was that I had grown to love Zoe. Not in a romantic sense, but similar to the way I loved my mother, even as a child when she asked me to do something I didn't want to do (like I had a choice in the matter) or as a teenager ready to lock horns and simultaneously lunge forward. It was a raw, unspoken kind of love rooted in simplicity, where just being seen by someone could knock the wind out of you.

The luggage I had drug around for nearly forty years toughened me up. The leather, once rigid and stiff like a new baseball glove that wouldn't close, had become worn and molded perfectly to me. Those leather bags had become so damn full it was like having ten pounds of history stuffed into a five-pound container.

Over a year ago, I decided I needed a therapist to clean out my closet, but there was no way I could trust a man with the kind of baggage I carried. There was no telling what the hell was going to be in there. Some strange guy asking me how that made me feel? No thank you. Being tough was hard enough even without the pressure of another man scribbling notes about my pain. Before I started therapy, I thought for a few weeks about the kind of therapist I would need. I envisioned what the whole process would look and feel like. Quite frankly, it scared me to death.

The thought of lying on a couch, baring my soul to a stranger, made my stomach come alive. Shedding a tear in front of a man? No way in hell was that happening. I hadn't cried in years. Growing up, crying got you two questions: "Is there blood?" "Is anything broken?" If the answers were no, you got, "Then you're fine." So, yeah, I learned how to suck it up. Swallow the pain. Hold it in. But holding it in for long enough starts to change a person. It tightens you up from the inside.

If I did happen to find the courage to twist the knob and push the door open, there would be no turning back. But I decided if I was going to do it, the best therapist I could get would have the softness of my dad and hardness of my mom, as if blending together a superparent. I wanted sympathy and understanding, and as strange as it sounded to me, I needed a woman to help.

So there I sat, across from Zoe, for more than an hour nearly every Tuesday and Thursday. Each week for over a year, Zoe's questions triggered a tsunami of emotions that had me running to higher ground. I had retreated so many times that the trail from uncomfortable to comfortable looked like a beaten-down cow path. Tuesdays were the worst days for me. Zoe referred to them as discovery days. Thursdays, on the other hand, were reserved for what Zoe called homework. We'd talk about the monsters that woke up from the Tuesday sessions, and before I walked out of her office, she'd smile and say, "Here's your homework for the weekend. I'll see you Tuesday."

Every weekend, I thought about the homework and what it would reveal in the warm and cozy room that felt like a safe space designed to lure my demons from the darkness. Deep down, I knew I wasn't perfect, yet my whole life I had heard countless versions of "Oh, you're just a perfectionist" to justify my actions. I wore those comments like a badge of honor in my early days.

I was the kid whose room was spotless and everything had a place, even if that place was shoved in a pile under my bed. Somewhere along the line, that perfectionism badge made room for an additional one: the "nobody's perfect" badge. That one typically followed a bout of frustration when I didn't get something "just right." I don't remember the exact moment, only that I was young, when I realized these shiny badges were actually boxes that left me gasping for air every time I found myself in one.

Each week, as I sat across from Zoe in that small therapy room, those boxes felt more and more suffocating. There was a window covered by slatted wooden blinds with a pull cord about ten feet away from where I sat. It appeared to offer my soul its only escape route, a gateway to safety, normalcy, and the life I knew.

Even on stormy days when thunder rattled the walls, light slipped through the slats and spilled across the floor like a promise. When Zoe's questions dug too deep, I'd fixate on that light. I'd imagine pulling the cord, shoving the window open, and diving headfirst into some other version of my life—one that didn't hurt so much.

By the third visit, I knew Zoe was the right one, as she repeatedly asked the same question: "So, Jason, how did that make you feel?"

"Like shit," I blurted. "I fucking hated it."

"I bet you did. I'd fucking hate it too." Her words came back across the room like a butterfly dancing above a meadow of flowers.

My chuckle turned up the corners of my mouth. I had come to grips with the fact that as I approached forty years old, I had to figure out what was wrong with me. I wondered if I had the courage to fully open up to confront my past. All of it had to come out, the bad along with the good. Zoe's five words, one of which I was forbidden to say as a kid, released the shackles of formality locked up in my spine.

As it turned out, Zoe's office wasn't devoid of judgment like I had initially thought. But the judgment I would have to face wasn't hers. I questioned how many of my circumstances were my fault and soon realized this was one of the answers she was going to help me find.

"Hope you have a lot of answers, 'cause I got a lot of questions," I said, with my arms folded.

Zoe nodded with a smile, the corners of her mouth curving gently under her soft eyes. With a tender Southern accent, she said, "Jason, you have the answers. Well, most of them. I'm just here to help you find them."

For months, Zoe had me crying with shame and disappointment as I explained who I let down or what I didn't live up to and how. I would get so angry at times that my head would throb for hours after a session ended, and countless times I struggled to see my life through her eyes.

And then she wanted me to make a list of everything I would change about my life if I could. My fingers clenched together behind my head as blue speckles of light shuttered in the darkness behind my eyelids, bringing some of my earliest memories to life.

"Okay, Zoe, I'll make the list."

2
THE SECRET

The first real and earliest memory that earned a spot on that damn list sizzled into my skin like a brand. I was ten years old at Fisher Field in my hometown of Lyndonville, Vermont.

Up until that day, my life was as good as it gets, but then the first "worst thing" I could remember happened. It started with a ground ball.

I'd seen thousands of them in my life. Dad had drilled it into me like scripture: *Charge the ball. Glove on the ground. Watch it all the way in. Two hands. Always two hands.*

It had worked until it didn't. I saw the ball coming, bouncing, and rolling across the infield toward me.

That's when it happened. I ate a leather baseball after a bad hop and tasted real fear for the first time. Sure, I had been afraid before, like when I was much younger and feared the scary witch who lived under my bed at night. I imagined her reaching her long, bony, green fingers up to pull me out from under my covers and into the depths beneath my mattress.

But this fear was different. Fielding a ground ball was simple, but the ball jumped up at the last minute, missed my glove, and slammed me in the face. My lip split open, instantly throbbing. The initial tears were from pain and surprise. As quickly as my mouth went from perfectly fine to swollen and bleeding, my fear shifted from the ball to what Dad was going to say. I tried to hold it back, but I whimpered as I watched him jog toward me on the field.

"Let me see it, son," Dad said, as my hands fought to keep my mouth hidden.

I didn't want him to see. I didn't want him to know how bad it hurt or how scared I was. But Dad pulled my hands away from my face, and I sniffed the running snot back into my nose, spitting blood on the infield.

"It's just a little blood," he said. "You're gonna be okay." He wrapped his arms around me. "You're gonna be okay."

Only, I wasn't going to be okay. It wasn't like a toddler stumbling while learning to walk. That kind of falling was expected. Nobody blamed you for tripping and falling then. This was different. I was ten. I knew how to field a ground ball. Or so I thought.

A few minutes later, Dad convinced me to return to second base. I had never walked onto the field with my head down, struggling to breathe. Not until that long trip from the dugout. For the rest of practice, whenever the ball came to me, I would take a step back and, at the last moment, slam my eyes shut, flinch, and turn my head away like an owl sitting in a tree. *What is going on? Why can't I keep my eye on the ball? It's the easiest part.*

The coach hit another ground ball to me, and as it bounced along the ground like it always did, I kept saying, "Watch the ball, watch the ball," but at the last second, I chickened out. I struggled not to look at Dad after every ground ball, but I couldn't keep it from happening. Every time my eyes hit his, my stomach felt yucky, and I hoped the coach would hit the next ground ball to someone else.

I hated being afraid of that ball. I hated how my body would tense and how the motions of fielding a ball, the ones I couldn't remember learning, suddenly became calculated and manipulated. I hated how that one bad bounce drove fear straight through my mouth and into my gut. I wished I were stronger, like the older kids on the team; they were fearless, and I couldn't wait to be their age.

My cleats dragged through the grass, weighed down by my slumping shoulders and heavy legs. I kept my eyes glued to the ground as Dad and I walked across the outfield toward the truck after practice. Dad's arm rested across my back, his big hand cupping my shoulder.

"You afraid of the ball, son?" he asked.

I was silent as my stomach feasted on my words before they could escape. The last thing I wanted to do was to admit I was afraid.

He pulled me closer as we walked and said, "It's a lot easier to catch the ball with your eyes open." His chuckle soothed my churning stomach. "We can fix it when we get home if ya want."

My eyes strained to see him as my head lifted slightly. "How?" I asked.

"It's a secret," he said, as he placed a finger across his lips. "It's okay to be afraid, son."

Dad and I arrived home that afternoon and spent the rest

of the day in the backyard. He rolled a ball to me from about ten feet away, at the gentle speed you'd use with a young child. Over the next few days, he gradually moved farther back, and the ball that once rolled softly across the grass began bouncing toward me with much more speed.

There I was, dressed in full catcher's gear: shin guards, chest protector, and helmet. The whole nine yards.

"You're not gonna get hurt, son. You have all that gear on," Dad said, tossing balls into every padded part of my body to prove his point.

One ball rattled off my face mask, causing me to slam my eyes shut.

"See what I'm tellin' ya, son?" he said with a grin, as if the rattling face mask was all the reassurance I needed.

"Is this the secret?" I asked.

"Nope. I'll tell ya when you're ready."

Every time I would flinch, close my eyes, or turn my head, Dad would chuckle and say, "Watch the ball go into your glove, son; you don't want me to tie a fishing line around your neck to a hook in your balls, do ya?"

I'd laugh, say no, and think, *He wouldn't really do that, would he?*

By the end of the week, I was fielding grounders thrown as hard as my dad could throw. While I admit I flinched a few times, whenever I did, Dad would grab a ball, walk in front of me, and toss it right into my face mask and say, "Watch the ball, son," and smile a gentle teasing grin.

The following Saturday morning, Dad and I loaded up in the truck for the short drive to Fisher Field for my first Little

League baseball game since the bloodbath at second base. I had told Dad the night before that I was ready to play, and when he asked if I was scared, I said, "Nope."

"Good for you, son. I'm proud of you." He kissed my forehead. But as soon as my butt hit the truck seat, my stomach felt a little uneasy. The truck puttered along as Dad talked me through how to field a ground ball, and with every movement of the steering wheel, my stomach would swirl a little. I was quiet, nodding and saying "yup" or "nope" as the ballfield grew closer through the windshield.

I climbed out of the truck as we parked facing the chain-link fence, and as soon as my cleats hit the outfield, my body started to stiffen and my stride shortened. Dad must have sensed my nervousness as his hand wrapped around my shoulder, pulling me toward him.

"Today's gonna be your day son," he said.

"What do ya mean?" I said, looking up at him.

"I got a feeling," he said.

Those words reached into my gut and yanked all the nervousness out of me.

"You afraid of the ball?"

"Nope," I said, as my legs bounced a little for the first time that morning.

"Ya ready for the secret?"

"Yeah," I said, with my eyes wide open. I'd been ready for the secret all week.

Dad stopped abruptly and spun me around to face him. He squatted down, rested one knee on the ground, and placed both hands on my shoulders. He looked into my eyes and said,

"You've worked hard all week. I'm proud of ya. Now ya got to ask for the ball, son."

Quiet, I simply stared at him as my eyes pinched together.

"Every time a batter gets to the plate, you smack your glove and say, 'Hit it to me. I want the ball.' Let me hear you say it," he said as his fingers gripped my shoulders.

Curling my fist tight, I punched my glove and said, "Hit it to me. I want the ball."

"Ya gotta mean it, son. Ain't no sense in sayin' it if ya don't mean it. Say it like ya mean it."

I gritted my teeth, smacked my glove, and said with a snarl, "Hit it to me. I want the ball."

"Just like that," Dad said, and he smiled. "Every single pitch. Say it out loud. Ya gotta talk to yourself out there. Smack your glove and say, 'Hit it to me. I want the ball.'"

The memory faded with my exhale as I looked toward the window in Zoe's office, trying to hold on to the courage of that boy on the field.

"I just wish it had never happened," I said, my voice low. "That ball . . . hitting me in the face. I wish I could erase it."

Zoe didn't respond right away. She let the words sit in the room.

"Well, how'd you play that day?" Zoe asked after a few moments.

"Good."

It felt odd to say it out loud, though, because as vividly as I remembered everything up to that moment, I still couldn't recall the game.

"All I can remember," I said, almost laughing, "is my dad

telling me I made eleven outs at second base without a single error. How is it possible I don't remember playing, as Dad would call it, 'The best baseball game of my life'?"

Zoe let my question sink into my own thoughts, tilted her head, and said, "Because your body remembered fear louder than your mind remembered success." She paused again. "Our brains are wired for survival, Jason."

"Before that day," she continued, "fielding a ground ball was routine. You were confident. You trusted your body, the ball, your instincts. And then suddenly, after one bad hop, it's gone. That trust, the joy, the freedom. All gone. Replaced with fear. Replaced with doubt."

I nodded. "Yeah . . . it wasn't just the pain."

"That's not uncommon. We don't always remember the moment things went right, but we never forget when something we love hurts us. The ball didn't just bruise your face, it fractured the innocence you had around the game. Around yourself."

I swallowed hard. "I didn't want to be afraid. I wanted to be fearless. Like the older kids."

Zoe's voice softened. "But fear isn't failure, Jason. It's a reaction. And what you did after, the drills with your dad, the catcher's gear, letting him throw ball after ball—that was courage. You were brave. You just didn't know it yet."

I sat on the couch and oddly felt heavier as my mind relived those early days.

"Your hometown sounds like a great place to grow up," Zoe added.

The statement seemed odd, almost out of place, but she

was right. My hometown had been an amazing place to grow up. It was the kind of place adults dreamed about raising their kids. More than half of the roads were dirt, winding through beautiful mountains like poetry written on the finest paper. The emerald-green landscape was dotted with charming old red barns and two-hundred-year-old covered bridges. In winter, snow glittered on the ground beneath the morning sun and filled the air with a stillness that felt sacred.

In the summer, I played baseball, kickball, tag, and any other game the older kids could conjure up in the middle of the street. Whenever a car came by, which was rare, we'd all step to the side and wave as it passed through the heart of our game.

Returning is what you did when you grew up in Lyndonville. As kids we returned to the street for another game, and graduating high school seniors would quickly return if they even left in the first place. You might leave for a short time, but if you did, you were simply going on a trip. Opportunity was vast, or so it appeared, only it led right back to town like a kid's yo-yo returning to her hand.

Zoe looked over at me and said, "Did you ever want to leave?"

"Never thought about it as a kid. Why would I want to leave? I had everything I ever wanted."

"Everything?" Zoe asked in a tone that challenged this thought.

"Well, maybe not everything."

I would go on to explain that the only keys I remember seeing as a kid were the ones that lived full-time in the ignition of my mom's used car and Dad's rusty green three-speed stepside truck. I remembered wanting my parents to have new cars, but only because some of my friends' parents had new ones. I wondered why we didn't, but those thoughts disappeared as fast as they revealed themselves to me. We had a big house on a corner lot with a white two-rail fence around the big backyard, and I had my own bedroom, which was great because I didn't want to share one with my younger brother.

It was rare that name-brand cereal boxes made their way into our cupboards, and when they did, they stood out like a beacon on a foggy morning next to the many cans of Campbell's soup. Our jeans weren't Levi's or Wrangler, and Mom kept them alive with patches she would iron over the holes.

Mom used to knit mittens and hats for us every year. There was this one hat that I remember most vividly: It had my name knitted vertically several times all the way around it. I thought it was so cool as a kid, but I was glad I didn't have to wear it by the time I made it to high school.

"Your mom sounds like quite a woman," Zoe said.

I smiled back at Zoe as I pictured my mom's dark hair and oval face. She stood five feet eight inches tall, slender and athletic, and yet I don't recall her ever talking about playing sports as a kid. As an entrepreneur and the breadwinner of our family, she was one of the hardest workers I would ever know. Yet sometimes I felt poor even though I didn't know what poor felt like. I remember thinking, *One day I am gonna be able to afford a Levi's jean jacket and not a generic one with ironed-on patches.*

When I needed comfort, my mom would wrap her arms around me. I remember this one time as a little boy I sat on the toilet in tears, unable to go to the bathroom, and there she was sitting right beside me on the edge of the tub. She was always there. She was the one I would run to when I was scared. Her hugs, while short on words, were long on feeling as her love poured into me like heat radiating into a room from the woodstove on a cold winter night. The power she held in her arms as they wrapped around me was immense. Her hugs weren't able to make all my problems and fear disappear, but they said, "You are not alone; I am here for you, by your side, and it will be okay."

Just telling Zoe about my mom made my heart happy, which was good because I hadn't felt that way in a long time. I hadn't talked much to my mom in years, but I knew soon enough Zoe would pry her words deeper into me. But at that moment, it felt good to have my mom's love wrapped around me once again.

"Yeah, my mom is quite a woman. So different from my dad," I said as I leaned forward.

"How so?" Zoe asked.

Mom didn't talk about the future much: hers, mine, or anyone's. She didn't talk about dreams or normal mushy mom stuff. Maybe that's because I was a boy. I didn't know. Dad, on the other hand, was as sappy as a maple tree in the spring. Standing over six feet tall, Dad was a giant. He taunted me often while playing hoops in the driveway, waving a basketball in one hand over my head. The Prendergast chiseled jaw bones, catcher's-mitt-sized hands, long back, and posture ran through the family tree directly onto Dad's branch and into mine. As a kid, I never saw Dad concerned about much. To me, he was the jolliest Green Giant I had ever known.

Dad's big dream in life wasn't to be rich, have a fancy degree framed on his wall, or make a living in a coat and tie of any sorts. Dad's big dream was simply to be a great dad. That's it. As simple as it was pure, as selfish as it was selfless. To pursue this dream, Dad sacrificed everything traditional society threw at a grown man in the 1970s.

I don't know if it bothered him that Mom was the breadwinner. I was too young to really know for sure, but my gut says he was just fine punching a time clock five days a week, clocking out at 3:30. His dream may have stemmed from his own experiences, as he didn't have a great dad, or even a good one, for that matter. This changed when my grandpa married my nana, who had divorced Dad's biological father when he was a young boy.

I leaned back and crossed a leg over my thigh and said, "Yeah, they were different, alright. Mom was tough, and Dad . . ." I paused, searching for the right word. "Was fragile."

"Sounds like you were lucky," Zoe said after her pen stopped moving.

"Yeah, I guess I was," I said, wondering what she had just written down.

"Would you say loved?" Zoe said.

"Of course," I said, offended by the question in her tone.

Zoe settled back in her chair and said, "What does love require?"

I uncrossed my legs. Elbows resting on my knees. Fingers laced, hanging. My head was bowed, not in defeat, but in thought.

The question didn't feel clinical. It wasn't diagnostic. It was something else, something that settled into the room and waited. It was as if she had asked this question of herself before.

A few moments passed. "Trust," I said after making eye contact.

Her face softened, just slightly, but enough to allow my chest to expand. The corners of her eyes relaxed, and her gaze held mine with something warm in it. Not pity. Not agreement just for agreement's sake. It was deeper than that.

She gave a small nod and sat quiet.

The silence between us held everything I'd said and everything I hadn't.

3

WALK THE TRACK

Identifying the first moment on the list created space for the next sequence of memories to come pouring in, each one a scene I wished I could rewrite.

My mind raced as the twisted knots in my stomach climbed into my throat. A few minutes ago, I nearly pissed my pants; then, sitting on the start line, it was all I could do to not puke. *Breathe, Jason, breathe.*

Where is he? I scanned the thirty of us lined up. *There he is. Number 88. You got this.* I moved my eyes back up the rut-filled dirt track. *Flip it—flip it!* The sign changed from 45 to 30. *Thirty more seconds, come on, you got this.* I took one last look at #88, the fastest rider. Come on, you got this.

Two fingers of my left hand gripped the clutch tight while my right hand twisted the throttle of my dirt bike. VROOOOOM, VROOOOOM. Shielded by goggles, my eyes briefly closed and my mouth shut tight to trap as much air as possible in my chest. *Come on, turn it, turn it.* The sign shifted sideways. Ten more seconds.

My dirt bike roared at a constant full throttle and drowned out the thirty other bikes on the start line, including that of rider #88.

My eyes, once blinking as fast as my heart, locked on to the stretched rubber band across my front tire, like a dam holding back my desires. The full twist of the throttle calmed my body, and the revving of my bike brought an eerie quiet to my mind. It was finally time. I was ready to go from sitting still to thirty-plus miles an hour in a few seconds.

In a flash, the rubber band disappeared. My fingers instantly released the clutch, my back tire gripped the dirt, and the suspension compressed as the torque of my bike pulled the seat down, causing my front tire to lift a foot off the ground. The race was on.

A hundred yards, as fast as I dared to go. Then a 180-degree turn. Then back up seventy-five yards before entering the track at the tee.

I started in second gear, shifting through third, then fourth as adrenaline rushed through my body, swallowing all the butterflies that once feasted on my stomach. I sped into the corner harder and faster than ever with a focus so intense that everything around me slowed down and I became deaf to everything except the high-pitched roar of my bike. Nearly blinded by the intensity, my eyes clearly saw exactly where I wanted my bike to go.

I usually jockeyed with other bikes into the first turn, but not this time. I squeezed the clutch and slammed down on the shifter with my foot to find second gear while my other foot stomped on the brake pedal. I laid my bike down to a 45-degree angle, turned the front wheel, and twisted the throttle. The back tire spun my bike around the corner of the wood-slatted snow fence protected by old car tires. The rear tire gripped the ground, the front wheel rose, and I cranked the throttle as far down as it would go. Moments later, I speed-shifted into third gear and then saw the tee and racetrack.

Oh shit!

My hand released the throttle, and the world crashed into my mind as I heard all the bikes behind me, and two flew past. I twisted the throttle again, squatted over my seat like a jockey in the Kentucky Derby, and followed the bikes after turning right onto the track.

I sat tall on my bike as I rode through the pit area after finishing in second place. I arrived at our camper, removed my helmet, and hung it on the handlebars, revealing a big smile.

A vertical winding river of smoke rose from my Grandpa Graves's fingers as he sat on his folding lawn chair. Grandpa Meehan (on my dad's side) had never smoked a day in his life. But Grandpa Graves (on my mom's side), the one that got us into racing, never went a day without a cigarette in his fingers. Grandpa Graves wore his patented oversized, unbuttoned plaid shirt—with a wad of money in one chest pocket and a pack of Winstons in the other—over his tee shirt while his hat, which was never on straight, sat perfectly cockeyed high on his head.

Our eyes met. "You had the hole shot," he said.

"Yup," I nodded.

"Well...? You went from first to third like that." He snapped his fingers.

My chin dropped. All the pride I had ridden through the pit area with left my body and soaked the ground at my feet as fast as that rubber band disappeared from the front of my tire.

"Mmmmm, I dunno," I said as I shrugged my shoulders.

"It's okay. What happened?"

I shrugged my shoulders again and said, "I . . . I . . . don't know."

I stood motionless, and Grandpa sat silent. It felt like a week had gone by before I could get the words out. "I . . . I . . . got . . . lost."

"You got lost?" His laugh caused him to cough and made me realize he wasn't disappointed.

My eyes slowly lifted. "I freaked out," I said as my shoulders swallowed my neck.

"We race here all the time," he said.

"I, I've . . . always followed someone. Never been in first," I said, talking through my wrists as I wiped my eyes dry with the back of my hand. "I couldn't remember if we were going left or right."

"I know what happened," he said with a smile. "We never planned for that."

"Getting lost?" I said.

"Nooo. For being in the lead. We never planned for that, did we?"

"I mean. I guess not."

"We're gonna from now on," he said. "Learn anything today?"

"Need to know where I am going?"

"Yes," Grandpa laughed. "Anything else?"

"I mean, I don't know."

He smiled at me. "You're fast. Fast enough to get the hole shot. Fast enough to win. You know who else knows you're fast?"

"Who?" I questioned.

"Number 88. Don't forget that."

Zoe peered over her pad of paper the following Thursday and said, "So that was the first time you ever remember being lost?"

She'd opened the session with: "Let's revisit exploring when you were a kid. Were you ever scared of getting lost when you went exploring?"

I remembered being ten or twelve and nervous out in the valley behind the house. My stomach pushed through the sole of my sneakers and my face went hot. My eyes darted around as my feet twisted my body back and forth. Dad had taught me about the sun's movement and the importance of paying attention to where it was at all times. A few seconds passed. I faced the sun, lifted my arm level with the ground, and said out loud, "Home's that way." As soon as those words hit, I was at ease.

I looked at Zoe and said, "No, not really. I mean, I got twisted around a few times in the valley, but Dad taught me how not to get lost in the woods. So no, not really."

Zoe jotted something down in her notebook, and before she finished, I said, "I do remember the first time I got lost, though."

Her eyes quickly lifted. "You do?"

After sharing the motocross story with her, she said, "Sounds like quite a day. What'd that feel like?"

"What. Getting lost? The hole shot or finishing second?" I said as my chest and head bounced with laughter.

"Any of them," she said.

I was proud to finish second. I had never won a race before, and second was as high as I had ever finished. Number 88 beat me that day, like he did most days, but I beat him off the start line for the first time ever. Going into that first corner in the lead was nothing like I had expected. I had envisioned myself with the hole shot every time I was in the start gate, but I had no idea that everything would be in slow motion. I was going faster than I had ever gone, and it felt like I was barely moving.

"What did your parent's think about you racing?" Zoe said.

"My dad loved it. He would take pictures of us at every race and talk to us about it on the way home. My mom on the other hand," I said, laughing, "she hated every single minute of it. She was scared to death I would get hurt."

"What about you? Were you ever scared racing?"

"Yeah, all the time," I said.

I went on to explain that I'd never truly overcome fear when I raced. I would teeter back and forth on the threshold of panic. Anxiety would rush through my body, forcing me to let off the throttle, and then a desire for speed would overcome me and I would twist the throttle as fast, as far, or for as long as I dared. Right up to the point that my body would tense up again.

I looked across the room at Zoe and said, "If someone says they don't get scared racing a dirt bike, they are either lying or not going fast enough."

Teetering between riding too slow and riding the edge, the edge of speed and disaster, was like standing on the edge of a cliff with the wind at your back.

In retrospect, one thing that surprised me most was how much I had mistaken speed for courage. In my comfort zone, everything felt predictable, but when I twisted that throttle a little more or held it for a little longer, that safety net disappeared, and so did the illusion. I was forced to relax and rely on instincts, resilience, and acceptance instead of preparation. I realized courage wasn't about going a little faster. Courage was about trusting myself even when I didn't.

Zoe tilted her head and said, "So, do you wish you had courage that day on the racetrack?"

I laughed. "I wish I knew where the hell I was going. I had no idea if we were going left or right, and when my eyes hit that tee in the track . . . I froze up tighter than a tick."

"So, you really were lost?" Zoe said.

"Big-time."

Zoe's feet shuffled, and as soon as she turned the page in her notebook, I knew it: She had sucked me right in. I quickly moved my eyes away from her and to a bookshelf and tried to read the spines, then to the floor, and then to her desk. The closer my eyes moved toward her, the louder I felt my temples pulsate.

"I hated the way it felt. Confusion sucked the confident me off my bike and left a whole different version of myself sitting there, lost and helpless."

That uneasiness pulled me inward like a turtle that just found himself on a busy road. Dad always told me to stay put if

I ever got lost in the woods, and someone would find me. I nodded my head every time and said, "I know, Dad." I had never been lost before that day, and panic rippled through my body as my mind went into overdrive and my body went into park.

My eyes lifted to Zoe's and I said, "That was the last time I ever got lost on a racetrack."

And I meant it.

Grandpa Graves had seen it too. He knew it wasn't about not knowing where I was but about not knowing where I was going. And soon enough, he'd show me how to never get lost again.

Arriving at Rider Hill, the week after getting lost on the racetrack, Grandpa said, "I want you to walk the track and figure out the fastest way around. And I want you to walk it backward."

"Backward?" I said. It didn't make any sense. Why would I walk it backward?

"Yes, backward. If you walk it forward, you aren't prepared for what will happen. All you know is where you've been, not where you are going."

"What?" I said, my eyes pinched together.

"When you go into a corner, how do you know if you should be on the inside, the outside, or in the middle?" he said.

"Ummmm," I muttered.

Grandpa looked at me and said, "What happens after the corner is important. Stand on the finish line, look back at the last corner, and ask yourself, what is the fastest line between the corner and where you stand? Look at everything: the ruts, the bumps, all of it. If you feel the track is faster coming out of the corner on a tight inside line, walk to that point and look at the next jump or corner. Stand at each point looking backward then forward. I want you to do that in every corner and at every jump around the track."

"Ahhhh," I said, finally understanding.

"Jason, be sure you go all the way back to the start line," he added, a grin tugging at the corners of his mouth. "Don't want you to get lost this time." He winked and puffed on his cigarette.

My last race ended up being the final time I ever rode a dirt bike. It was also the last time I walked the track backward.

One of the saddest days of my life turned into one of my mom's happiest. But fear didn't disappear for me or Mom. Fear evolved; it hid in plain sight.

4

HILLS

The cool evenings of late August brought a warm glow to the Vermont landscape, along with the arrival of the Caledonia County Fair. Soon, Mother Nature would add her signature to the Northeast Kingdom canvas, transforming the Green Mountain State's hills, mountaintops, and valleys into vibrant collages of red, orange, and yellow.

As a boy, the cooler nights meant one thing: The fair had come to town. But as a teenager in 1985, it signified something even more special: One of my dreams might just come true.

It's strange how our childhood dreams can weather the test of time. After all the moments I'd spent feeling directionless, the one thing I always returned to were my dreams.

"I want you to spend the weekend thinking about your dreams," Zoe told me in our last session.

"Oh, that's easy, I have lots of them. Ones I had as a kid or an adult?"

"All of them," she said.

I remembered Mom coming out of the house one day eyeing the makeshift ramp I'd built in the driveway out of a split piece of firewood and a board.

"I'm Evel Knievel," I said proudly.

I was maybe eight, pedaling my Huffy bike as fast as I could, launching myself off that rickety ramp and flying through the air as if I had cars lined up beneath me.

When Mom came back out, my jump had grown from one piece of wood to several. She made me go inside and put on her Ski-Doo helmet, which was far too big. She strapped it up as tight as it would go, but my head still wobbled inside. I ran outside, hopped on my bike, and jumped over and over again. I was fearless.

A few days later, I came home crying, and my face was all bloody. I had made the biggest jump ever built by an eight-year-old, and the jump fell apart as my bike rode up the ramp and I found myself in a heap on the paved driveway.

Mom cleaned me up and scolded me for not wearing my helmet. The next day I was back outside, staring at the broken ramp, trying to figure out why the jump wasn't any good and why I crashed.

"How was your weekend?" Zoe asked as I sat down the following Tuesday.

"It was great. I laughed a few times thinking about my dreams as a kid."

"They made you laugh?" she asked, already looking up from her notes.

"Yeah, some of them were pretty funny. I wanted to be Evel Knievel when I was young."

"Evel Knievel?" Zoe repeated with a slight smile forming.

"Yeah, I don't know how long it lasted . . . a while, I think. Crazy thing is, my parents were okay with it. I mean, I crashed my bike a bunch and bloodied my face once. Whose parents don't try to stop an eight-year-old wanting to launch himself off homemade jumps like a stuntman?" I laughed.

"No helmets, no elbow pads, knee pads, or any of all that. Just imagination and road rash back in those days."

Zoe chuckled softly. "Did you dream about anything else?"

"Yeah, lots of stuff."

I went on to tell Zoe about the time the Pittsburgh Steelers drafted me as a nine-year-old to play quarterback in the backyard of my childhood home. Dad and I watched football on Sundays. As I sat on the living room floor (too close to the TV, Dad always said), he sprawled out on the couch behind me. I watched the football players file off the field, and I couldn't help but notice how filthy their jerseys had become: smeared with dirt, streaked with sweat, and some stained with blood. There was something raw and honest about those stains, like a visual badge of toughness.

In my backyard, I became the whole team.

Standing at one end of the yard, I called a pass play while I huddled with myself. I squatted as if under center, with a football in hand. I moved my head from side to side, surveying the imaginary defense.

"Down. Set. Hut!"

I'd snap the ball to myself, drop back three steps, and plant my foot just as I had seen my hero, number 12, Terry Bradshaw do countless times. I tossed the ball high into the air. I sprinted across the yard, transforming into another hero, Lynn Swann, and tried to catch the football. Sometimes I'd have to dive, and other times I'd catch it midstride while I dodged imaginary defenders. I would run across the makeshift end zone and spike the Nerf football into the ground as the crowd cheered at the game-winning touchdown.

I would play this game for hours, imagining myself on television and picturing myself winning a Super Bowl. I remember Mom looked at me after one game and shook her head as I barreled into the house.

"Another hole in your jeans?" she said.

I looked down at myself. Grass stains ran down the sides of my cotton T-shirt and spread across my thighs, and sure enough, one of my knees was showing. The dirt was ground in deep, the green smudges vivid against the fabric. But instead of feeling dirty, I felt proud. Those stains meant something. They were proof that I had played hard, given it my all, and left everything I had out there. Just like those football players on TV. I looked up at Mom and shrugged my shoulders.

"Did you win?" she said.

"Yup," I said with a little smile.

I had finally grown up and was old enough to attend high school. My shiny white cleats would dig into the lined turf for the first time in a few weeks. I was finally old enough to suit up.

The days of wanting to be Terry Bradshaw in the backyard were over long before I turned fifteen and entered high school. By then, the days of the green synthetic rope pressed against my body, keeping me confined outside Lyndon Institute's football field and dreaming about playing football, were also over.

Still, before then, I just hoped I was good enough to play.

My family often ate dinner together around 5:30, and one night, Mom and Dad sat on one side of the table while my brother and I sat far too close together on the other. Halfway through dinner, Dad broke the golden rule of not talking with your mouth full. "Talked with the Coach ta-day. You can practice with the varsity team."

Silence slammed into the dinner table.

"The varsity team?" I said, as I looked up from my shepherd's pie. "Why would I do that?"

"Freshman practice starts in two weeks. Wanna make the team, don't ya?"

"Yeeeah."

"Best way to make the team is ta be ready," Dad said as he shoveled a forkful of food into his mouth.

"Var . . . varsity?" I said through the stiffness of my body as my mind flashed through game film from years past. I remembered standing against the green rope. The sounds of the players all as big as Dad grunting and groaning after the loud crash of helmets and pads. *The varsity team? He can't be serious.*

Dad looked across the table at me. I was as white as the mashed potatoes on my plate. "What are you afraid of?" he asked.

"Ahhh. I mean. Have you seen how big they are?"

"Bigger doesn't mean tougher," Dad said as he lifted food to his mouth again. "Toughness is in here," he said, pointing to his temple.

Yeah, right, I thought. All I could see in my mind were players barreling down the field at me, their eyes as big as baseballs staring through the bars on their helmet, about to plow into me.

"If you practice with the varsity team every day for two weeks, who's gonna be ready for freshman tryouts? You, or everyone else? Who's gonna be in better shape? Who's gonna be more prepared?"

I sat bolted to the wooden bench, looking back at him.

He paused to gulp down half a glass of milk, which he jokingly referred to as "heifer sweat," before he continued. "Whose legs gonna be cramping? And whose ain't? Who's gonna be throwin' up and gasping for air? And who ain't? Best way to make the team is to be ready for tryouts. Best way to be ready is to practice when no one else is," he said before pausing again.

"They're faster than me," I said, interrupting and pleading my case.

"Wanna make the team, don't ya?"

Wanna make the team? Of course I wanted to make the team. I had dreamed about playing high school football for years. But I didn't know I would have to practice with the varsity team.

I sat across from Zoe, my shoulders slumped just slightly, as if the words I'd just spoken carried more weight than I expected.

"I don't know," I said. "Even now, sometimes I just wish I didn't have so much doubt. I wish I could just . . . believe in myself all the time."

Zoe tilted her head slightly, always patient. She waited for me to finish, not just the words, but the thought behind them.

I continued: "The truth is, I don't always have to dig that

deep to figure out what I'm really feeling. Doubt's more buoyant than confidence, you know? Especially when someone comes along and stirs the pot a bit. It rises fast, faster than anything else."

Zoe smiled at that. "That's a good way to put it."

I nodded. "Yeah. And emotions . . . they have this way of floating to the top when someone else gets involved. It's one thing to wrestle with something in your own mind, but when another person steps in, especially someone who matters, it's like everything inside just bubbles up."

"And someone who believes in you," she said gently, "can make all the difference."

"Exactly. Dad always told me that believing in myself was important. I agree. But when someone else believed in me? It was different. It was like flipping a switch or kicking into overdrive when I didn't even know another gear existed."

Zoe sat forward.

"That kind of strength doesn't come from nowhere," I continued. "It's a gift, really. And Dad had it. Mom did too, in her own way, but Dad . . . he just knew how to say the right thing. It was like he wasn't just talking to me. He was talking to the version of me I hadn't become yet. My future self."

Zoe raised her eyebrows. "That's a beautiful thought."

"Yeah," I said, my voice quieter now. "It was like he was having a conversation with the voices in my head. He always seemed to know when I needed reassurance in the moment . . . and when I needed to be pushed hard."

Zoe leaned back in her chair. "That's a rare kind of love, Jason. Not everyone gets that. To be believed in like that, it shapes how we carry ourselves. How we handle our own doubts."

I looked away for a moment, blinking against the stinging in my eyes. "Yeah. Maybe." I continued with my story.

I spent the next two weeks practicing with the varsity team, which meant a lot of running, running, and more running. The hills were the worst. We had to run up the hill and then back down, only to run back up and down again. Over and over.

Running the hills felt endless, as if they became taller and steeper each time. My legs felt like they were rooted to the ground when I reached the bottom, my arms locked straight, hands pressing into my thigh pads as I gasped for air.

Dad was there every day, cheering me on from the sidelines. Occasionally, I glanced at him, blinking the salty sweat away. Our eyes would lock, and his nod meant one thing: *You're doing great, son.*

In bed one night after practice, I flipped over, side to side, looking for comfort like a fish searching for water in a boat. My eyes would close momentarily, then snapped open from the pain shooting through my legs.

I lay there, staring into the darkness, feeling the same fear as a young boy being afraid of the dark and wanting my mom to lie beside me to protect me from its dangers.

What is it about the darkness that gives rise to monsters? Not the monsters that live under the security blanket of light, but the ones that live inside us?

Hope flooded my aching muscles as my mind flashed back to being a kid playing football in my backyard and to that older kid pressed against the green rope, watching the varsity team play football.

I tried to see myself on the football field, but I could never find my jersey. I'd snap my eyes open to reset the image and shut them again. But I never showed up. The thought of not making the team pressed on my chest, taking away the hurt in my legs.

As I sat in the truck on the way home from practice one afternoon, I looked over at Dad and said, "Tackling drills suck. Every time I line up against someone, all I can think about before the whistle blows is getting knocked into next week. No matter what I do, these guys run me over. Told you they were tougher than me."

Dad pulled the truck to the side of the road and twisted toward me. "You're playing scared, son."

Feeling my eyes well up with tears, I had lost the battle to hold them back, and a tear slipped down my cheek.

No shit: I was playing scared, and it was for good reason. These guys were bigger, faster, stronger, and older than me. I didn't feel like I belonged on the field with the upperclassmen. My body felt the same as it did after being smashed in the mouth with that ground ball when I was ten.

"Look at me, son," Dad said, as he gently wiped away my tears with his thumb.

I pulled my stare off the floorboard of the truck to meet his eyes. Dad always taught me to look a man in the eye when he was speaking to me, especially if I was in trouble. But the tone in his voice this time was filled with compassion, not disappointment.

"Ya gotta show them how tough you are," Dad said.

"I'm trying," I said as tears fell again.

"I know ya are, son. I'm proud of ya. After you get tackled, I want ya to jump up. Get up faster than the other guy. They may be bigger than you, but toughness is in here, remember?" he said, pressing his fingers to his temple again. "The guy who gets hit is the one who gets hurt. You understand what I am telling ya, son? Don't wait for them to hit ya. I want you to start hitting them. Ya understand?"

"Yeah, I guess." My crackled whisper broke the silence in the cab.

"Tackle their feet and get up fast. You may get run over, but ya win if ya get up first. Earning respect on the field is about getting up fast. Ya understand what I am telling ya?"

I nodded as fear and doubt battled my faith in his words.

"I am proud of ya, son."

"Am I gonna make the team?" I said as I wiped my face dry.

"You'll make the team if ya keep working hard," he said, and then he paused. "Know what I noticed today?"

I shook my head from side to side.

"When coach starts a new drill—sprints, hills, or anything—the same few guys are always first to line up."

"Same guys?" I said.

"Same guys. Those are the leaders of the team. Leaders go first. Think you can stand next to those guys?"

I shrugged my shoulders. "I'll try," I said softly.

Dad paused, as he often did when he talked with me, and said, "When you run hills, get in the first group and run your ass off. Dig deep; the more tired and sore you are, the deeper you dig. Some people do the minimum, some work hard, and some dig deep. Who are ya, son? Ya gotta decide. I can't do it for you. It is up to you."

"That's a big decision to make as a fifteen-year-old," Zoe said.

"Yeah, at the time it was," I said.

"At the time?" she questioned.

Dad knew I wasn't fast, but it wasn't about winning a race or game or being the best on the team. It never was. For him, it was always about encouraging me to push myself to become better. Even if I were the best on the team, it wasn't about being better than anyone else. For Dad, competing meant only one thing: pushing myself to get better.

The atmosphere on the ride home after a game was always the same, whether I won or lost. Of course, Dad wanted me to win—what dad doesn't? But for him, the focus was always on preparation and outworking everyone else. It was about proving to myself that I could hold my own against bigger and better players. It was about believing I belonged. It was about facing my monsters, monsters that looked just like me when I looked in the mirror.

Dad was on a two-week mission to help me discover a part of myself that I had never encountered before. He understood that standing next to the freshmen on the football field would be much easier if I could earn my place among the big boys on the varsity team. He knew me well enough to realize I wanted to stand beside those who went first.

"Keep your head up and show them what you're made of," Dad would say. "They may be bigger, faster, and better than you, but you can't control that, son. Focus on what you can control. You'll make the team if you're coachable, run harder, and work harder than everyone on the field."

"Nervous?" Dad asked as I climbed into the truck the following Monday. The time had come for me to stand next to everyone else who hadn't stepped foot on a practice field yet.

"I don't know. Kinda. You think I am going to make the team?" I said, searching for a yes in his eyes.

"I don't know, son. Either way, I'm proud of ya. You've worked hard. What do you think?"

"Hope so," I said, shrugging my shoulders.

"When you walk on that field today, you need to remember you've been practicing for two weeks with the varsity team, and the coaches will know too."

"They will?" I said.

Dad nodded. "Yup. You've worked harder than everyone else showing up today."

My eyes scanned the freshmen clustered around the coaches. It wasn't until that moment that my dad's words finally sunk in. I'd been competing with the varsity squad for the past two weeks, and in many ways, I'd become a part of that team. I was determined to work harder than every single one of the guys. I stood at the front of the line during practice, shoulder to shoulder with the best football players in our school. The same guys I told my dad I was afraid of just two weeks earlier.

The coach's whistle cut through the nervous chatter of the freshmen on the field. "Everyone who wants to try out for quarterback, stand here," he said, as he pointed left.

I jogged toward the designated spot without hesitation, followed by a few other guys. I'd been practicing to be a quarterback in my backyard for years, and now it was time to play in real life.

"Running backs here, receivers here, and linemen here," the coach instructed, gesturing to different places on the field. "Welcome to freshman football."

"Quarterback, huh?" Dad said as we drove home after tryouts.

"Yeah," I said with a little smile.

"The quarterback is the leader of the team, ya know." Dad smiled under his mustache.

"Yeah."

"Up for that?"

"Yeah," I said.

"If you are going to lead the team, you have to work harder than everyone. The leader pushes everyone to get better. Ya need to know what everyone is doing on the field on every play: where they stand, who they block, what routes they run. You ready for that?"

I nodded.

"When the shit hits the fan and the game is on the line, everyone is going to be afraid of losing. You can't be afraid of losing, son. You afraid of losing?"

"I mean . . . I don't want to lose."

"No one wants to lose. Not wanting to lose and being afraid of losing are different."

My eyes narrowed, wrinkling my forehead, and then I locked eyes with Dad.

"To win, ya have to be willing to lose. If you're not willing to lose, ya play scared. And ya can't win playing scared. A leader plays to win and wants the ball. Ya want the ball, son?"

"Yeah, I want the ball." I slammed my knuckles into the

palm of my hand.

"Good for you, son," Dad said as his big hand smacked down on my thigh, gripping my leg. "I am proud of ya, son. You've worked hard."

Dad never told me that every player trying out for the team would make it. He knew this all along. I didn't know it until years later. Dad's little secret introduced me to this new person inside of myself, one tucked away deep within me. A person I hadn't met: my future self.

I was lucky to have both of them in my life.

5

DIRT ROADS

The light through the window slats in Zoe's office waved good morning to me as I sat down on the couch. I gave a nod. Something about the sunlight burned into the carpet differently. It was brighter than I recalled.

Zoe and I had talked about several things over the past couple of weeks. We'd discussed the pressures and impact middle school had on me as I began to think about my place in the world. When she asked about my favorite part of the day, I explained how I had mastered the art of shoving my things into my backpack while slinging it over my shoulders at the sound of the lunch bell. I sprinted down the hall, through the tall wooden front doors, and around the side of the school to where my bike rested in the steel bars of the bike rack.

I was twelve when I convinced Mom I was old enough to ditch the school bus for my bike. My legs pumped the pedals of my ten-speed as I raced across the park toward Gram's apartment for lunch. I had never wanted a ten-speed until just before middle school. Ten-speeds were for old people out for a leisurely ride. As a kid, I needed a bike that had knobby tires and could handle a jump. A big jump. But I wasn't a kid anymore.

Once I reached Gram's apartment, I leaped up the stairs two at a time and called out, "I'm here, Gram!"

This was my grandmother on my mom's side. She had a large white bathtub, the kind with clawed feet at the bottom, and it sat off to the side in the biggest bathroom I had ever seen. The walls were covered with pictures, but the one I remember most vividly showed two birds in flight with these words: "If you love something, set it free. If it comes back, it's yours. If not, it was never meant to be."

I turned the water on in the white porcelain sink and inspected my hands to see just how dirty they really were. After washing my hands, sometimes with soap, I walked to the kitchen counter where Gram's blocks lived. Each day, a new message was spelled using dice-sized blocks with letters instead of numbers. Sometimes, the message would read, "Are you hungry, Jason?" The best ones were when the message spelled "Happy birthday" followed by your name. It felt so good inside, like your whole body was smiling when you saw your name in Gram's blocks.

Large, poster-sized maps of Italy, France, Alaska, and other places Gram had visited were pinned to the walls of her second-story apartment, accompanied by photographs she had taken during her travels. The maps seemed to come alive as my eyes followed the yellow or green highlighted paths she marked on each one. Gram had been to so many places, but I didn't ever remember her being gone.

The lunch menu was always different, but my favorite cuisine was when canned baked beans and hot dogs waited for me on the TV tray set up in the living room. Gram and I would compete to guess each puzzle as we watched *Wheel of Fortune* before I hugged her and flew down the stairs to return to school. Looking back, it is amazing how two wheels and ten speeds introduced me early in life to independence and trust, and that little bike gave me the opportunity to fly to a place of freedom with my grandma.

The next few weeks with Zoe were good, as she had me reliving many of my happy memories of my childhood. Somehow, though, I knew it would soon change.

Walking into her office reminded me exactly how I felt once as an eighth grader paired up with a couple of friends for an end-of-year project, when the three of us had decided to interview at the Hoffman house.

Mrs. Hoffman lived in an old farmhouse that was known to be haunted. As we interviewed her, she showed us through the old farmhouse and said, "One of the rooms upstairs is where the spirit of Daniel Calhoon Sr. lives. It's where he died in 1811. You boys tell me which room you think is haunted."

We walked around the house with a camcorder on our shoulder, taping the interview. As we climbed up the stairs, Mrs. Hoffman said, "Daniel was gored by a bull while trying to save a child's life and died in one of these rooms." We walked into a yellow room, then a red room, and a blue room. They were all decorated like the rooms in the Western movies my dad used to like watching. We walked into the green room, and I immediately felt sick to my stomach and my face started to burn up. Nauseous, I stumbled to the door. As soon as I reached the hall, it was as if I had jumped into a cold lake; I was instantly fine.

That's how I felt sitting on the couch looking at Zoe. Something was about to happen. I knew it. My eyes hit the sunlight on the floor, which ricocheted them to the pull cord on the window.

"Jason, let's talk about your parents some more. Are they still married?"

I felt my feet touch the green room floor in the Hoffman house. Zoe went quiet, and the silence hit me like Daniel Calhoon's spirit did so many years ago, forcing my eyes back to the pull cord hanging in the window.

"Boys, come down here . . ." My father's voice walked up the stairs and entered our bedrooms.

Garett, thirteen, and me, fifteen, stepped into the hall. We stared at each other, each of us velcroed to the carpet. This phrase had been shouted up the staircase many times, usually after a fight between us. But this was different. Neither of us had ever heard this tone before.

"Are we in trouble?" Garett whispered.

"I don't know," I said, shaking my head. "I hope not."

As we crept down the stairs, the living room came into view. Mom's perfect posture was slumped as she sat on the couch, and Dad sat in the chair, his elbows resting on his knees with his head down.

"Sit down, boys," he said as he raised his head to look at us. "Your mother and I have something to tell you."

The eerie silence in the room lingered as Garett and I

sat motionless on the couch. My eyes darted back and forth between my parents, trying to understand what was happening.

"Are . . . are we in trouble?" Garett's soft voice tested the silence.

"No, you aren't in trouble," Dad said, looking across the room at Mom. "Your mother and I are getting a divorce."

The room become a blur as Garett and I both started to cry.

"Is this my fault? I promise not to fight anymore. I promise," I pleaded.

"You boys did nothing wrong. It's not your fault," Dad said.

"Are you putting us up for adoption?" Garett asked, through his tears.

"Of course not," Dad said. The first tear I had ever seen on his face rolled down his cheek. In fact, until this moment, I had never witnessed *either* of my parents cry. I didn't try to hold back my tears, and even if I had, there was no way possible.

"I want you boys to know I love you very much. I am always going to be your dad. That doesn't change. I am so proud of you boys," he said.

My body tightened as I wrapped my arms around my knees. *What's going on? Why is this happening?* So many questions flooded my thoughts as I tried to make sense of the moment.

"Boys, I am leaving," Dad said.

"Leaving? When? Where are you going?" I uttered through my tears as I rocked on the couch.

"I have to leave now. You boys are going to stay with your mother."

"Where are you going?" Garett stammered. "Are you coming back?"

"I'm not going far, boys. No, Gar. I'm not coming back."

"Ever?" I asked.

"Not to this house. I'm sorry."

"Will . . . we . . . ever . . . see . . . you . . . again?" Garett pieced together between his sobbing.

"Of course, I promise," he said, walking over to us, kneeling on the floor, and pulling us into the tightest hug he had ever given us.

"Why, Dad? Why?" I said, with my head shoved into his neck.

"I'm so proud of you boys. I love you both," he whispered.

Dad pulled away from us, then he looked me straight in the eye. "No more fighting. You hear me?"

I put my arm around my brother, my hand on his shoulder, and pulled him to me the same way Dad had done to me many times.

"You boys be good to your mother," he said as he stood up. "I love you boys." He turned toward the door.

"Don't leave. Please don't leave," Garett and I both pleaded.

"You'll be okay. I'll call you, I promise. I love you both," Dad said. Then he disappeared behind the closing of the front door.

Mom walked over to the couch, sat between us, and pulled the three of us together.

"Why, Mom? Why?" I pleaded.

"It's gonna be okay," she said. "It's gonna be okay."

"Does Dad still love us?" I said.

"Yes, he still loves you both," Mom said. "We both do."

I looked up at Zoe, and sad tears flowed from my eyes for the first time in years, maybe decades, as my head fell heavy in my hands. I had shed plenty of prideful tears during a movie when a kid overcomes some obstacle and perseveres in the end. I cry every time in those movies, and Disney movies are the worst. But those tears weren't meant for me.

"Divorce ripped its way through my family, Zoe," I said, wiping the tears from my eyes.

"How'd that make you feel, Jason?"

"The divorce, or my dad leaving?"

"Both," she said.

When Dad walked out of the house, it felt like he took all the parts of himself that he had cultivated inside me with him. It felt like all the things he was to me had been sucked from my body, leaving this gaping hole that nobody could fill, not even Mom. As she sat between Garett and me, it was as if she was leaving too. Her hug felt different, the same way Dad's felt different.

I wanted so much to be mad at them both. I had been mad at them for things like grounding me for talking back or fighting with Garett. What I wanted to feel was anger because I knew what would happen after I felt anger. I would feel remorse, then sadness, and then I would feel their arms wrapped around me, and my heart would feel their "I love you" as they whispered the words in my ear. I wasn't allowed to be disrespectful or hurtful to anyone, but I was allowed to be mad and angry as long as I processed those emotions.

Being angry at that moment meant the emotions were both going to be there later and they were both going to be there in the morning. I had never felt that kind of scared. I imagined myself sitting next to the phone as I waited for Dad to call. I imagined myself making up some bullshit lie as to why my parents were getting divorced after one of my friends asked where my dad was.

I wanted to be anything but scared, only there wasn't room in my body for anything else. I was filled with the emptiness fear leaves behind as it evacuated my body to form a cage around me. Anything but scared, that's what I wanted to feel.

But I was so scared. My whole life changed in those moments. My parents had never lied to me before, which meant that when Dad said he was leaving never to return to this house, it was true, and I believed him. When he said he would call, I wanted to believe it, but I had a hard time being a hundred percent sure, and I didn't understand why.

My family imploded, leaving nothing but fragments of what we once were. This wasn't a ground ball that I could fix with a helmet. There wasn't a fix for this problem. I looked at Garett, who hugged the other side of Mom and saw a shield being constructed around him too.

I looked over at Zoe, shook my head, and my body heaved slightly as I huffed and said, "That moment changed my life forever."

6

THE CALL

I found it hard to focus the following week as I prepared for my meeting with Zoe. She had asked me to think about the days and weeks following my parents' divorce, but the aroma of warm, sweet, and buttery pancakes and smoky bacon that morning kept flashing my mind back to the Miss Lyndonville Diner back home, where I had eaten so many times.

The harder I thought about those days after Dad left, the more blank they became, and the emptiness kept eating my insides. I tried to remember what it felt like the first night going to bed knowing Dad wasn't coming back. I squinted my eyes and looked at the ceiling as I searched for specific memories, but my mind was as blank as the tiles overhead. The nothingness was unsettling.

I sat across from Zoe after breakfast and said, "Well, I did what you asked. I thought about it."

"And?" she said, with that dagger of a pen in her hand hovering over the paper on her lap.

"I got nuthin'."

"Nothing?" she repeated.

"How is it possible I don't remember what happened after one of the most impactful days of my life? Is this like forgetting the best baseball game I ever played?" I paused. The deeper I dug for answers, the more I questioned the absence of my memory. Was the divorce really as bad as I made it out to be?

Zoe sat quiet.

"I am sure I was eventually mad, angry, ashamed, lonely, you name it. I mean, that would be normal, right? But the more I thought about it, the more I thought, 'I'm just making this shit up.'"

Zoe looked back across at me, her eyes fixed on mine, and said nothing. Not only did she not say anything, she didn't move a muscle. It was like she was sitting there sound asleep with her eyes open. That dagger in her hand, it didn't move either; it didn't spill a drop of blood on the paper in her notebook. She would be still and quiet like this from time to time, and I had come to learn that I wasn't done talking yet and I just didn't know it. But this time, her nothingness felt different from those before and the nothingness I had felt earlier at breakfast. Her nothingness felt . . . well, it felt like . . . like it was full.

Zoe's eyes held mine in that familiar way: calm, patient, but always searching.

"Do you remember what you told me last week," she said, "about that Little League game after you got hit in the face with the ball? How we talked about fear being louder than success?"

I nodded.

"Sometimes we don't forget because something wasn't

important, we forget because it was too important. Because it impacted us in a way we didn't know how to handle."

I nodded slowly, finally saying what I had been thinking out loud. "The deeper I dig, the more I wonder, was the divorce really as bad as I made it out to be? Or have I rewritten parts of it without realizing it?"

Zoe's voice was calm. "That's a natural question, Jason. But here's something to consider: Just because a memory is missing doesn't mean the pain wasn't real. Sometimes our bodies remember what our minds can't. And the fact that you remember everything up to that moment tells me that mattered."

"You didn't just forget the baseball game. You forgot the part where you kept going, even after being hurt. That says a lot. Maybe it was too hard to believe that you were still capable of doing something good after something bad had happened."

I stared down at my hands. "So you're saying . . . I might've forgotten the game because I didn't believe I deserved to play well?"

"Possibly. Or maybe the pain, the fear, and the pressure of being okay too soon was too much to carry at once. So your mind held on to what hurt and let go of what proved you were stronger than you thought."

I swallowed, feeling her words dive into me. "Maybe that's why I keep second-guessing the divorce, too," I said. "I remember the pain. The hurt. But I don't remember enough of the in-between. The good parts. I question whether it was really that bad . . . or if I just fabricated my own story."

Zoe smiled gently. "It's okay to question the story. But

don't forget, your body was there. Your heart was there. Just because your mind can't pull up every detail doesn't mean your experience wasn't real. The missing pieces don't invalidate what shaped you. They just remind us how human you were through it all."

For the first time, the silence didn't feel like a void. It felt like a place I could breathe. After what seemed to be several minutes I said, "You know what I do remember as vividly as the divorce?"

"What's that?" she asked.

"Well, let me tell ya," I said and leaned back.

Months after the divorce, I found myself in a Spanish class my sophomore year of high school. Although I was already bilingual and fluent in English and Vermont Redneck, the school, with all its collective wisdom, believed I needed to become even more well-rounded. I remember thinking, *More well-rounded? For what?* I knew how not to get lost in the woods, and I had mastered starting a fire with a single match. I knew how the sun moved, how to skin and quarter a deer. I mean, they didn't teach those classes in school.

But like so many times in my middle teens, I was mistaken, or at least, that is what I was told. When I asked my counselor if I could take something else instead, she went on to explain all the benefits of a foreign language and then went into something about being more valuable in society or something. I stopped listening as soon as she didn't answer my question. At some point I started paying attention again, and I learned I had three options: Latin, French, and Spanish. I laughed, thinking, *I'm never gonna visit those places.*

I looked at her and thought, *Ain't no way she looked at my report card from last year.* If she had—or better yet, if she had talked with my teacher—she would have known there was no way I would pass a foreign language class. I barely made a C in English last year. I was pretty sure the C stood for "Congratulations, you passed." And not a congratulations as in, "Hooray," but more like, "You're welcome." Had she done any investigation whatsoever, she would have known a foreign language was a bad idea.

I couldn't envision anything positive to come from a Spanish class, nothing at all. Seriously, when would I ever need to speak Spanish in Lyndonville, Vermont? It wasn't like I was ever going to leave.

One Thursday, as I left Spanish class, my friend Rachelle, who was like a sister to me, grabbed my backpack and spun me around. "Hey, Kathleen likes you. You should call her."

"Ya sure she likes me?" I said, as my eyes broke away from Rachelle's and I thought, *No way.*

"Yup, she thinks you're cute."

"Seriously?"

"Call her," Rachelle pleaded.

"Ain't got her number," I said, and shoved my hands into my pockets.

She rattled off a string of digits, and it took me a moment to realize she had just given me Kathleen's number. "Call her after school," Rachelle said, as she started to walk away.

"Wait," I said. "And say what?"

"Ask her out."

"Hmm . . . I don't know."

The Call

"She's gonna say yes. Just call her."

Kathleen was a year younger than me, and I had never talked to her before Spanish class, but I knew her older brother, Brian, from the ski team at Burke Mountain.

Rachelle disappeared down the hall, and the words "Call her" echoed off the lockers. I stood there for a second, stuck somewhere between disbelief and the sudden rush of something that made my insides tingle. The hallway around me moved, but I wasn't really in it. As I headed to my next class, my mind wasn't on the usual stuff—football, where my buddies were, or what was happening after school. It was all scrambled now. I kept hearing Rachelle say, "She thinks you're cute."

Seriously? Me?

With every step, I felt like I was walking through a fog of what-ifs. My stomach had that weird feeling of being light and heavy at the same time, the one where part of you wants to sprint and the other part wants to hide. I kept seeing Kathleen's smile, those soft curls brushing her shoulders, her eyes that somehow looked like they were made to hold secrets and sunshine at once.

And now, I had her number. Those digits felt like a map to a place I wasn't sure I had the courage to go. I didn't know what I'd say, didn't know how to sound cool or even like I knew what I was doing. But I trusted Rachelle, and that counted for something.

Still, as I slipped into the seat of my next class and stared ahead, pretending to listen, all I could really think was: *Could this actually happen? Could she really like me?*

On Thursday afternoon, October 1, 1987, I paced the kitchen

for an hour, wearing a path in the linoleum floor while holding the mustard yellow rotary phone. Rachelle's voice saying, "'She's gonna say yes. Just call her," echoed in my head, pushing and pulling me with every step. I had started to dial Kathleen's number several times but hung up before reaching the last digit.

What if Rachelle was wrong? Why would Kathleen even like me? She didn't really know me. How would I ask her out if I couldn't even dial her number? Come on, Jason, just dial the damn number.

The tip of my index finger had slid into the hole above the 8 on the phone, and with each turn of the dial, it felt like breathing through a balloon. I snapped it to the stopper, quick and sharp, and let it spin back. Again with the 9. I'd done this dance before, always stopping short, always one number away from hearing her voice.

My lungs filled with a sharp breath, air rushing through my nose like I was gearing up to dive underwater at the pool and stay under until it was at the other side. I stared at the phone like it might give me a sign. My finger hovered over the 4, the last number. I pulled the dial, tight, hard, then let it go. That's when it hit. The sweat started first, thin and cold against my skin. My stomach twisted itself into a knot even a sailor couldn't untangle. The fear didn't scream, it crept in, quiet and hot, like molten metal poured into a mold. I could feel doubt hardening inside me, taking shape, slowing my breath.

What if she doesn't wanna talk? What if Rachelle was wrong? What if this is all a joke? The phone rang once. Doubt screamed at me to hang up, but some other part of me told me to wait. Two rings. I held my breath again. I wasn't sure if I was terrified of hearing her voice or terrified that no one would pick up at all.

"Hello," a soft voice answered.

"Ahhh, is Kathleen home?"

"This is Kathleen."

"This is Jason. Rachelle said I should call you."

"She did?"

"Yeah. So, ya like Spanish class?" I said.

"Yeah, it's pretty good. You like it?"

"It's okay."

"Hey, aaahhh, ya wanna go out?"

"Sure."

"Okay, cool."

I hung up the phone and stood in the kitchen as fear escaped my body with a loud, deep exhale. I had been knotted up since the moment Rachelle hurried away from me down the hall. It had taken all I had to dial her number. All my breath and every bit of nerve I could scrape together. It wasn't just a phone call, it was me stepping out of whatever safe, quiet corner I had been hiding in for the past few months.

Had Kathleen laughed, or hesitated, or said she wasn't interested, it would've hit me like a wrecking ball, confirming every quiet doubt I'd had about not being enough. Rejection, in that instant, would've meant retreat. Back to silence, back to watching from the other side of the gym floor, back to keeping feelings to myself because putting them out there clearly didn't end well. And the scariest part? I wasn't sure I'd be able to tell myself it didn't matter. Because it would have. A lot.

The molten metal of doubt flowed through my veins, slowly hardening into a new form. Kathleen and I were together; we were one. I was infatuated with everything about her. She was beautiful and intelligent (undoubtedly smarter than I was), and her heart was kind. When I was with Kathleen, the rest of the world ceased to exist: My parents' divorce . . . gone. School . . . gone. Sports . . . gone. Everything in the world disappeared, leaving only her.

I could feel my eyes smile at Zoe when I finished talking. I paused a few moments as the whirlpool of memories slowed and said, "I was in love for the first time in my life. I don't know when that happened. I don't even remember falling in love. When I look back on those years, I simply don't recall ever not being in love with her."

Zoe's face lit up as my happiness reflected off her skin.

"She changed my life, Zoe. You have no idea," I said.

Her feet pushed the stool under her chair and said, "Let's talk about that next time."

7
THE GRAFT

I stood outside The White Market, our local grocery store, one Saturday the following April, 1988, as the sun, finally strong enough to push out Old Man Winter, hit my face. Patches of snow, once pure white, fought to stay frozen in Bandstand Park across the street. Mother Nature was thawing out. The dirt roads had been releasing four feet of frost for the past few weeks, and the once frozen dirt roads had become a muddy, washboard mess. Kathleen, whose parents owned the place, came around the corner of the store and said, "Hey honey, my mom says I have to pump gas. But I don't wanna. You wanna do it for me?"

Pumping gas wouldn't be my first real job if I said yes. I had worked part-time as a dishwasher, or, as I liked to call it, a ceramic technician. I had recently spent the previous summer, the one before meeting Katleen, working as a laborer on a construction crew building a custom home with my dad in Marlborough, Massachusetts.

When I met Kathleen's parents for the first time, I was nervous, and I asked her, "What should I call them?"

"Everyone calls my dad George and my mom Mom," Kathleen said.

"Okay." That was way better than calling them Mr. and Mrs. Nichols, like my mom told me to do.

When I walked into Kathleen's house for the first time, my insides were jumping around. I saw them sitting at the kitchen bar. Before I even got out the words I had been practicing for the last fifteen minutes, George said, "Ahh, you must be Jason."

"Yup," I said, which was so far from the "Hi, George, I'm Jason" that I had scripted.

Kathleen's mom smiled at me over the top of the stove, which butted up against the counter where George sat. I smiled back, lifted my hand, and gave a little wave.

I was able to avoid calling Kathleen's dad George during that first visit, but I didn't escape her mom. Kathleen had asked me to get something from the kitchen at one point, and I walked in and froze. My eyes bounced around, not knowing where to start looking, and my throat tightened. "Ahhh, Mom," I muttered, "Kathleen wants water. Where are the cups?"

Kathleen's mom turned around, unfazed. "They're in the cupboard," she said, pointing to my left.

I didn't truly understand the significance behind the words "Mom" and "Dad" until I considered assigning those titles to someone else. My mom and I were fighting more than we weren't during that time, but something didn't sit right calling someone else "Mom." The feeling of betrayal ate at me for a few days. I had a mom, and it didn't seem right to call someone else Mom, so I settled on Ma.

"Well, do you wanna work for me?" Kathleen asked again

as we stood outside The White Market.

"Sure, why not?" I said.

Kathleen and I walked into the office at Speedwell, her family's business, to let her mom know she didn't want to work, but I was excited to pump gas for the first time. Ma explained that George was out of town, which was rare for him, and said, "Come on, I'll show you what to do."

Located at the corner of Route 5 and Red Village Road, Speedwell was the largest gas station in town, just a few hundred yards from the interstate exit. It exemplified the old saying about location, location, location.

In addition to gas pumps, Speedwell featured the only drive-through car wash in town, refilled propane grill bottles, and delivered home heating oil. It was more than just a mom-and-pop business, it served as a daily stop for many people, even when their gas tanks weren't running low. George was the face of Speedwell, manning the pumps every morning before climbing into the cab of the home delivery fuel truck, making sure his customers didn't run out of heating oil on those cold Vermont days. As for Ma, she made everything happen behind closed doors.

George stood about 5'10" and had dirty-blond hair and longish sideburns that framed his face and smile. Some people you meet have an aura about them, a presence that draws you in. That was George, a man who made you feel special when you were with him. George smoked Winstons and drank warm Miller Lite in the summer and cold Miller Lite in the winter, often saying, "It's not good to shock your stomach."

George had a unique way about him. He was different from

other adults I knew. He would pump someone's gas with the handle set to slow, lean against the car to chat, wash their windshield, and check their oil. Great with people and frugal with his money, George employed accounting methods that made Ma cringe. The wad of bills in his pocket followed a simple system: Bills facing one way were from gas sales, money turned upside down was for paying off someone's account (marked with their initials on the bill and the amount), and cash facing the opposite direction came from propane sales and car washes. The wad of money in his pocket would often grow to a few thousand dollars, and he'd wait until it became too bulky before he'd take it to Ma.

Occasionally, a money bag sat on the floorboard under his truck seat for a few days before he deposited it, which was strange since he loved visiting the ladies at the bank. I remember him telling Kathleen that the deposit needed to be such that all the bills faced the same way, heads up, and in order, saying, "That's how the ladies at the bank like it."

Ma, much more sophisticated than George, was his pearl in the oyster. She dressed in nice clothes, but nothing too fancy. She had a quiet yet strong and confident presence about her. Although Ma didn't talk much, you listened when she did.

My parents' divorce split the family apart like a metal wedge being driven into a block of oak. Mom and I weren't talking much, and the silence echoed through the house, striking me in the gut with every step I took toward the even quieter solace of my bedroom. When Mom and I did communicate, our stubbornness clashed, with her battling for dominance and me fighting for attention.

The Graft

Mom sold the house shortly after the divorce, and we eventually settled into a new home. This new house didn't know who I was or who our family used to be. I saw Dad everywhere at the old house, but in this new one, he wasn't just gone: It was if he hadn't existed. Maybe that's what Mom needed—a fresh start. It didn't feel like a fresh start to me. It felt more like a story that had ended midsentence.

Suffering from attention dehydration, I rebelled like many teenagers experiencing a divorce, struggling to understand my life and my place in the world. Dad, my emotional rock, was not by my side. For the first time, he wasn't there in person to guide me. When I was eight years old, he took me deer hunting in the mountains of Vermont. The snow was so deep that I struggled to keep up, lagging far behind. Realizing how hard it was for me, Dad said, "Just walk in my tracks, son." Now, almost sixteen years old, there were no more tracks to follow, and life was becoming as challenging as the deep snow I faced that day when I was eight.

I loved Speedwell because it provided me with a place to escape the loneliness of my new bedroom in my mom's new home. Dad lived four hours away in Massachusetts, and my mom slept just down the hall from me. Yet on most days, I felt further away from her than I did from Dad.

At this new home, the silence had a sharp edge that pressed in from all sides, compressing until it exploded with an argument. The kind of quiet where even the floorboards seemed reluctant to creak, like this new house itself was trying not to get in the way. The dinner table wasn't our old table. The clink of forks against plates made more noise than it should have, like the room was trying to remind me of what was missing. Mom's eyes often seemed tired, somewhere else, and mine were usually fixed on my food or the clock or the walls of my bedroom where I had smuggled in remnants of Dad and our old life as a family.

But at Speedwell, it was different. There, the days had activity and happiness; people had names, and I had purpose. George greeted me every time I arrived at work with a nod, a smile, and the words, "How's your day going?" before filling me in on what I needed to do.

Customers came through with their routines: going to the same pump, offering the same small talk, coming from the same place, and going the same direction. And over time, I wasn't just "the kid helping out" or Kathleen's boyfriend anymore. I was part of the place. Sometimes, George would ask about my day before I even had one. Ma always smiled when I walked into the office, asked how school was, or what plans Kathleen and I had that weekend.

It wasn't loud, this sense of belonging, and it didn't need to be. It was in the way George let me top off the tanks he had started or in the way Ma once quietly left a pair of work gloves on the counter near the register for when I filled propane bottles.

At my new home, I was surrounded by a newness I didn't want. At Speedwell, I was surrounded by acceptance and purpose. Kathleen's family was the kind of family that shows up when you need one. And in those long, slow hours at the pumps just before closing after a busy day, I realized that sometimes the place that feels most like home isn't the place where you sleep.

One morning, Kathleen's brother, Brian, wheeled into Speedwell far too fast as his right arm lifted flat over his head. His signature wave.

"What's up, Brian?" I said as I walked over to his red Ford F-150 truck.

"Haying," Brian said, hopping out from behind the wheel. "Could use some help. What time ya off?"

"Ah, three," I said.

"Shit, that ain't no good."

"What's no good?" George said, as he walked toward us.

"Jason off at three. Could use some help haying."

George lifted his chin toward me said, "I got it; go help Brian."

Brian had taken a liking to me soon after Kathleen and I started dating. That was after I didn't run away following his big brother lecture. During that calculated conversation, Brian explained exactly what would happen to me if I ever disrespected his sister.

Brian and I spent the afternoon in the hay field. He drove the tractor; I threw and stacked hay in the wagon he towed. Back at the barn, Brian loaded the hay bales on the escalator that was leaned high up into the hay loft, where he taught me how to stack the hay bales a dozen high so they wouldn't combust.

Every once in a while, Brian would yell up to me, "You stackin' 'em right?"

"Yup, cut side up," I'd yell back down.

Brian tossed me an ice-cold Coors Light after I stacked the last bale. The cold can hit my hot and sweaty underage hand, and a feeling of being older ran through me. I had never worked so hard, and I felt like an adult in that moment.

"Ain't got time to take ya back," Brian said. "Need ta start chores, might's well learn how ta milk."

"Works for me," I said, and the two of us sat on the truck's tailgate. As the oldest of two boys, I hadn't grown up with an older brother. The beer slid down my dry throat, and I thought, *This is why my younger brother, Garett, always wanted to hang out with me.*

Foam formed at the top of Brian's beer can as he popped the top of his second beer, and he said, "Ahhhh, the sound of my favorite author: Pull Tab to Open," just before he lifted the beer to his mouth.

Although I didn't grow up on a farm, I tell people I did because it's simpler than explaining the whole story. The truth is, my branch had just been grafted into the Nichols family tree, and it was as if I had been born again. A second life that started the day I met Kathleen and solidified the first day I threw hay, milked cows, and shoveled shit.

I didn't forget about my old self and my old life as Kathleen and I grew closer, but rather I pushed it aside to make room for a new one. Ma and George welcomed me deeper into their lives. Working on the farm with Brian, pumping gas with George, holding Kathleen's hand, and eating Ma's good cooking felt like life used to. Different, but similar.

Over the next several months, I kept busy with school and sports, working at Speedwell, and helping on the farm. Finding transportation to work was often challenging since I relied on my own two feet, which my dad humorously called "the shoe leather express." Mom had an extra car sitting in the driveway most of the time, but I was grounded from using it more often than not, which made getting to work even more difficult.

Kathleen's alarm would go off on many weekends around 4:00 a.m., but it wasn't for her to get ready for work. Instead, she would pick me up in her pajamas and drive me fifteen minutes to the farm so I could do chores and then return home to crawl back into bed.

Getting to the farm was more challenging after school. Sometimes, Kathleen would take me, or Brian would pick me up. When neither of those free taxi rides was available, one of my teachers, who lived near the farm, would drop me off on her way home. Blazing my path through life often felt uphill, with what seemed like never-ending challenges piling up like heavy, wet snow against my legs, but somehow everything always worked out in the end.

I played football in the fall, and Ma and George traveled to nearly every game, even when I sat the bench as a backup quarterback in the early part of my junior year. George would ask me if I was colorblind after a bad game when I had thrown a couple of interceptions. His needling felt comforting in a weird way. I ski raced in the winter, but I had stopped playing baseball my freshman year. Mom and Dad never let me quit anything growing up, saying, "If you start something, you gotta finish it." I finished baseball my freshman year, never to return to the field in high school after the coach sucked the baseball life right out of me. His yelling and constant beratement style of coaching might have worked for some, but not for me.

If sports had begun to feel like pressure and disappointment, the sugar woods gave me a quieter purpose without the yelling. Vermont is known for many things, but one of its most iconic products is Pure Vermont Maple Syrup. In January and February of 1989, Brian and I spent hours running miles of plastic sap lines through the woods and tapping thousands of maple trees in preparation for the sugaring season. The sap, which typically ran in the middle of March, used to drip into buckets hung on a tree. Now, however, it would get vacuum pumped straight to the sugarhouse. Sweet white clouds of steam would gather in the rafters of the sugarhouse before escaping through the ventilation panels like smoke from a steam locomotive barreling down the tracks. After countless hours of preparation in the sugar woods, the process of boiling the maple sap into syrup began.

Work stopped feeling like work the moment I said yes to Kathleen's question outside The White Market. I didn't even see it coming; I just saw her, my girlfriend, standing there, looking at me like I was someone worth asking. And after that, everything changed.

Whether I was pumping gas at Speedwell, milking cows long before the sun woke up, shoveling shit out of the barn, running sap lines through the woods, or shearing what felt like an endless sea of balsam firs into perfect Christmas trees, I'd catch myself thinking, *Is this real?* Not the work itself—that was always real, always hard—but the life I was living, which was unlike anything I could imagine.

I'd be up to my elbows in hay bales sneezing or bent over with pine needles down my back, and still, this quiet kind of joy would settle in. I had found something in this thing called work, and it made everything feel less like a job and more like . . . life.

Something I wanted to show up for. Something that looked forward to seeing me every day. Something I didn't want to miss.

This had become my life, and I cherished every single moment. The Nichols graft had healed, and my branch had became part of the Nichols family tree.

We spent the rest of our session with Zoe digging deeper into my feelings about my dad, the divorce, and my mom, as well as the introduction of this new family and Kathleen. Zoe brought me right back to those days, and it felt like I was in Florida, where it rains one minute and sun shines the next.

Zoe looked up at me after writing something down in her notebook and said, "Sounds like the Nichols family took you in."

"They did. I didn't like life much back then unless I was with Kathleen or working."

"Why's that?" Zoe asked.

"My mind always found a way to focus on what I didn't have. The only place I wanted to be was at work or by her side," I said.

Zoe jotted something down and said, "Sounds like a great place to start next time."

8

A SNAKE'S NEW SKIN

I arrived at Zoe's the following Thursday, my foot bouncing on the floor as I sat on the couch, twisting my watch back and forth on my wrist.

"Good morning, Jason, how are you?" Zoe asked.

"Yeah, I'm good," I said, nodding my head. "I've been busy at work, so that helps."

Zoe quietly nodded, as she had done so many times before.

"Know you wanted to talk about work and Kathleen," I said, pausing as my eyes hit their familiar place on the floor. "Work is a good thing for me. Has been ever since Speedwell."

My mind flashed through thousands of days I had spent working over the past two decades. I'd been afraid Zoe was going to try to convince me otherwise, saying something like, "Work is a job, a place you go to make money so you can pay the bills." Sure, work did those things, but I didn't have many bills in my early days at Speedwell. It paid the bills now as an adult, but even so, I couldn't remember the last time I went to work for a paycheck.

"Work's a good place for me," I said, making eye contact with her. "That's not a bad thing."

"No. No, it's not," Zoe said.

I let out a big sigh and nodded, looking back at the outline of the window on the floor.

We talked about work and Kathleen for several minutes, and somehow the topic of my eighteenth birthday came up, causing me to go quiet. But so did Zoe. My stomach felt like it used to when I sat on my dirt bike before a race, only more intense.

"I should probably tell you about that day," I said.

A couple of months before my eighteenth birthday, after a bonfire-sized fight with my mother—one I started, like I always did, with a match pulled from the endless book I carried in my back pocket—I threatened to move out. I meant it, too. Or at least, I wanted to mean it. The divorce had scorched through our family like a barbecue grill, first with a roaring flame as the lighter fluid burned and then as a slow glow as the coals heated up. While it hurt all of us, I was convinced it had burned me the worst. I was about to turn eighteen, old enough to tell myself I didn't need this anymore, especially not a mother who seemed more like a stranger with every passing day.

But beneath the anger, beneath the shouting and slammed doors, was something quieter and harder to admit. I wasn't just mad at her. I was lost. Everything had changed when Dad left, and instead of falling apart all at once like I thought I had done, it had continued in slow motion. Day by day, our house, which wasn't even my home, grew colder. Mom and I barely spoke unless it was to fight. And I didn't know how to reach her, or if she even wanted to be reached. So I did what I could to protect myself: I acted like I didn't care.

But I did care. I loved her. She was my mom. Of course I loved her. I cared so much it made my soul cry some nights, lying in bed, staring at the ceiling, wondering what I had done wrong. I wanted Mom to choose me over anything and everything, regardless of how big or small they may have been. I carried that pain like weights in the gym I couldn't put down, and every time my mom and I argued, it was like I was trying to unload them on her, hoping she'd finally understand what it felt like to be me.

When I threatened to move out, I wasn't just trying to win the fight. I was testing the world. I wanted to know if anyone would try to stop me, especially her. I wanted to prove I was strong enough to walk away, but deep down, I was terrified that those steps would mean disappearing completely. That if I left, she wouldn't come looking. That maybe I really didn't matter.

Staying meant facing the silence as I screamed inside. It meant waking up in a house that would never feel like home, pretending things were fine when they weren't. But leaving? That meant risking the connection I still had with Mom, broken as it was. I didn't know what I wanted more: to be an adult or seven years old. All I knew was that something had to give. And on that day, I decided it had to be me.

"No, you are not moving out. Not until you are eighteen," Mom's voice elevated.

"What are ya gonna do about it?" I quickly said, standing firm as we locked eyes.

Seriously, what was she going to do, spank me? I remembered how the one-inch-thick, eighteen-inch-long stick covered in masking tape hurt like hell on my ass when I was a kid.

I remembered the last time that stick found my backside, how I stood there, squeezing my eyes so tight, trapping the tears as they formed. I remembered it hurting like hell, but I stood there and took it, and that was the last time Mom or Dad ever used it on me.

"I'll send the cops to pick you up. That's what. Go ahead. Try it," Mom said.

"You're gonna send me to jail?" The thought of my hands squeezing the cold steel bars trapping me from the outside locked my body up tight, as if she had just slammed the jail doors shut.

Would she seriously send me to jail? Could she even do that?

"You're not leaving until you're eighteen. Not a day sooner," Mom said.

"That day can't come quick enough!" I yelled, storming down the hall. "What is the difference between today and a few months from now?" I slammed my bedroom door shut.

"Be careful what you wish for." Her voice traveled its way from the kitchen, down the hall, through the solid wood door and into my room.

Be careful what you wish for. I had heard this a few times since the divorce. I had wished for many things, but they never came true. I wished the divorce never happened and for my life to return to what it used to be, but that never happened. I wished for my dad to still be around, but he was gone, living four hours away, and wouldn't be moving back. I wished my mom would love me like she used to, before the divorce, when everything was normal. None of that would come true. Be careful what you wish for, no shit.

My moment came on the morning of Saturday, May 6, 1989. I woke a little after 7:00 a.m., still wrapped in the calm of sleep, those last few seconds where everything feels okay because life hasn't caught up to you yet. But then it did. The chaos of loneliness was having coffee with fear, waiting for me wake up. The silence wasn't peace anymore; it was emptiness. My eyes opened to a bedroom stripped bare; the walls, marked only by thumbtack holes where posters of athletes, dream cars, and models that once brought the room to life, looked gutted and abandoned. That room didn't just look empty. It mirrored exactly how I felt inside.

I was finally able to leave. I had packed up everything I owned a few days prior. Not that it took very long or more than a few boxes. Today was the day. It had finally come. I could finally get the hell out of that place.

I could finally leave, and I wanted to do so—but more than anything, I also wanted Mom to try to stop me. Not because I was eighteen and officially responsible for my own life, but because she didn't want me to go. This wasn't something I had planned in all the conversations I had imagined over the past few weeks. Up until that moment, the desire to leave reminded me of the tides at the beach: Some days I couldn't wait to get out of there, and other days that feeling would retreat back to sea, pulled by the forces of fear. But not today. Today, the anchor that kept me tethered to this place had been cut loose.

My door squeaked as it swung open, and I took methodical steps down the hall, as if I were in trouble. It felt like my lungs had shrunk overnight, barely holding any air. The moment was too strong for the muscles in my neck, and my eyes remained fixed on the carpet as I crept across it and into the kitchen, where Mom stood with her hands in the sink. I placed my hand on the doorknob a few feet away from her, pulled it open, and looked at her.

I wanted Mom to say something. I wanted her to say, "Don't go." I wanted her to say, "Please stay." To say, "I'm sorry." To say, "You're ready. You can do this. You're a grown man."

But I wasn't a grown man. I had simply turned eighteen years old, as if this was some magical moment in my life. I wanted her to say, "Good luck; I am always here for you." I wanted her to say, "I love you." But even though she said nothing, Mom's quietness wasn't quiet.

She had been right all along when she said, "Be careful what you wish for." How does the momma bird know when her chicks are ready to fly? Death is inevitable if she pushes her young out of the nest too early, and her quietness was shoving me out the door.

I planned to leave no matter what she said, but I wanted my mom at that moment. The mom who tucked me in at night as a child. The mom who comforted me when I was scared. The mom that fought off the monsters in my room and sat beside me while I cried. I wanted that mom, not this one.

A part of me hoped she would break down and cry, asking me to stay. What child wouldn't want this from their mom as they prepared to leap into the deep end of life without a lifeline? Just because I wanted to soar didn't mean I was ready to fly. A battle commenced in my mind between my future self (who was telling me, *Walk out the door, you can do this*), my old childhood self (telling me to crawl back into bed and Mom would come lay down with me), and my current self (mustering up the courage to cross the threshold).

My hand rested on the cool aluminum handle of the storm door, my fingers slightly open, delaying the tension building inside me. I knew that if I pushed the door open, it would trigger something within me. I looked at Mom again, and our eyes connected like metal to a magnet, but hers seemed hollow.

Was she hurting inside like I was? Why was she letting me go without saying anything? I didn't like her much at that moment, but I loved her. She was my mom. Of course I loved her. I would always love her.

My future self, the one begging me to take that next step, said, *She's your mom, of course she loves you. She wouldn't let you go if something really bad was going to happen. Come on, let's go.*

My fingers curled around the handle like a newborn's hand around a finger. With a push, the door swung open onto the porch, and I stepped out into the real world for the first time.

My slow, short gait gradually sped and lengthened as I walked toward Brian's red farm truck, which I had parked in the driveway the night before. The truck's rusty, bent-up hinges said, "Good morning," as I pulled open the door and hopped inside.

I had just climbed into the front seat of life's journey, gripping the wheel with both hands. I had a few hundred dollars, two jobs, and a girlfriend I loved more than anything, along with her family, whom I had come to adopt as my own.

The truck inched out of the driveway, and I was out of there like a snake slithering out of a skin that had gotten far too tight. I had spent the past few months preparing for this moment, knowing it could go one of two ways: Either I'd make

A Snake's New Skin

it on my own, or I wouldn't. But one thing was certain: I wasn't going back home with my tail between my legs. No way in hell.

As I pulled away, I heard my mother's voice in my head: "You made your bed; now you have to sleep in it." I hated that saying more than any of the others she used to throw my way, but this time, she wasn't wrong. I'd been talking a big game for a long time. Now it was time to prove to her and to everyone, but mostly to myself, that I could fly.

A couple of weeks earlier, I had sat down with my ski coach and science teacher, David Williams ("Dub-yah," as I called him), and told him I was planning to leave home. Without hesitation, he offered me a place to stay while I finished high school. Dropping out had never been on the table. My parents had raised me with one unshakable rule: If you start something, you finish it. Quitting wasn't an option, and I didn't want to—I actually liked school. The only time they ever bent on that belief was when I was twelve, after my first basketball game. My dad had looked me in the eye and said, "You don't have to play basketball if you don't want to." He knew it wasn't my thing.

I didn't fly very far on my maiden voyage, as "Dub-yah" lived only a few miles away. He had turned a tiny room, barely the size of a walk-in closet, into a space just big enough for a mattress on the floor and a few milk crates for my clothes. It wasn't much, but it had a roof, warmth, and most importantly, it was a branch to land on and launch from. There was fear in all of it, no question. But there was also something else, something I hadn't felt in a long time: hope. The kind that whispered, *This is going to work.*

I sat in front of Zoe, my eyes dry and my heart full of a mixture of sadness, hurt, and pride as I reflected on that birthday.

I inhaled, and my head shook a little from side to side. My eyes blurred, and the room disappeared, Zoe along with it. I could feel my breath work back in through my nose and fill my lungs. I held it for a moment, then my chest heaved upward as I forced more air in and pushed it down to my toes, as I had learned in yoga. I waited as long as I could and slowly felt my breath leave my toes and travel up through my feet, legs, hips, torso, and back out through my nose as the room and Zoe reappeared.

"Everyone kept telling me, 'Your mom loves you no matter what,'" I said. "I knew she loved me. But why didn't she say anything? Why didn't she stop me?" I looked away. "It felt like I was screaming, and she couldn't hear me."

Zoe leaned forward, her tone gentle but firm. "I don't think she couldn't hear you, Jason. Maybe she didn't know what to say. That's a different kind of silence. She was grieving, too."

I nodded. That day had crept back into my body, and I sat motionless. "Yeah, I'm sure she was. I didn't see it. I couldn't see anything except what I was going through," I said.

Sadness pushed its way into my heart as I thought about my mom and her stubbornness, her toughness, her loving heart. She had been hurting, too.

Zoe sat quiet for a moment and said, "What if your leaving wasn't about giving up on her but finally choosing to bet on yourself? Maybe, just maybe, that wasn't the end of something broken but the beginning of someone who became brave enough to walk into the darkness of the unknown."

"I've learned to always bet on myself," I smiled. "Always."

"And look at what you have accomplished."

I smiled again and nodded.

9

THE ENVELOPE

A month after moving out of Mom's house, I was sitting on a silver folding chair placed on the fifteen-yard line of the football field, facing the makeshift stage that had been set up in one end zone on graduation day. I remembered the young boy that pressed his chest up against the green rope circling the field, dreaming about being a football player. I remembered how vividly I could see that dream in my head after every football game. It was so real I could almost touch it.

    I looked over and saw my buddy and laughed to myself as I remembered the biggest football game of my career as a junior against our rivals. Thirteen seconds after the opening kickoff, we were already down six points. I remembered the looks of defeat through the face masks as I entered the huddle and took a knee. Dad asked me in the truck after freshman tryouts if I was ready to lead the team. If I wanted the ball. I said yes. Partly because that was what Dad wanted to hear me say, partly because that was what I wanted to say, but mostly because that was who I wanted to become.

I looked at the guys in the huddle, their faces screaming defeat, and said, "Well, that fucking sucks." I called the running play and looked at Lefaivre, a senior running back who was team captain, and said, "Lefaivre, run their ass over!"

He gave me a nod, and I shifted my eyes to the linemen and said, "Let's open a damn hole, whaddya say?"

Someone said, "Let's do it!"

The team broke the huddle with more excitement than we had had the night before at the pep rally. I could still hear the sounds of helmets and pads colliding on that first play of the game as I sat there during graduation. The team huddled up for the second play of the game and one of the linemen said, "Come on guys, we can do this. They ain't so tough."

A few plays later, I threw the best interception of my life. The ball sailed forty yards in the air to one of my running backs sprinting down the field and was intercepted by my wide receiver, who was supposed to run a flag route to the corner, but instead he ran a post route to the middle of the field by mistake. The ball was just out of reach of my running back and landed in the outstretched hands of my wide receiver. Our rivals never lead again after the extra point.

Sitting in the folding chair, I took a deep breath. So much had happened since those days pressed up against the green rope, wanting to be inside, wanting to be living my dream.

Moments later, I walked across the stage, shook the headmaster's hand as he handed me my well-rounded diploma, and exited the stage. That piece of paper was supposed to signify accomplishment, a chapter in my existence, the keys to the vehicle of life, but as I sat back down in my chair, something was missing. I looked around the football field and saw my classmates, families, and teachers. I looked for Mom and Dad. They were there somewhere, but I couldn't see either of them anywhere on the field. The emptiness was still there, calling my name, and then I realized what was missing. There wasn't a green rope anywhere to be found.

What do I want to do with my life? How do you even go to college? Where do you start? I had so many questions, and they all seemed to lead to the same answer: *I don't know.*

Can a guy who scored far less than 1,000 on his SAT even get into college? Will a college accept you when your wallet is so thin that you can't even feel it when you sit down? The questions looped in my head like the track around the football field, each time tightening the knot in my stomach. My chest felt heavy, like when I got the wind knocked out of me on that touchdown pass as two defenders drove me in the turf. I sat on the folding chair, staring at the track that circled the football field, waiting for the answers to go sprinting by.

Mom had been saying, "College is what happens after high school," which was ironic because neither of my parents attended college. Mom said this is what happens, but she never taught me how. My friends seemed to have a plan, or at least a direction, it seemed. Me? I had questions. So many questions. And they all circled back to the same dead end. I kept returning to one big one: Could a guy like me, who didn't sniff a 1,000 on the SAT, actually get into college? Was that even a real option?

Would a college even look at me? Would they care who I

was? Or would they just see the three-digit number on the SAT report and the goose egg in my bank account and move on?

The pressure buzzed in my ears. I could feel my heart in my throat, pounding out every fear I had about the future: *What if I fail? What if I never figure it out? What if this is as far as I go?* One of the happiest days of my life—or that's what I thought graduation was supposed to be—had more fear hiding in it than anything.

But underneath it all, buried under the rubble of doubt and the noise of not knowing, there was a flicker of something else. Not confidence. But a voice, the same voice I heard from the porch weeks earlier, begging for me to walk through the door and into life. My future self said, *There's a way. Don't quit.*

Dad had told me once, "Find something you are good at and love, then figure out how to make a living doing it." While I enjoyed milking cows and pumping gas, or being a petroleum transfer engineer as I called it, I knew I didn't want to do either for the rest of my life.

Going to college, as Mom said, would give me the best chance at success. But success at what? How was I supposed to know what I wanted to do for the rest of my life? I had just experienced the rest of my first life when I walked out of Mom's house, never to return. This was a brand-new life, one void of direction and green ropes. It felt like I was looking up into space, my eyes reaching for the edge of the universe, knowing that every direction pointed to someplace different, and it was overwhelming.

What am I good at? I thought. I was good at math and science, and I liked them both. According to Dad's philosophy, the answer was hidden in those two subjects.

I needed some help and thought about all the people in my

The Envelope

life that I could call upon for advice. I knew a lot of people from my time pumping gas, but I didn't know many who had gone to college, or at least I didn't think they had attended. How can someone give you advice on something they have never done before? Did Kathleen's parents go to college? I didn't recall them ever talking about it. Brian went to a technical college, but he went for farming. Was that even the same thing? My Uncle Tom fought in Vietnam, so I didn't think he went. My list was as long as the number of celebrities I had met: zero.

I knew there had to be someone who could help me, and then it struck me. If anyone would know how to get into college, it would be Dwight Davis, the headmaster of Lyndon Institute that had days before handed me the keys to my future. Surely, Mr. Davis would help me.

"Mr. Davis, I'm thinking about going to college, but I need some help," I said.

"That's great to hear."

After sharing the age-old advice from my mom and dad, Mr. Davis suggested I consider environmental science at Lyndon State College, located in town. I don't remember ever discussing this degree's career opportunities, how much money I could make, or whether it was even a wise decision. All I knew was that pursuing environmental science at Lyndon State College gave me a plan. Most importantly, attending college would give me a place to live and food to eat, and I desperately needed both of those.

One of the great things about growing up in my hometown was that "everyone knew you—everyone." However, the downside was that your personal life could feel like the steel ball in a pinball machine, bouncing from house to house. As the score increased with every ricochet, so did the story about you and your life.

"I don't have any money. Can you even go to college if you're flat broke?" I asked.

"It's possible," he said. "There are programs in place for people like you."

"That's good. So, how much is college gonna cost me?"

"Lyndon State is about seven thousand dollars."

My eyes widened. "Seven thousand dollars?" How the hell would I come up with seven thousand dollars? "I ain't got that kinda money," I said.

"You don't have to. Most people don't at your age."

No shit, I thought. Only rich people had that kind of money lying around. I didn't even know what that much money looked like. "So, ah, what do I do?" I said.

"You apply for loans and grants," Mr. Davis said.

I knew what loans were, but I had never heard of a grant before. "Grants, what are those?" I said.

"Grants are free money that you don't pay back."

"Free money. Let's get those," I said.

"It isn't quite that simple, but given your situation, you should qualify for many of them."

Mr. Davis explained the application process and asked, "Would you like me to write a recommendation letter on your behalf?"

"A recommendation letter?" I questioned, confused as to what that even was.

"Yes, I am willing to write one explaining your situation.

The Envelope

Colleges use your parents' income to determine how much financial assistance you will receive, and a letter of recommendation could help you."

I sat there in front of Mr. Davis and thought about this letter he was willing to write. I couldn't imagine a way for him to say anything that would look good—for me, Dad, or Mom. How did he plan to explain what had happened in my life? What would he say? That I walked out of my house the day I turned eighteen without much of a plan? Boy, that would look good.

Would he say that I had had a job milking cows and pumping gas, but I'd most likely need to quit one or both to attend college? How could he explain that I was a good kid worthy of having someone give me thousands of dollars for college when I didn't even know what I wanted to do with my life? I sure hoped he wouldn't tell them that half the reason for going was so that I had a place to live and food to eat.

"My dad doesn't have any money," I said. "I don't know if my mom does either, but I ain't gonna ask for her help."

Mr. Davis wrote the letter, and I received very little special treatment. Between the standard grants and loans I qualified for, there would be just enough money to cover my freshman year at Lyndon State College. How I qualified for a dime was beyond me, but I wasn't asking any questions.

Little did I realize that college would be harder than high school. I had never applied myself academically, as it required minimal effort to be an average student. My parents had been happy with my grades, which was good enough for me.

My minimal effort in the classroom worked most of the time, but it was far from foolproof. I had to write a paper once about Lenin in a history class. Like clockwork, I started a couple of days before the paper was due. The teacher lectured us all about the importance of paying attention in class and reading the assigned chapters in our textbook as she handed back the papers and said, "One of you wrote about Lennon—John Lennon, the musician." I still remember the laughter as my own breath got stuck in my throat.

I quickly learned that environmental science wasn't for me. Maybe it wasn't just the major. Maybe college in general wasn't right for me. I enjoyed college algebra, zoology, and botany. Invertebrate zoology was my favorite, as I discovered there is a life beneath the surface of everything I could see with my naked eye. But this wasn't high school, and the strategy that had earned me average grades didn't work anymore. This had to be one of those experiments like basketball as a kid, only Dad was there to tell me I didn't need to play anymore. Now, I had to make that decision for myself.

So, I tasted the glue on the back of a stamp, stuck it on my environmental science curriculum envelope, left the return address blank, and mailed it in for the remainder of my freshman year. A career in environmental science wasn't in the cards for me.

My life horizon was up close and personal. We stared each other down like two heavyweight prizefighters before the opening bell. Me on one side, and everything I was afraid to admit on the other. I had built this image of myself, this perfect plan that somehow defied logic: I'd go to college, make something of myself, and prove to everyone and myself that I could beat the odds. But the truth was written in the numbers

The Envelope

I couldn't escape: a cumulative GPA of one-point-something.

The idea of having short-, mid-, and long-term goals for my life was hard to wrap my head around. Some of the smartest people I knew stood in front of classrooms, preaching the importance of goal setting like it was the key to everything.

But how was I supposed to set goals when I didn't even know what I wanted to do with the rest of my life? Hell, half the time I didn't know what I was doing the next day. Make small, simple goals and start checking them off your list, they'd say. Once you hit one, set another, then another. It sounded easy when they said it, and it was, but even then, it felt more like putting a Band-Aid on my leg when I needed a tourniquet.

I remembered Gram's apartment, how her walls were covered with maps, each one marked with bright, highlighted trails showing where she'd been and where she might go next. But a map only mattered if you were actually going somewhere. The map that hung on my wall was of Lyndonville, and the highlighter ran from the Nichols family to the unique mixture of gasoline and cow shit.

10
A CLOVER PATCH

A couple therapy sessions later, and with what looked like a new notebook and pen, Zoe said, "You've talked a lot about Kathleen, her parents, and her brother." She paused a moment. "Your adopted family, as you call them."

I nodded, wondering where this was going.

"Were there any other people in your life, besides them, that gave you a similar feeling?"

"Of being adopted?" I questioned.

"Yes. That adopted feeling?" she said.

"Yeah, there were."

"Would you like to talk about them?"

"Yeah, we can do that." I paused. "I'm not sure how to explain Uncle Stan and Aunt Deb," I said. "You know, so you would understand."

"Why don't you share a story about them with me. Do you have one?"

"Yeah, I have a lot of 'em."

A Clover Patch

As a child, I grew up at Uncle Stan's hunting camp, in a way. I wasn't related to Uncle Stan or his wife, Aunt Deb, but they were like family, and I don't remember a time when they were not in my life. Aunt Deb and my mom were inseparable when I was young, and she was the one that taught me how to hunt for four-leaf clovers. I remember the first four-leaf clover she showed me. She held it between her fingers, rubbing the stem as the petals twirled. I remember thinking how cool it was, as I'd never seen one before. She told me how special and rare four-leaf clovers were and that they were good luck charms. When I asked where she found it, she said, "Over there," as she pointed to the side of her house.

My eyes sprinted as if to see one from where I stood.

"Want me to show you?" she asked.

There we stood, bent over with our hands on our knees, staring into the emerald-green patches of clover scattered across the yard. I looked so hard that my vision became blurry, but we didn't find one. I remember being so disappointed I wanted to cry. I was maybe six years old.

Aunt Deb saw the look on my face and said, "Jason, there aren't many four-leaf clovers alive, and you don't find one every time you look. That's what makes them so special."

Those words helped, but I was still disappointed.

Several days later, Aunt Deb helped me find my first lucky charm. We were hunting them together on the lawn at her house when she said, "Jason, there's one right here, I can see it."

"Where is it?" I ran over to her, excited, and looked to the ground and then back up at her. "Where is it?"

"Look and see if you can find it," she told me. "It's right

down there." She pointed to the ground.

I was thrilled. My eyes bounced around as I looked and looked. I looked at every clover in front of me, but nothing had four leaves.

"I can't find it," I said, with defeat in my voice.

"You have to keep looking if you want to find it. It's right there, I promise," she said.

I looked for what seemed like hours and and then yelled, "I found it! I found it!" I pulled it from the ground and ran toward her.

Aunt Deb would explain to me that finding four-leaf clovers (or anything rare or worth holding on to, as I would realize later in life) was never really about luck. It was about focus, about learning to look past the obvious and paying attention to the details hiding in plain sight.

She would say, "You have to want to find one and believe it's possible," even if I'd searched a hundred times and come up empty.

At that point in my life, I was just a kid scanning the grass for a good luck charm.

In retrospect, Aunt Deb was teaching me something bigger, whether she knew it or not. She showed me that finding something special took more than just looking. It took intention. It meant seeing beyond the everyday, beyond what everyone else walked past, to notice what was right in front of me if I was willing to slow down and look.

Using a microscope in college reminded me of hunting for four-leaf clovers as I peered down the scope. Things looked totally different when you really examined them. Aunt Deb

A Clover Patch

introduced me to patience and the kind of muted hope that keeps me searching, even when I have no idea what I might find.

Many years later, I was hunting four-leaf clovers on the hillside behind my cabin in Mississippi when something didn't look right. My eyes were deep in the clover patch, and there was a pattern I had never seen before. I reached down, broke the stem, and pulled it to my face. A six-leaf clover? Seriously? I didn't know this existed, even after all these years of hunting. I smiled and thought of Aunt Deb, wondering if she had ever found one. Minutes later, in the same patch of clover, I pulled my first five-leaf clover out of the ground, and then a four-leaf one. I had found a six, a five, and a four in less than fifteen minutes. I stood on the hillside and laughed at myself. I laughed at how silly I must look, in my forties, hunched over looking at clovers. Then I wondered: How many fives and sixes had I missed in my life because I was looking for fours?

But that lesson didn't stay in the backyard. It showed up again in the woods in the form of my uncle. He, whom I later nicknamed "Doc," after Doc Holliday from *Tombstone*, would cough up a lung three or four times a day while his Camel non-filter cigarette was lodged between his fingers or burned in the ashtray beside him.

I never saw Doc hunt for a four-leaf clover, but he lived for deer season. While the number of "official" seasons in Vermont is up for debate nowadays, it never was for Doc, who would say, "There are only fifty weeks in a year" when discussing the two-week-long whitetail deer season.

I would sit and listen for hours to Doc's stories about tracking deer in the snow, sometimes for miles, before ever laying eyes on the animal. He would describe old hunts as if they had happened yesterday, sharing tales of deer backtracking, following them in the brook for a few hundred yards, and accounts of deer actually walking backward. He once told me, "If you are going to track a deer, you must be willing to spend five hours on the track before you see him. You can't be worried about where you are going or getting lost. And if you aren't willing to sleep in the woods, you are wasting your time." Doc was known as one of the best hunters around, and I never outgrew the desire to sit close enough to hear him talk.

Uncle Stan's son was also named Stan, but everyone called him Grease or Greaser, including Uncle Stan and Aunt Deb. Greaser was a logger, and the name fit him well. His muscles bulged through his dirty, always torn up T-shirt, and he had a strut to his stride. Every time I saw him, I tried to picture myself growing up to look like him. Greaser often lumbered down to the pond's edge at Uncle Stan and Aunt Deb's house, where I would fish for hours and ask, "They biting?" I always liked it when he sat on the bank with me for a few minutes, but he never stayed as long as I wanted him to.

Sometimes, I would fish so long I could still see the red-and-white plastic bobber floating in my mind when I tried to sleep. I was eight years old, and Greaser nine years older than me. He looked like Rocky Balboa, he was the coolest guy I knew, and I wanted to be just like him.

Uncle Stan's hunting camp, an A-frame, was perched a few feet off the ground, with scabs of plywood covering the annual holes porcupines had gnawed. I saw those holes for the first time as a young boy, maybe six or seven, when my parents took me to Uncle Stan's camp in the summer for the day. When we arrived, I asked Dad what the holes were in the walls, as it looked like something had chewed its way in or maybe even out.

Dad said, "Oh, those are porcupine holes. They eat the wood."

I remember tiptoeing inside, scared they would still be there, waiting to attack me. Mom promised they weren't and took me by the hand to show me as I walked cautiously with half of my body behind her. She was right: nothing there except lots of mouse poop.

Behind the camp, there was a small A-frame outhouse that had weathered many a nor'easter, with a toilet seat screwed to the bench above the deep hole in the ground. I would be in my late teens before someone would devise the clever idea of hanging a second toilet seat above the woodstove for those frigid, below-zero mornings during deer season.

Zoe's face puckered a little as she pictured the outhouse. I could see her imagination was running wild, which made me smile.

I remember being sixteen years old, feeling the camp's emptiness seep into my body as I watched taillights disappear through the trees down the camp road as everyone headed to the bars. The quiet surrounding me as I stood on the front porch of the A-frame was broken only by the wind rustling in the darkness. There were a couple of hard-and-fast camp rules: no store-bought meat after the opening day of deer season, and no radios. I was left alone, accompanied only by my thoughts for the next few hours. *Why did they always have to leave? Why didn't anyone stay to keep me company?*

After they left, I would guide the beam of my flashlight

fifty yards downhill through the trees to the spring. A dented eight-inch soup pot hung from a branch next to a makeshift funnel created from an old two-liter bottle of Sprite. I scooped water from the shallow spring, careful not to stir up the dirt, and filled two red five-gallon gas cans. Many times I had tried to carry both thirty-five-pound water jugs at once, but I could never make it back to camp without stopping. I'd get so far up the hill and then have to stop. I'd look for the nearest tree, stump, or low-hanging branch to mark how far I had gone. After resting a minute, I'd pick them both up and trudge a little further before I had to stop again. Fetching water was one of my jobs, but I didn't mind. Having a job at camp made me feel important. It made me feel like one of the guys.

Once back inside, I would clean off the kitchen table, throw the empty beer cans in a trash can, clean the kitchen, lug in firewood, and finally sweep the floor, with hours still needing to pass before anyone returned.

Doing the camp chores while everyone was out drinking kept my mind busy, but then, the stillness of camp wreaked havoc on my mind. I was mad at my parents for divorcing. I was angry at Dad for moving away. Why did he have to go so far? I was mad at my mom for being so distant when she was so close. I missed him. I missed her. I missed the way it was.

Once I was alone and my chores were done, I'd grab a pen from the old coffee cup that sat on the counter. Then I'd find a brown paper bag that had once held someone's groceries and sit at the table. I'd unsnap the leather latch of my buck knife, the one looped through my belt, and slide it out. It was the same six-inch, black-handled buck knife Doc

A Clover Patch

and Greaser carried, worn in the same spot on my hip as Greaser wore his.

The yellow propane mantle above me gave off a soft *whoooing* sound, casting a dim glow and throwing my shadow across the table. Each time I ran the blade through the paper bag, I felt a little surge of pride rise in me. Doc had taught me how to sharpen that knife, and I could still hear his voice saying, "It ain't sharp if it don't cut paper."

Then, I'd write a letter to Kathleen. I wrote about my time in the woods, what I saw, and how things were going at camp. I shared my frustrations about my mom and how much I missed my dad. I loved Kathleen with all my heart, especially the broken pieces, and I would tell her all about it. I pictured our future together: married, with kids, maybe working in the family business. I longed for the kind of life I had before the divorce, a happy family under one roof.

When I ran out of space on the paper bag I had cut into a square, I ended the letter with, "I love you, sweatheart," not knowing it was spelled s-w-e-e-t. Then, with a twist of the lever on the propane light, camp would go dark, and the emptiness inside the A-frame tucked me inside my sleeping bag.

In the morning, Doc always woke up first, and it wasn't long before he started banging the broom handle on the ceiling, disrupting the orchestra of snores. Making breakfast, he would sit on a block of wood next to the barrel woodstove flipping the bread that toasted on the hot metal. The smell of instant coffee had already begun to drift through the camp, pulling everyone out of their sleeping bags.

Greaser had worn two layers of Duofold long underwear,

the outer layer turned inside out to cover the holes in the first. He pulled his Herman Survivors leather work boots down from the nail above the woodstove, where they had been drying out from the day before. Mother Nature was calling, and Greaser lost the silent tug-of-war the rest of us were still playing. He trudged through the snow, the exposed steel toes of his boots dragging the laces through the snow toward the outhouse. That morning, he was the one who had to knock the ice off the toilet seat. A few years still had to pass before he would be carrying the warm toilet seat from above the woodstove.

Zoe looked down at the notebook for a moment and then back up at me. I expected her to say something, but as usual, she just waited.

"I've been pretty lucky, I guess," I went on.

Zoe nodded and smiled, "Yes, you have been. Sounds like there are a lot of people that love you."

"Then why do I feel like this? I don't know how to explain it. It's like an emptiness, but not really. I don't know, it's like no matter how hard I work or what I do, a piece of me just doesn't fill up or something."

"What would you like to fill up?" Zoe asked.

I sat silent, my head feel and hit my hands, "That's just it. I don't know. I mean, I look back on my life and I was lucky at times, but man, I had some shit happen that just sucked."

Zoe didn't know it yet, but the worst was still inside me. It had taken all I had to share what I had so far. It was hard for me, a grown man, to talk about being afraid even if the times I chose to share were when I was a kid. That baseball woke up the fear inside me, and it hadn't ever left. The divorce, walking out of my house, my failed attempt at college—it was all I could do to share that stuff. I had told her things I hadn't ever told anyone.

Several times I went home after our sessions exhausted, feeling like I did running those hills in football practice. I wouldn't be gasping for air, but my body would feel beat to death, only from the inside out. There were so many things in my life I wished didn't happen. So many things that seemed to compound and run me over like a freight train.

"Why did the bad stuff have to be so bad?" I said, hoping she would have a brilliant answer so obvious it would be like the three-leaf clovers I ignored.

"That's a really good question worth asking," she said.

I looked at her and could tell she could see the desperation in my eyes.

"This emotion you are feeling is understandable, Jason. It's okay to feel it, and you are brave to acknowledge it."

Hearing those words didn't fix anything, and they didn't come close to answering my question, but I felt a little relief and sat back on the couch, hearing Dad's voice: "Emotions are real, son, but they aren't always justified." I still wasn't sure if I totally agreed with him or not, but he was right about one thing: They were real.

"Would you like to talk about what happened after you discovered environmental science wasn't for you?"

"That's fine," I said. "A lot happened, that's for sure."

"Great, let's talk about that next time."

11

HEADS OR TAILS

After five months in college, the smell of freshly cut balsam filled the Nichols house with the scent of Christmas, and I had a much-needed break from a degree I wanted to love but didn't even like. The tree in the living room, one Brian or I sheared that summer, reminded me of the ones from my childhood, the ones that drank water from a red metal base on the floor, with crayon-colored lights strung through decorations and upside-down fishhooks of peppermint.

    As a boy, I was filled with curiosity looking into the fireplace, wondering how someone as big as Santa could fit through it. The questions never stopped coming, and my mom would lie next to me at bedtime, trying to answer them all. But these days, the answers seemed to flow like maple sap below freezing. That Christmas, my childhood bed was replaced by the couch at Ma and George's while I was on break from Lyndon State College.

    As a child, the only thing I had to wait for on Christmas morning was Mom and Dad's coffee to brew, which always took forever. I would stand in front of the presents, my feet running in place, begging my parents to let me start. Much to Kathleen's disliking, she had to wait too, only for her dad's return from Speedwell. He would always say, "People need gas on Christmas Day, too."

It later became Kathleen and her mom and George waiting on me to finish pumping gas and Brian to wrap up chores. Life didn't pause for holidays. Not at Speedwell. Not on the farm. The gas station, like the farm, was open 365 days a year. By the time Brian was running Speedwell Farms, a fourth-generation enterprise dating back to his great-grandfather in the late 1800s, blending life and work had become second nature for all of us.

"Good morning, Dee Dee," George said as I followed him through the door.

Our table at Oscar's Bakery sat to the left. It was the same one we sat at yesterday and the same one we'd sit at again tomorrow. I grabbed the top of my chair, tilted it slightly, and pulled so the wooden chair skidded toward me. Dozens of people would sit there through the day, but at 5:00 every morning, this chair knew it would see me.

George sat to my left, and soon, all the chairs were reunited with their faithful owners as our table filled with tradesmen.

I eagerly anticipated the first few minutes of every day, as each person would either make eye contact and say, "Morning," or glance my way, nod, and say, "Jason." Those first few moments performed CPR on my spirit and felt as good as the steaming cup of caffeine I cradled in my hands.

Tobacco two-stepped with coffee beans above the table, swirling together in the awkward tango of a middle school dance. Like a thirteen-year-old awkwardly standing in the corner of a school gym at homecoming, my eyes danced to the beat of their conversation: local politics, construction projects, and the news of the town.

The smell of wheat toast and butter never got old as Dee Dee placed my plate in front of me. She didn't ask anymore, and I wouldn't have changed my order now even if I were starving.

"Thank you," I said, smiling.

"You're welcome," Dee Dee replied, gliding around the table with her coffee pot like a vulture circling the treetops, searching for a hidden scent in the trees below.

I sat silently, listening to the varying opinions on whatever topic had taken over that morning. As the conversations grew more intense, I could feel the firmness of my chair pressing against my back, the tension crawling up my spine. I turned my eyes toward George, waiting for his opinion, something to latch on to so I could quietly agree with a head nod in approval or disagreement and relieve the mounting pressure building inside me.

Every morning, the roller coaster ride lasted the same amount of time, and I knew exactly what was about to come.

At 5:50, George looked at me and said, "Heads or tails?" with a quarter balanced on his thumb. The loser went to work, and the winner got to stay for one more cup of coffee.

"Heads," I said as the quarter flipped into the air. My eyes tracked it, rising, pausing, then plunging back down, while I held my breath.

"It's heads," George said with a smile, like he'd just won instead of lost. He stood up, pulled a wad of cash from his pocket, and dropped a five-dollar bill on the table.

The guys around us called out their goodbyes as he pushed his chair back. George looked at me and said, "I'll go open the station. See ya at work when you get there."

"Yup," I said, settling in for one more hot cup, and the feeling, however fleeting, of belonging at the table tightened my insides.

Sitting at the table without George gave me that same sinking feeling I had in trigonometry class: proud to sit up front, but praying not to be called on because I didn't understand a sine, cosine, and tangent. The others carried on like usual, but to me, it felt like the star player on my team had been pulled from the game. I sipped my coffee, trying to look calm, while silently voicing opinions I'd never dare say out loud.

Still, it was hard not to enjoy winning the coin toss. Being at that table with the blue-collar elites made me feel like I belonged, even if no one spoke to me or seemed to notice I was there. I listened closely, soaking in the swirl of talk, the mix of breakfast and smoke, and the heat of my own awkwardness. Maybe they didn't see me, or maybe they did. Either way, I was there.

The conversation about inflation cut off a story someone was telling about current events, and I felt my spine straighten as heat rushed through me like morning rush hour traffic. I didn't know much about inflation, just that it meant things cost more. But I did know that it meant the price of fuel would go up because George talked about it all the time.

He'd say, "We lose money when the fuel prices go up. Can't raise prices as fast as they raise them on us. We gotta make our money when the prices go down by going down slow."

My eyes blinked rapidly. *Say it. Just say it,* I thought. My gut was full of the words, the way my childhood bug jar used to be packed with fireflies. I took a deep breath and leaned forward. The only problem was, when I opened my mouth, nothing came out. I inhaled again, glanced around the table, exhaled, and finally managed to say, "Inflation sucks."

But before the words could settle, someone jumped in with, "Hey, did anyone catch the news last night?" And, just like that, the topic of inflation was dead, and my opinion died on the table.

Later, when I got to Speedwell, George asked, "Well, what'd I miss?"

"Not much," I told him.

"Learn anything good?"

"Nah. We talked about football, how much snow we're getting this year, and someone mentioned something about hornet nests being high."

George laughed. "Hornet nests?"

"Yeah, makes sense," I said.

"That's an old wives' tale. Hornets die in the winter."

They die? Really? It actually made sense, but I still felt a little foolish. Trying to steer the conversation somewhere safer, I added, "Oh yeah, we talked about inflation too, 'bout how much stuff is costing these days."

"That's true. Fuel's going up," George said.

Most days, I'd pump gas until two o'clock, then head to the farm for chores. After finishing milking around six, I'd head back to Speedwell. Many nights, George would have the fuel truck, Old Blue, already loaded and waiting. Our first stop was always the Miss Lyndonville Diner, where he'd buy me dinner to go.

One December night, I jolted awake around midnight to find George standing over me.

"Get up, Jason. We gotta go to work. Jim Sully's out of oil."

When we got to Speedwell, I asked, "How much ya want me to put in?"

"Might as well fill 'er up," George said.

Jack Frost had danced all over Old Blue's windshield, and her engine slugged as I turned the key. As the cab slowly started to warm, I remembered the first time George asked me to fill up Old Blue on my own. I said, "Okay," and walked slowly away from him. I had seen him drive Old Blue before, plenty of times, and I knew how to drive a standard transmission.

I'd been driving one since I was about twelve on the horse farm Gramp Graves, the one who got me into motocross, used to caretake for. All I could think as I approached Old Blue that first time was, *Don't grind the gears whatever you do.*

Old Blue's joints creaked, and her stiffness eased as I released the clutch and pressed the stubborn gas pedal, moving her from where she was parked to the fuel pump. Like me, Old Blue had just been awakened, and we were both glad to see each other.

Misty clouds escaped from my mouth like morning steam rising off a pond in the fall as I stood on top of Old Blue. I watched as the two-inch pipe filled with home heating oil poured warmth into Old Blue and into me.

"She's full," I said ten minutes later, climbing down the ladder fixed to her side.

We pulled up to Jim Sully's house, and I hopped out of the passenger seat. We were a team, and our roles rarely changed. My unspoken goal was always the same: Drag the two-inch-thick rubber hose from Old Blue's belly to the fuel pipe on the side of the house and be waiting before George could yell, "Okay, she's ready." I never told him, but it meant a lot to me when my voice crystallized in the icy air just before his. It was my way of showing how much it mattered that he brought me along.

With the hose looped over my shoulder, I headed toward the house. As I reached the edge of the driveway, my leg sank deep into a snowbank, and I faceplanted into the snow. Struggling to get up, I heard George laughing from behind me. "You okay?" he called out.

"I'm good," I muttered, flopping around in the snow, trying to free my leg.

When I finally stood up, I looked like Frosty the Snowman. "Damn, that's cold," I said, shaking my jacket free of snow.

George's job was easy. He'd put a ticket in the meter, set the dial for the fuel volume, and yell to me when he was ready. Once the pump shut off, I'd pull the nozzle from the pipe leading into the house, spin the cap on tight, and yell back, "Okay, reel 'er in!"

That's where the hard part started, for George, anyway, as he pushed the button to automatically reel in the hose while I walked it back.

"Come on," he said, walking toward the house. "I'll show you how to start the furnace."

Jim Sully met us at the front door as we stamped the snow

off our boots. George said, "We put a hundred gallons in. We'll go start your furnace for ya."

We crossed the worn hardwood kitchen floor and stood at the top of the basement stairs.

"The switch is on the left," Jim's voice called from behind us. My body tensed as I descended, my shoulders nearly brushing both walls of the narrow stairwell, and my feet turned sideways to fit on the skinny treads. It reminded me of my nana's house in Rhode Island where my dad grew up.

George walked me through the steps to bleed the fuel line at the furnace, making sure all the air was out. I hit the red reset button on the burner, and with a roar, the furnace ignited.

As we climbed the stairs, Jim called from the kitchen, "Thank you guys for coming out so late. I really appreciate it."

"Of course. We're happy to do it," George said, shaking his hand.

After five minutes of talking about nothing important, George and I made our way to the door.

"Thanks again," Jim said, shaking George's hand again and then mine.

"You're welcome. Call us any time," I said, releasing his hand.

Mother Nature's breath hit my lungs as we stepped off the porch. I turned back just in time to see Jim's breath crystallize in the winter air as he said, "Merry Christmas to the family."

"Merry Christmas to yours, too," George replied.

Once we were back inside Old Blue, George looked over at me and said, "Might's well deliver fuel on the way home, don't ya think?"

"Sure, why not?" I said.

But the truth was, I felt like a ten-year-old again and Dad had just asked, "Wanna go look for some deer after dinner?" Who was he kidding? Of course I wanted to deliver fuel on the way home.

A few minutes later, we made a right-hand turn onto a one-way street.

"We're going the wrong way," I said.

George smiled. "You can go any way you want at 1:00 a.m."

I laughed. "It's nice when nobody's in the way, isn't it?"

"Sure is," George replied. "Sure as hell is."

No-heat calls were common in the dead of winter, and heading straight home was rare. After we filled a house one night, I asked, "Why do we deliver fuel on the way home?"

George smiled. "It costs a lot more money to go home," he said.

"What?" I questioned, shifting toward him in my seat. "How's it cost more?"

"It costs the same amount of money tonight to stop and fill them up as it does to drive by and go home."

Old Blue's cab went quiet. Moments passed like hours as I tried to make sense of what sounded like nonsense.

"Ever heard the phrase, 'Time is money'?" he asked.

"I've heard you say it at Oscar's before."

"That's what it means," he said.

Finally, it made sense. "Gotcha. It saves money to deliver fuel on the way home," I said.

"Nope. Doesn't save money. Allows us to make money tomorrow."

"What?" I asked, and paused a moment. "Ahhhh, now I get it. So what you're saying is, if we deliver fuel on the way home, we get to deliver more fuel tomorrow to different people. If we go home, we have to come back here tomorrow," I said, sitting taller in Old Blue's passenger seat as if I had just passed a trigonometry test.

George smiled. "Time is money, Jason. Time is money."

"I've heard Brian say, 'Gotta make hay while the sun shines' lots of times. That the same thing?" I asked.

"Yeah, kinda. What Brian means is you gotta get hay in the barn when ya can, and that's when the sun is shining, and it's not always shining. Know what I'm saying?" George said.

"Yeah. We ain't hayin' in the rain," I said.

"No, we're not."

A few days later, I pulled into Speedwell after finishing chores on the farm. Before my truck door even shut, George called out, "Order some dinner; we have a long night ahead of us."

"We do?" I asked.

"Yup. Getting fuel in the morning. Price is going up."

The smell of my bacon burger and fries escaped the now-greasy Miss Lyndonville Diner to-go bag and filled the cab of Old Blue. "So, I got a question," I said, shoving fries into my mouth.

"What's that?" George asked.

"We make more money when someone is on automatic delivery, don't we?"

"How's that? The price is the same whether we put them on automatic or they call," George said.

"Well, we gotta make more money if we can deliver to who we want, when we want, not when they want us to, right?" I said, taking a bite of my burger and wiping my hands on my barn pants, stained with cow shit and gasoline.

George looked at me and smiled.

Looking back at him, I said, "So, we gotta figure out the fastest way to deliver the most amount of fuel possible. 'Cause time is money, right?"

"That's right," George said, still smiling.

We stopped at one house around midnight, and George said, "We're putting fifty in."

"Why only fifty?" I asked, puzzled. A hundred gallons was the minimum, and fifty was a first for me.

"This guy struggles to pay his bill. Gonna save him some money," George said with a little smile.

"We're gonna deliver fuel to someone who struggles to pay their bill, and we are going to sell them the cheaper fuel?" I said.

"That's right," George said. "They're having a hard time, and we're gonna help 'em out. Fifty dollars isn't going to last them that long, but a small bill is easier to swallow than a big one."

I understood what he was talking about. I recalled the crushing feeling I experienced when my wallet, filled with two tons of nothing, fell on top of me as I tried to enter Lyndon State College. It was like finding myself thrown overboard a cruise ship named *Life*, flailing my arms in the water, yelling for help. The life preserver Lyndon State College threw me wasn't filled with buoyant foam; instead, it was weighted with future obligations.

As George handed me the ticket, he said, "Put this in the door."

I trudged up the driveway, my shadow cast by Old Blue's headlights guiding the way. I opened the screen door, and under the porch light, I noticed something written on the fuel ticket. It read: *"We were driving by, and I knew you were close to being out of fuel. The price is going up tomorrow, and I wanted to save you some money. I hope we didn't wake you up. Pay me when you can. —George."*

I stood there for a moment, staring at that ticket.

As we pulled out of the driveway, I looked over and asked, "Think they'll pay us?"

"Yeah. Eventually."

"How much did we save him? Like five bucks?"

"If that," George said, pausing. "It's less about how much we save him and more about the fact that we were thinking of him."

I didn't say anything, but I knew I'd remember those words for the rest of my life.

George often said, "A business needs customers, and I want loyal ones." The first time he told me he didn't want people to buy their fuel from Speedwell, I was baffled.

When I asked why not, he replied, "Because I want them to buy from me." He said it as if it was the most obvious thing in the world, like he was simply stating that the sky is blue and the grass is green. My teenage mind couldn't quite grasp it at the time. If they didn't buy from Speedwell, why would they come back? I thought about it more, and the more I turned it over, the more it seemed like one of those puzzles that should've been simple but wasn't.

But as the years passed, the answer started to unfold. It wasn't about the fuel or the money. It was about George. Speedwell wasn't just a place where people got gas, it was an extension of him. He wasn't just filling Old Blue's tank with heating oil; he was giving people a piece of himself. The truck, the service, the way he knew every customer by name—it was all part of him. People didn't buy gas and fuel oil from Speedwell because it was cheap or convenient: They bought it because they trusted George. They bought from him because they knew he'd show up, no matter the hour, no matter the weather, because that is what family does: They show up.

I began to see that the value of a customer wasn't in how much profit you made from a sale. It was in the bond you built with them over time. It wasn't just about what they spent on a tank of gas or a fuel tank of home heating oil, it was about how much they trusted you to show up, to care, to be there when they needed you most. The stronger that bond, the more they came back, and when they did come back, they bought from George, not Speedwell.

George only offered deals to customers who purchased in large volumes. The price was fixed and not negotiable. He believed that supply, demand, competition, and the market would determine that price. George taught me that while you might lose some customers who tried to negotiate for a lower price, it was crucial to stand firm. He would say, "If you give in to their pressure, you risk losing all your customers once they find out you're selling the same product to others at a cheaper price. The word gets out."

I sat in my usual spot, and Zoe was in hers. She rested her pen on her notebook and said, "The note George wrote on the ticket, the one he asked you to put in the door—who was that for?"

I looked at her and laughed. "You think that note was for me, don't you?"

Zoe tilted her head slightly and said, "What if it was as much for you as it was for the homeowner?"

I sat silent, and she said, "He taught you how to show up for people."

I smiled and said, "He sure did."

"And what do you think George meant when he said, 'The word gets out'?"

"It's not just about business or reputation. It's about trust. Integrity. Doing right by people, even when no one's looking," I said.

Zoe leaned in slightly, nodded, and said, "George wasn't just protecting a business. He was protecting something bigger. A name. A legacy. And you absorbed that, not because he told you to, but because you saw it, lived it. It was his way of saying that your choices don't exist in isolation. That they ripple out."

My body felt heavy with gratitude as I sank into the couch. My eyes left Zoe and focused on nothing important in the room.

When my eyes found Zoe again, she said, "There's a difference between living with integrity and living to prove it."

I didn't say anything. Just stared at the floor where the grain in the wood escaped the edge of the rug. It suddenly felt too complicated, like it might twist itself into something I couldn't follow.

She sat back. "You're not responsible for controlling the story other people write about you. But you are responsible for telling your own."

I thought about how hard it was to isolate myself from my external life. My internal and external lives collided so often that they seemed to blend into something indistinguishable.

12

THE AIRSTREAM

Kathleen and I fit together as naturally as peanut butter and jelly. My love for her ran so deep it felt embedded in my bone marrow. We didn't talk about our future often, and when we did, it was usually me doing the talking. But we didn't need to say much. We were in love, and her family had taken me in as one of their own. In my mind, there was never a question of *if* we would get married, only when.

She had saved me, carrying a torch through the darkness I had stumbled into after my parents' divorce, showing me the way forward. Destiny is a beautiful destination, and it felt like a place we were traveling to together. Everything associated with that teenage love, the unforgettable moments and all the "firsts" we went through, became etched in my heart and imprinted in my mind. I hadn't realized how fragile my heart was; it had never loved that deeply before and didn't yet know it could be broken.

Kathleen and I had broken up once before for a couple of days over the typical teenage drama. But this time felt different. She told me we needed to break up because she was leaving for college, and it wouldn't work.

The undercurrent of that one sentence—"It wouldn't work"—had me drowning again.

Who was she kidding? *Of course it would work.* I would wait for her. Of course I would wait.

But deep down, I couldn't shake the fear that if she went away to college, she might find someone else to replace me. Some guy who would have no idea how lucky he was. Someone whom Ma and George would love just as much as they loved me. What if she did find someone? What would happen to me? Did she no longer love me? If she did love me, why was she leaving?

Standing in a meadow filled with sunlight and bright colors after exiting that dark cave, she let go of my hand. She didn't disappear; she was still there, but not like before. We were now two jars: one peanut butter and one jelly. One with the lid on tight, and one with it off.

I realized that love, real love, didn't always mean safety. It didn't always mean permanence. The warmth and certainty she once gave me began to feel like borrowed light. Letting go of her hand felt like losing the grip of the thing that led me to her family, to a place I belonged.

I began to question my worth as someone deserving of being chosen and held on to. If the person who pulled me from the darkness could let go so easily, then maybe I wasn't meant to stay in the light. I had built my sense of safety around her love, and now, with that thread fraying, I felt exposed again, like I had stepped into the open without armor. Love no longer felt like shelter; it felt like risk.

I slithered away from my house the day I turned eighteen to face the world on my own. The truth of the matter was, I hadn't been alone. I'd had Kathleen and her family right by my side the whole time.

A naïve heart is as vulnerable as the weakest animal in the herd. No matter how much those who loved me had tried to shield me from pain, it was only a matter of time before I discovered the truth: Sometimes, love breaks your heart. The feel-good hormones that had once pulsed through me, bringing life and joy, vanished in an instant, leaving behind a hollowness I hadn't known was possible.

I was about to finish my second and last semester at Lyndon State College, in a program I didn't care about, just weeks away from being evicted from the dorm, and now this.

What did it all mean? Did this mean no more farming? What about Speedwell? Would Ma and George still want me around, or would they break up with me, too? And Kathleen—were we really going to stay friends? What if she never spoke to me again?

The questions circled me like a pack of hungry wolves, and I had no answers, just the dizzying fear that everything I had come to rely on might be slipping through my fingers all at once. I couldn't sit still, but I had nowhere to go.

I blinked and found myself back in the depths of the cave, blinded by the darkness once again. It felt as though Kathleen had taken me by the hand, led me into the warmth and beauty of the sunlit world, only to let go and say, "I'm not meant to be with you."

Was this what Mom and Dad had felt like when they divorced? Had their hearts been torn apart too? Life didn't feel fair, not then, not now. Why wasn't my heart strong enough not to break?

A soft voice called out through the void.

It was Ma's voice. "Kathleen is going to college and needs to go without you. It is unfair for you to wait for her and unfair for you to ask her the same. You're a part of this family, and that doesn't change."

I shivered as Ma's words surrounded me like a blanket. "It doesn't?" I asked, my voice trembling as tears began to flood my face.

"No, it doesn't," she said, wrapping her arms around me in a hug I hadn't felt in a long time.

"I don't want her to go, Ma. I—I don't want her to go."

"I know you don't. It's going to be okay."

She gently pulled back and looked at me. "You finish school in a couple of weeks. Do you have a plan?"

"I—I don't have one," I whimpered, feeling like a little kid again.

"Why don't you come back to Speedwell full-time until you figure it out?"

"I can do that?"

"Of course you can."

"I don't have anywhere to live, Ma. Ya think I can live with Brian again?"

"I'm going to fix up the Airstream for you," she said. "You can sleep there, eat with us, and use the shower and the bathroom whenever you need it. You're going to be okay, I promise."

She pulled me back into her arms, and I fell limp against her, finally giving way to the comfort I'd been needing.

Was this what that saying in Gram's bathroom really meant? "If you love something, set it free, and if it comes back to you, it was meant to be." Was Kathleen setting me free? Letting me go? Of course I would come back. Of course I was hers. I couldn't imagine loving anyone else. But if I let her go, would she come back? And what if she wanted to, but I was gone? What if I never knew?

I held tight to the torch Kathleen had once used to guide me. I wouldn't let go, not yet. Even though the flame had dwindled to a mere glow, it still flickered with hope. There was still a chance. A chance that she would go off to college and come back without replacing my love. The warmth and light of that torch would only vanish completely when she said "I do" to someone other than me. Until then, there would still be hope.

A few days later, Ma said, "I have the Airstream ready for you."

"Can we go look at it?" I asked, trying to hide the mix of anticipation and excitement.

"Of course," she said.

We walked across the lawn and up the small hill above the driveway. Ma paused and tilted her head toward the door. "Go ahead," she said, motioning for me to open it.

I stepped up and pulled the door open. White curtains hung neatly in the window above the table she had already set. A clean towel draped from the handle of the little stove. A blue comforter was perfectly tucked under the mattress in the corner, and a thirteen-inch black-and-white TV with rabbit ear antennas waited on a small table.

Emotion rose in my throat. I turned and gave her a hug. "I love it," I whispered. "It's perfect. Thank you so much."

I sat across from Zoe, my eyes wet as my body and mind relived those few months. The desire to hurl myself through the blinds and plate glass window had lessened over the past few months, but it was still there, looming to my left.

"How did that make you feel when you saw the Airstream?" Zoe asked.

I explained that my heart instantly became heavy, but it didn't fall. Instead, it simply swelled in place. They gave me a home again. I reached into the Nichols family, latching on to all of them, including George's sister, Aunt Rachel, and Ma's parents, Bob and Calista, having called them Gram and Gramp early on. It wasn't until after Kathleen and I broke up that I realized they had adopted me, too.

The heartbreak with Kathleen left me raw, like new skin after a sunburn, but as I stood in the doorway of that little Airstream, I realized I hadn't been abandoned as I feared.

I looked down at my crisp golf shirt, khakis, and brown loafers and smiled. "That was the summer I learned how to play golf," I said.

"How old were you? Eighteen or nineteen?" Zoe asked.

"Yeah, nineteen. Hard to believe."

13

FIVE DOLLARS OF GAS

Life in the Airstream over the following weeks helped me settle back into my old self. I threw myself into work on the farm and my work at Speedwell with George more than ever. That summer, like the ones before, George would leave the station a couple of times a week to play golf.

When he returned, I'd always ask how he played, and he'd tell me what he shot for eighteen holes. One day, he said, "Pretty good—shot 82 today." Then, out of the blue one Thursday in June of 1990, George said, "I'm playing in a golf tournament this weekend. You wanna caddie for me?"

"Sure," I told him, not knowing what that actually entailed.

That weekend, I rode beside him in the cart as he played the event. A caddie is supposed to carry the player's clubs and offer advice on where to hit the ball. But caddying for George mostly meant riding along in the cart while he spent the day saying things like, "Jason, stand there," or "Don't walk through the bunker," and "Shhhhhh" whenever someone was about to swing.

Five Dollars of Gas

Years later, someone told me, "You could fill a book with what I don't know about golf." Well, that weekend, I was reading that book, one page at a time.

George scored eighty-something for the eighteen holes, and not knowing whether that was good or bad, I asked on the drive home, "Why'd you miss so many short putts?"

"Didn't miss on purpose, ya know," George said, half laughing, half defending himself.

"Some were only this long," I said, laughing and holding my hands up like a kid being asked how big his fish was.

He chuckled and shook his head. "Well, it ain't as easy as it looks. You wanna play sometime?"

"Sure, why not?" I asked.

George took me to play that week, a nine-hole course carved out of old pastureland by a dairy farmer in Barton, Vermont. I climbed out of George's truck in my boots, blue jeans, and a shirt that had all worked just as hard as I had, with two or three days' worth of cow shit stains and gasoline since they last saw a washing machine.

Perched on my head was a green Marlboro Tennis Courts hat I'd stolen from my dad years earlier. The clasp in the back had long since broken and been replaced with a short piece of an old boot lace, and three half-inch strips of duct tape folded neatly over the curved bill held the visor together.

I looked like I was ready to muck a barn, not walk the fairways of a golf course. The round ended, and I scored a 66, thirty shots over par for nine holes, and that was only because I stopped counting at ten strokes when the hole was bad.

"Why'd you keep missing those short putts?" George said,

laughing as we drove home. "Not as easy as it looks, huh?"

I shook my head, grinning through the embarrassment. "Yeah, a little harder than it looks," I said. "When can we play again?"

George usually took me to Barton Golf Club in the afternoons because it had a much more laid-back atmosphere than St. Johnsbury Country Club, where he played with all his business buddies. Only the rich folks in town could afford the $350-a-year membership at St. Johnsbury, and I definitely wasn't one of them.

But the following summer, in 1991, George signed us up to play in a season-long tournament at St. Johnsbury Country Club. I don't remember much about the matches from that summer, but one hole stuck with me: the ninth hole.

"What is that?" George asked.

"What?" I said.

"On your driver? What is that?"

"Oh, that," I said, grinning. "It says, 'Let the Big Dog Eat.' I wrote it on there to remind me to swing hard and fast," I said, laughing.

George shook his head. "How about you just hit it in the fairway?"

"Watch this," I said as I teed up my ball. "I'm about to let the Big Dog eat." Then I swung as hard and fast as I could. The ball shot up into the air, curving hard to the right before disappearing behind a stand of trees.

When we got to my ball, George stood next to me and said,

Five Dollars of Gas

"What are you doing?"

"I'm gonna hit it over the trees," I said confidently.

"Turn around and look at the tee box," he said, pointing back up the hill.

"Yeah?"

"Now, look where you are."

I looked down at the ground, then around my feet, confused. "Whaddya mean?"

George laughed and said, "Look where you are. You're not even on the same hole you started on," pointing behind me to the fifth green, which was just a short distance away. "You're not good enough to hit it over the trees. If we tie this hole, we win the match, and you get two shots because of your handicap. If you make a six and they make a four, we win. Hit the ball back into the fairway," he said, pointing to the left. "Then go for the green."

I looked up at the trees, my grip tightening on the club. I hated the idea of backing down, but I knew he was right. Shaking my head, I gave in and hit the ball forty yards sideways into the fairway.

Two shots later, George approached me as I stood over my ball, roughly twenty feet from the hole. He said, "Okay, they made four. If you two-putt, you make six, and we win."

I nodded, took a deep breath, and rolled the first putt. It stopped just short of the hole. I walked up and tapped it in for a double bogey six.

As we walked off the green, George put his arm over my shoulder and said, "Sometimes punching out of trouble is the right choice. Great playing."

Golf reignited a competitive flame in me, and I found myself counting down the hours until I could play again the moment a round ended. There was something about the game's difficulty, its maddening precision, its silent mental battles, that pulled me in like nothing else. Golf didn't come easy, and that was exactly why I loved it. I hadn't loved something that much since Kathleen.

Zoe leaned back in her chair, one leg crossed over the other, hands lightly folded in her lap. "You know," she said gently, "I don't think that story was about golf."

I gave a short laugh. "No?"

She smiled. "No. I think it was about being seen. About being guided without being pushed. About someone believing in you quietly, without needing to say it out loud all the time."

I stared at the floor, letting her words hang in the room. My throat tightened just a bit.

Zoe continued, "You said something earlier that stuck with me, about wishing your mom had tried to stop you from leaving, that you wanted her to say something, anything, when you walked out that door."

I nodded slowly. "Yeah."

"George didn't say much either. But he stayed close. He created space for you to grow. He gave you structure and a voice of reason. And unlike what you experienced after the divorce, his guidance didn't come with volatility or emotional strings."

I shifted in my seat. "Yeah, but it's not the same. He wasn't my mom."

"No," she agreed, "he wasn't. And that's what makes this so complicated. You can be incredibly grateful to George and still heartbroken over what you didn't get from your mom.

Both can be true."

I looked up at her. "Sometimes I think I keep trying to prove I'm okay now so I don't have to feel how much it still hurts."

Zoe nodded. "And maybe golf gave you a safe place to compete with yourself instead of your past. A place where failing didn't mean rejection."

I thought a moment. "You know, he would laugh when I messed up sometimes. I'd be frustrated, and he'd say, 'Golf's hard. You think you're gonna hit where you want to every time?'"

"And isn't that what you really wanted after the divorce? To mess up and not be cast out for it?"

I blinked a few times, feeling the tightness in my body.

Zoe continued, "You talk about that moment on the ninth hole, when George told you to punch back into the fairway instead of going for the risky shot over the trees. You listened. That was trust. That was love, too."

I nodded, "Yeah . . . I trusted him."

"And you learned to trust yourself a little more in the process," she said. "Even if just in the smallest of ways."

Silence filled the room for a moment. I finally exhaled. "It wasn't just a golf story, was it?"

Zoe smiled softly. "Not even close."

Kathleen had etched herself deep in my soul. Her handprint on my heart reminded me of how fulfilled my life once was. She owned that part of me, and it was forever hers. But in the time that followed being boyfriend and girlfriend, I had to begin asking who I was without her. That question followed me everywhere, like a shadow even on a cloudy day.

It's common to assume that what seems obvious is actually

true. In those moments, I didn't have to make any assumptions. My heart was trying to heal. Instead of introducing me as "Kathleen's boyfriend," Ma would sometimes say, "This is my son," especially when we ran into people at the golf course where stories were too long and explanations felt unnecessary. "It's just easier," she'd say. "They don't want to hear the whole story." I liked it when she called me her son. But deep down, I didn't want to be her son or even Jason; I wished I was still Kathleen's boyfriend.

My daily routine grew from breakfast at Oscar's with George before daylight to lunch with him at the Miss Lyndonville Diner. I never had to ask if I could go. George always got there first, tossing out a casual, "You hungry?" or "Ready for lunch?" like it was the most natural thing in the world. For reasons I didn't fully understand then, he wanted me around as much as I wanted to be around him. There was no formal invitation, no plan. It wasn't something we talked about. It just was.

Lunch at the diner was mostly the same as breakfast at Oscar's, but with a few differences. We didn't have assigned seats like we did at Oscar's, but somehow we always ended up at the counter or a table in the front. In all the years and hundreds of meals I shared with George there, I couldn't remember ever once sitting in one of the booths in the back.

The crowd was different too. At Oscar's, I'd been surrounded by blue-collar guys: carpenters, plumbers, loggers. They looked like me and talked like me. But at the diner, the seats next to us were filled by bankers, sales associates, and businesspeople in crisp button-downs and even a few suits. I had thrown away every tie I owned after high school, all three

Five Dollars of Gas

of them, including the skinny white leather one I loved. These people spoke with a Northern accent like mine, but their words were more polished, their sentences more sophisticated. Their handshakes were firm but soft, not like the calloused grips I was used to trading over my first cup of coffee.

At Oscar's, George had always seemed like the one with the most to say. He told stories and made people laugh. But at the diner, I began to notice something different: how often he asked questions, and how curious he was. He drew people out and seemed to listen more. He didn't dominate the room, he orchestrated it. And I sat there beside him, taking it all in.

I had watched George over the years as he serviced multiple people at once at Speedwell, a master of timing and attention. Sometimes, he would even pump gas slower on purpose, easing the handle back just enough to buy himself time to finish up with someone else. He manipulated the speed of the pump depending on how much gas a customer wanted, stretching out five dollars just long enough to wash a windshield, check the oil, or simply have a conversation.

I often stood beside him, listening in. I paid close attention to how he spoke to everyone, from construction workers in muddy boots to bankers in dress shirts, from local salespeople to out-of-state travelers. Each person got George, the George I had come to know. Regardless of who was in front of him, he always remained himself.

Every day, people from Canada stopped in to fill up. We were right off the interstate, only about forty minutes from the border. George would walk right up to their car windows with a friendly smile, asking about their trip. Where in Canada were they from? How long were they staying? Were they planning to head back the same way?

I asked him once why he always asked so many specific questions. "I'm trying to get to know them," he said, like it was the most natural thing in the world.

One morning, bellied up to the diner counter after a busy morning, George said, "I saw you taking care of Charlie this morning."

"You did?" I asked.

Nodding, he said, "I did."

"He drives me crazy," I said, shaking my head. "He gets five dollars of gas every day."

George sat quietly, food resting on the fork in his hand.

"Every day. Five dollars, check the oil, wash the windshield. And it's always when we're busy. I just don't get it."

George slowly swiveled toward me, bringing his coffee cup to his lips. His eyes met mine over the rim of the mug.

"Why doesn't he just fill up?" I said.

After a few seconds, George said, "I don't want him to fill up."

"Really?" I said. That didn't make any sense. Confused, I looked at him and said, "We make more money if he fills up."

"Family is more important than money," he said softly.

"What does family have to do with it?" I asked, confused.

George's voice dropped, "Did you know he's all alone? Lost both his parents a couple years ago and lost his brother last year."

"No, I didn't," I said, my voice barely above a whisper.

"He gets five dollars every day because we are his family," George said gently. "You like seeing Ma every day, don't you?"

Five Dollars of Gas

"Yeah, of course."

"Do you want to see her once a week for an hour, or every day for fifteen minutes?"

"Every day."

"Of course you do. Charlie wants to see us every day. We give him purpose, and he gets to see your smiling face each morning. He knows he has someone waiting for him when he wakes up."

"I had no idea," I said, my voice quieter now as a sick feeling of guilt twisted in my stomach.

He looked over at me. "If Charlie fills up, we don't see him as often. If he fills up every time, he will need gas somewhere else at some point. We're his family. I want him to come in every day. We make a difference in his life. Every day. With five dollars of gas."

Zoe jotted something in her notebook. "How did it make you feel, hearing George say that Charlie is our family?"

"It stopped me." I paused. "It felt like . . . like someone turned the lights on in a room I didn't know I was sitting in."

Zoe's quietness pushed my eyes toward the window and then down to my hands. "Embarrassed. Even guilty that I hadn't seen it."

She nodded.

"Zoe, I can remember sitting on my stool, staring blankly at my plate of food. I remember my mind drifting back to the note George had written on that fuel bill, the one he asked me to tuck into the door that said, 'I hope we didn't wake you up. Pay me when you can.' How good those words had made me feel. How they must have felt for the homeowner the next morning."

I couldn't believe I had missed it when it was right in my face, clear as day.

Zoe rested her pen. "You didn't miss it. You didn't know to look for it. It's hard to notice someone else's need when you're still trying to understand your own."

"Yeah, I guess you're right," I said and gave a soft laugh. "You know, funny thing is this: I share this story with my team all the time. One of my assistants will be sitting in my office and another will overhear pieces of a conversation and walk to the door and say, 'Are you telling the story about five dollars of gas?'"

Zoe's face lit up with a smile. "You tell your team?"

I nodded. "I do."

I went on to tell her about one of my members that called the golf shop every day. Several times a day, in fact. My staff would get frustrated and avoid the phone when his name showed up on the caller ID. When they did talk to him, I could hear the fakeness in their voice.

"It bothered me and sent my mind right back to Charlie," I said. "So my team, all of them, hear about five dollars of gas on one of their first days of work."

"So it wasn't just about Charlie?" Zoe said.

I shook my head. "I thought it was at the time, but I was wrong. George was teaching me to see people. Five minutes and five dollars at a time."

I thought back to those days as I sat there on the couch, to the moment I realized that everything George said had purpose. How everything he did had purpose and how that had shaped who I had become.

Five Dollars of Gas

I remembered him asking me, "What do you think people want when they pull into Speedwell?"

It felt like a trick question. "Gas?" I answered.

"Of course they do," he said, and I could see that little smirk on his face as he shook his head and said, "We don't sell milk."

That was the first time I learned not to say, "Can I help you?" but instead to put a smile on my face and say "good morning" or "afternoon." I heard George's voice say, "Ask them how their day is going. Anything, just make it about them. They'll tell you how you can help if you just talk to them."

At the time, it seemed like a matter of semantics, too simple to be profound. But maybe that was the point. It was simple and I'd been missing it.

I blinked a few times and looked at Zoe. "George told me once at the diner, 'We talk differently to people we care about than we do to strangers.'"

She nodded.

"I realized it wasn't in the words I used, but in the intention behind them. I needed to start caring, really caring, about the people in front of me."

I went on to tell her that later that night, I lay down in the Airstream. So much about my life resembled a bed of clovers I was standing over. The past few years, I had been crouched over, hands on my knees, searching the ground, scanning what I could see in search of myself.

I remembered Aunt Deb saying, "There aren't many four-leaf clovers alive, and you don't find one every time you look. That's what makes them so special." The disappointment I had that first day hit me again, only this time I didn't want to cry. I just felt more defeated.

Then, I remembered what Uncle Stan told me once after going days without seeing a deer during deer season: "You're walking too fast. Slow down, Jason. Every step in the woods reveals something you couldn't see before." I pictured him sitting on his block of wood, his red hunting cap with a narrow circular brim sitting high on his head. The little smirk on his face was as if he had known for days that this was my problem. I lay there in bed and laughed. Then Aunt Deb's voice broke into the Airstream and said, "Look again, Jason." I remembered when she told me to look again after I told her I didn't find a four-leaf clover. I looked again and still didn't find one. But I had done it countless times in my life, looking in the same patch of clover more than once, and found one I had missed.

Zoe's pen stopped moving, and she said, "That's a powerful realization, Jason. And when you say 'really caring,' what does that mean for you?"

I looked down at the floor for a moment. "I think it means . . . slowing down. Seeing people. Listening with intention. Not brushing past them because I'm too wrapped up in what I think matters more."

"There's something else in what you said, too, that quote from George. 'We talk differently to people we care about.' When you talk to yourself, who are you talking too?" she asked.

I huffed and shook my head. I knew exactly what she was asking.

The room was quiet for a couple of minutes, and then Zoe said, "Did Charlie show up the next day for his five dollars of gas?"

"He sure did. Let me tell you about that . . ."

Like clockwork, Charlie pulled into the station, and I said, "Good morning, Charlie. How are you feeling today?"

"I'm good, Jason, how are you?"

"I'm great, Charlie. It's good to see you. You want the usual?" I said as I spun off the gas cap, slid the nozzle into the tank, and set it on slow.

Charlie smiled and nodded. I knew what that smile felt like. It felt like the one I had had only an hour ago when Dee Dee slid my toast in front of me at Oscar's. We chatted as I washed his windshield, and after hanging up the pump, I smiled and said, "See ya tomorrow, Charlie."

He smiled, nodded, and said, "Okay Jason, I'll see you tomorrow."

14

A NECK-DOWN

"Have you figured it out yet?" Dad asked one day during that summer I lived in the Airstream.

"Figured what out?"

"What ya gonna do for a living."

"I don't know, Dad."

"Why don't ya move out here and go into business with your old man?" he said.

"Maybe."

"Think about it, son. Gotta get your ducks in a row."

In a strange way, my bond with Dad had grown stronger once the initial shock of the divorce wore off. The deep conversations we used to have with his arm draped over my shoulder were replaced by his voice in my ear through the coiled cord of the phone. Those days of riding the dirt roads "looking for deer" were behind us, and long-distance phone calls became our new connection.

Dad had talked passionately about the West when I was a

A Neck-Down

kid. Living on a horse ranch out there somewhere seemed to bring life to his eyes. I remember the way his voice changed when he talked about it, like he was already standing under that wide-open sky. That dream—well, most of it—eventually came true after he married his second wife. Together, they packed up and moved to Oregon.

The horse ranch never happened, though. That part of the dream was traded for something more practical. Instead of raising horses, he began working as a carpenter, "pounding nails," as he liked to say. It wasn't the vision he painted for me as a boy, but it was a new life, and he found peace in building something with his hands.

Thinking back to the summer of 1986, I remembered one hot afternoon when my socks and shirt were glued to my body with sweat from lugging sheets of plywood onto the roof. Mom and Dad were recently divorced, and I was spending the summer with Dad in Massachusetts, working as a laborer on a construction crew.

How many nails does it take to put all this plywood down? I wondered as I climbed the temporary staircase, carrying the sheet of plywood. The sixty-pound sheet slammed onto the roof with a heavy *thud,* and I started counting a sheet already nailed down—one, two, three, all the way to thirty.

Damn, that's a lot of nails.

"Hey, Dad," I yelled from the roof. "How many sheets of plywood in one of them there stacks?" I pointed to the piles on the ground below.

"Maybe fifty," he said.

"Fifty?"

You gotta be kidding me. That's a hundred and fifty sheets. Thirty nails per sheet . . . I thought, doing the math in my head. "Damn!" I said out loud.

Later, sitting on my red-and-white Igloo cooler, my dirty hands wrapped around the sandwich I'd made when they were clean that morning, I looked over at Dad and said, "Gonna be over four thousand nails in the ruff."

"What?" the foreman called out, his eyes squinting like he didn't hear right.

"Yup," I said, taking a bite. "Over four thousand nails. That means over four thousand holes in the ruff."

I caught Dad looking at me across the bench seat of his truck on the way home that afternoon. I'd seen that look plenty of times before: half amused, half about to teach me something.

"Son, ya know what a neck-down is?"

I tilted my head. "Nope."

"A neck-down is someone hired from here down," he said, placing his hand at his throat. "No thinking allowed. You're a neck-down. Ya hear what I'm telling ya?"

I nodded quietly, already feeling the lesson coming.

"Just do as you're told," he said, shaking his head, "and don't tell him how many holes are in the damn roof." His laughter finally cracked the serious tension in the cab. "Over four thousand nails, huh?"

"Yup," I said, laughing back. "Not countin' them shingles. Ain't no way it don't leak."

A year earlier, I had found myself contemplating my future as I prepared to enter Lyndon State College. I had followed

A Neck-Down

Dad's advice to "find something you love and make a living from it," but that approach hadn't worked out the way I'd hoped. Now, I was back at square one, asking myself the same question: *What do I want to do for the rest of my life?*

My brother, Garett, had moved to Oregon with Dad a few years earlier, and living out there was starting to sound like a good idea. What would I do if I stayed in Vermont? Milk cows and pump gas forever? No, that wasn't what I wanted. I could see working with the old man in Oregon happening. But being a neck-down? No way in hell. I wanted to be more than just a laborer. Then I remembered one of my buddies had gone to college to become a carpenter. Maybe I should do that too.

A couple of weeks later, I heard, "Sign here." The financial advisor pointed to the bottom of the page. *How much money have I borrowed so far? I'm gonna have to pay this all back eventually.* But I pushed the thought aside. *No need to worry about it now*, I told myself.

The pen hovered for a second before I pressed it to the paper. My name curved across the line in ink. I had officially entered Vermont Technical College (VTC) that fall, enrolling in the one-year Building Trades program.

I handed the form back to the advisor, my fingers still curled like they weren't ready to let go. Outside, the late summer air felt different, or maybe I was just noticing it for the first time.

I walked to the parking lot alone, the sound of my boots trudging across the pavement, the burden of that signed form resting heavy in my back pocket. I didn't pump gas that afternoon. I didn't stack hay or milk cows. Instead, I sat on the tailgate of my truck, staring out across the fields that framed the edge of campus with the sun hitting my face.

The voices in my head started up again. *What if you're no good at this? What if you hate it? What if you just wasted more money you don't have?*

I didn't know if I wanted to be a carpenter like my dad. I didn't know if swinging a hammer would lead me anywhere worth going. But it was worth finding out. For the first time in a long time, I had made a move that felt like my own.

The months that followed were nothing like my time at Lyndon State College. I liked my classes and loved the feeling of creating something as we built walls, installed roofs, and cut staircases. I spent Thanksgiving break at Uncle Stan's camp hunting with the guys. During Christmas break, I cut fresh trees for people on our Christmas tree farm, as well as pumping gas at Speedwell and delivering fuel with George and helping Brian with farm chores.

The wheels hit the tarmac in Portland with a jolt that shook my whole body forward in the seat. As the plane taxied to the gate, I stared out the small oval window and wondered if I would call this place home. My Building Trades certificate was in Vermont, tucked inside a fancy folder, the ink still fresh from graduation a week earlier.

When the door opened and the line started moving, I stood, and a surge of adrenaline shot through my body. I hadn't seen Dad in a long time. The air in the terminal was different from Vermont—I couldn't determine how, just unfamiliar. I scanned the crowd until I spotted Dad waiting near baggage claim. His big hand waved and I saw his grin, which hadn't changed a bit.

It was as if he'd never left Vermont as his arms squeezed me and he said, "Great to see you, son."

"You too, Dad."

"How was the flight?" he asked.

"Good," I said, reaching down to pull one of my bags off the carousel.

"That your bag, son?"

"Yup."

"Are you serious? What is that?"

"Blue Seal grain bag," I said, grabbing the duct-taped, twisted end of the one-hundred-pound plastic sack that, just last week, had been full of grain.

Dad stared at me, baffled.

"What?" I said, as if hauling a feed bag all the way across the country was the most natural thing in the world.

"They let you check that?"

"Yeah . . . what?" I said, giving him the same baffled look he was giving me.

"How many grain bags ya got, son?"

"This is it," I said, grabbing the second bag and slinging it over my shoulder.

"Did ya at least empty the grain out first?"

"What do ya think? I needed something to put my clothes in," I said, and shook my head in disbelief.

Dad stood there, silently belly laughing, shaking his head as people walked past us and glanced at my makeshift luggage. A couple of them even slowed down, probably wondering what kind of guy traveled with duct-taped Blue Seal grain bags.

But I didn't care. If anything, I stood a little taller, smiled and nodded as people walked past. Those bags weren't much to look at, but they held a lot of what I owned, and everything I had worked for. Clothes I'd worn through school, pumping gas, and milking cows. Those grain bags had seen as much of my life as anything else, and now they were seeing me off into whatever came next.

"You ready or what?" I said, adjusting the bags on my shoulders with a bit of swagger. "Where's the truck at?"

"Grain bags, son? Seriously?"

"It's all I had," I said, grinning as I walked ahead of him through the airport. "Gotta run what ya brung, Dad."

We started a roofing project the following morning. Dad worked from the roof while I stayed on the ground, stationed near a pile of lumber and a saw. I watched as he made his measurements, but something about the way he marked the board didn't sit right with me. He tossed the piece of wood down, and his pencil lines looked more like chicken scratch than anything readable.

Dad and I worked all morning together, both of us trying to prove to the other we knew what we were doing. We managed okay until I saw him measuring the valley.

"What are ya doing? That ain't how ya do it," I yelled up to him. "That ain't how ya measure for the valley."

"Just cut the damn thing already," he said, tossing the board down to me.

"What's this?" I said, twisting the piece of wood around that he had drawn on.

"Just cut the damn thing," he said, looking down at me with his hands on his hips.

"Okay, ya want me to cut it, I'll cut it. But it ain't right," I said, grabbing the Skilsaw. "Here," I said, leaning the rafter up to the roof after I finished.

"What the hell is this?" Dad said, staring down at me after he pulled the rafter up. "This ain't right."

"I told ya, it wasn't right," I said.

Sitting on the back deck that evening, Dad said, "You've been fighting me all day. I've been doing this a long time, son. I know what I'm doing. Just do what I tell ya."

I nodded. I'd heard that tone before, plenty of times. That was the tone: I am your father, and you'll do what I tell you. Only I wasn't a kid anymore.

But I knew what I was doing, too. And I knew one thing for certain: I wasn't moving out here, that was for damn sure. I loved my dad. He was the best dad a son could ask for. But working with him wasn't in the cards for me.

I realized that evening that Dad needed to be my dad that day on the roof as much as I needed to be his son. He needed me to see who he'd become, to be proud of him. After the divorce had chewed him up and spit him out, I think he was still finding pieces of himself, still trying to glue it all back together. He had been broken too, just like the rest of us.

In his eyes, I was still fifteen. Still the kid I'd been when he walked out the door for the last time. We both had versions of each other we carried around. But I wasn't that teenager anymore. He hadn't been there to see me mature and witness the impact of the choices I'd made turn me into the person I was becoming. And the truth was, he had grown and changed too. We just hadn't quite caught up to each other yet.

"How'd that make you feel when your plan to move out there changed?" Zoe asked from her chair.

"Things got easier that week once I realized I wasn't staying. I was sad. But it was like I released this internal pressure or something. I don't know."

Zoe waited.

"I just . . . just let myself just be there. With him. You know. It was just the two of us, laughing, joking, working side by side. The rest of the trip felt like those old evenings in the truck, just before dark. He was just my dad. I had lost my dad once, and I didn't want to lose him again."

"And what about returning home to Vermont? How did you feel about that?" she asked.

"I was actually good. I was sad to leave, but . . . but good. Maybe I wasn't ever going to move to Oregon, I don't know. I really liked being a carpenter, and I started a new job pounding nails a few days after I got back," I said.

My eyes hit the floor after those words hit the air, and I went silent. Zoe sat patiently, and the room became dense with quietness. I lifted my head, exhaled deeply, and said, "It was a good thing I was home."

"A good thing? Why's that?" Zoe said.

I inflated my chest and looked at my watch. Our time was almost up, and that seemed to help slow my heartbeat. "We don't have enough time," I said.

Zoe nodded and said, "Next time."

15

TWO DUCKS

The sweet smell of pure Vermont maple syrup plumed out of the pot and signaled the ring of the dinner bell in July 1991 as Ma lifted the lid off her homemade baked beans. The warmth of dinner at home with Ma and George reminded me of my childhood dinners with Mom and Dad. Steam burst out of the baked potato on George's plate as he cut it in half to scoop out the insides, a necessary process to transform the skin into two bowls, each begging for a slab of butter.

"Ya wanna play golf after dinner?" I asked, glancing over at George.

He tilted his head to peer out the kitchen window. "Looks like rain," he said.

"Nah, it looks fine. Come on, let's play nine holes."

"I think you should go play," Ma said, sending me a smile across the counter.

I usually walked when I played golf, unable to afford the cart fee, which cost more than double my less-than-four-dollar minimum wage. But not that night. George was playing, which meant we were riding. He never walked and never let me pay for anything.

"Load us up," George said as he headed toward the St. Johnsbury Country Club golf shop.

"Load us up" didn't just mean putting the golf clubs on the cart.

"Okay," I said, my ear nearly touching the truck's floorboard as I reached under the front seat. I grabbed the six-pack ring, now missing four beers, and dragged the warm Miller Lites across the dingy floor mat. Then I snatched his cigarettes off the dash.

"We ready?" he asked, walking out of the golf shop.

"Still don't know how you can drink warm beer. It's nasty," I said.

"It's not good for your stomach to drink cold beer when it's hot outside," George replied.

"It ain't good for ya to drink warm-ass beer anytime," I said, laughing.

The air hung heavy with a gentle mist as we approached the sixth hole, a par five with a hill tucked into the dogleg. George dropped me off at my ball and drove the cart farther down the fairway. When I returned to the cart, I noticed him sitting slightly hunched over.

"You okay?" I asked.

"Yeah, indigestion. I guess I ate too much of Ma's good cooking."

"It's probably that warm-ass beer. The truck is right there," I said, pointing to the parking lot two hundred yards away. "We can go if you don't feel good."

"I'm fine. We're almost done."

I pulled up a seat at the table in the diner the following day—our new morning watering hole since Oscar's had shut down.

"Where's George?" one of the guys asked.

"I gave him the morning off," I said with a grin, lifting my coffee cup. The days of my opinions always living in my head had passed. I wasn't leading the conversation or changing the topics, but I had involved myself in the dialogue.

For George, a morning off didn't mean sleeping in. It just meant he'd show up at Speedwell around 7:30 or 8 a.m. instead of his usual 6 a.m.. He used to tell me that some of the most important conversations happened before 8 a.m.

"It's essential to be at work early," he'd say. "I need everyone heading off to work to be able to say hi."

It was almost 9 a.m., and George hadn't shown up yet. "I'm going to call George," I told the guy working with me. *Where the hell is he?* I thought, walking into the office.

"Good morning, Ma," I said, leaning back in her chair at the desk, the phone tucked between my ear and shoulder. "Is George still home? We're supposed to play golf at 9:30."

"Hang on. He's in the bathroom. I'll ask."

"George, Jason is on the phone. He wants to know if you are still playing," I heard in a muffled tone.

"Yes, he is still playing," Ma said moments later.

Before I could say anything, a loud crash rang in my ear as Ma dropped the phone.

Then her voice: "Call the ambulance! George is having a heart attack!"

Flying forward, I frantically searched for the number to the ambulance, but there wasn't an emergency sticker on the phone like at home.

The operator quickly answered after I dialed zero. "I need an ambulance; it's an emergency!"

The operator gave me the number, and I slammed the phone down, picked it up again, and dialed.

"I need an ambulance! George Nichols is having a heart attack! Hurry!"

"Where is he?"

"At home. Hurry!"

Emergency 911 didn't exist in our hometown in 1991. It was good that the person who answered the phone at the emergency response center knew George and where he lived because I hung up the phone and never gave them an address. Despite having lived at the house for years and having drove by the response center where the ambulance was parked every day, I didn't know the address of our house.

"Where the hell is the ambulance?" I said as I accelerated down the driveway and across the lawn. "Ma, where are you?" I yelled, running through the door.

I turned the corner into the living room to see Ma's petite body thrusting up and down on George's chest. Ma's face, frozen by fear, was pale white. She looked like I felt during a bad dream when I tried to scream for help, but nothing would come out.

Just as I reached her, I heard the ambulance pull in and sprinted back to the door. I yelled, "He's in here! Hurry!"

I held Ma tight as we stared at George's motionless body, tangled in tubes and wires, hooked up to machines that beeped and clicked around us. The sight of him like that felt wrong, like I was caught in some nightmare I couldn't wake up from. *This isn't real. This can't be real. What happened? How did I beat the ambulance home? How the hell did I even get home?* My mind raced in every direction, struggling to piece together the moments that led here. I couldn't remember how I even got to the hospital. The questions kept coming, but none of them made any sense.

"We need to call Kathleen," Ma's voice sobbed, pulling me from my thoughts. She was right. Kathleen was in Colorado and would need to get home as soon as possible. We needed to call Brian, too. We needed to call so many people.

"I'll call her," I said, but my voice didn't sound like my own.

Much of that day remained a blur, as blank as the expression on Ma's face when I first saw her giving George CPR. After urging the ambulance to hurry, the events felt like they vanished into the fog of my mind. I had no recollection of how I got home or how I managed to outrun the ambulance. I couldn't remember driving to the hospital or the words I spoke to Kathleen. The only thing I could hold on to was that Kathleen was in Colorado, thousands of miles away, and I was the one who had to break the news to her. I was the one who had to tell Kathleen that her father had a heart attack.

Ma sat leaning into the hospital bed with her fingers tucked gently into the hand of the love of her life when I returned. Her shoulders sagged and her back curved like a branch covered with too much snow. Every muscle in her body seemed frozen, except for her thumb, which was moving in small, trembling circles over George's hand.

"I talked to Kathleen," I said, lowering myself beside her.

Her eyes shifted toward me, glassy and distant, and her lips parted just enough to let out a fragile "Thank you," as though speaking took more strength than she had left.

I laid my arm across her back. "I just quit my job, Ma."

Her head turned, and then, without a word, she laid her head on my shoulder. Her breath hitched, and one of the strongest people I knew sobbed. Our world was unraveling.

When Ma laid her head on my shoulder, something inside me cracked open too. I held her, but I was barely holding myself together.

My mind drifted to Speedwell. I could still smell the gas, feel the cool handle of the pump in my hand, hear George's voice talking to a customer like they were the most important person in the world. That place had been more than just a job. It was where I learned how to be part of something. Where George taught me what it meant to show up, to care about people, to notice the little things. It was where I began to understand who I was.

But as I sat there in that sterile room, I felt helpless. Like the gravity that held my world together had let go. I needed to get back to Speedwell for him, for Ma, for me. For everyone that would be stopping in once they heard the news.

I didn't know what the next few days would look like, but I knew where I needed to be. Or maybe it was where I wanted to be. Speedwell wasn't just Ma and George's place anymore—it was mine too. This family had been there for me every day since the moment I met them, a high school kid fumbling his way through teenage love and the dark moments of his parents' divorce. They took me in, fed me, listened to me. George had always been there for me. He was the kind of man you could count on even when everything else felt like it was falling apart, and I wanted to be that kind of man now.

But George wouldn't be at Speedwell tomorrow. Or the next day. Or any time soon, for that matter. That place wouldn't sound the same without his voice echoing across the pumps. I wanted to stay by his side, to be there for him, for Ma like they had been for me more times than I could count. But something pulled me toward Speedwell. I kept seeing the station in my mind: the pumps, the counter, Charlie wanting five dollars of gas, and all the morning regulars pulling in looking for George's grin and his cheery good morning.

What would they do when he wasn't there? What would I do?

The idea of leaving Ma alone twisted something in me. She sat beside George rubbing his hand as if to send life and hope into him, like if she let go for even a second, he would slip away. But I also knew George would've wanted someone to show up at Speedwell. The customers were his family too.

I hugged Ma shortly after Aunt Rachel, George's sister, arrived. She gave me a soft nod, as if she knew without asking where I was going. I leaned down and kissed Ma on the forehead.

"I'm going to Speedwell," I whispered. "I'll be back after work."

Hope eroded with the passing of each day, and by the fourth day, the family made the painful decision to remove life support. There was never any progress, no signs of return—only machines doing what George's body could no longer manage on its own.

Death spurred a battle between what once was and what was now about to be. The end of something tangible—his voice, his laughter, the way he leaned on a counter and sipped his coffee—triggered the beginning of something invisible and impossible to hold. Grief doesn't have a face, but it stared deep into me and never blinked. The quietness of death wasn't silent: It screamed in every corner of my mind as I updated everyone stopping in at Speedwell.

And yet, I hadn't done anything wrong. None of us had. Still, I kept asking the same question, over and over: Why? Why did death have to take someone who cared about so many people? Why George?

There was no answer. Just the pain that lingered, haunting me in the days that followed, and in the ones that would come after that.

"Visiting hours are Saturday at five," Ma said.

"I . . . I don't think I can go," I replied, my voice trembling.

"Are you sure?"

"I just don't think I can do it. I just wanna go to work."

"Okay," she said softly, pausing before adding, "but I want you to go if you want to. It's okay not to be at work. You know that, right?"

I nodded, but the moment made it hard to breathe, let alone speak. I wasn't sure what scared me more: seeing George like that again, or not going and having to carry the guilt of it. Work felt easier. Familiar. Safer. Grief, on the other hand, felt like stepping into a room I didn't know how to be in.

"Yeah," I said with a nod. "I just want to work. That okay?"

"It's okay," Ma said, pulling me into a gentle hug that

carried understanding and sadness.

Grief had always felt too big, too messy, like a rushing river I didn't know how to swim through. Work, on the other hand, always felt like a place I belonged. There was always something that needed doing, something that made me feel useful, even when I felt lost inside.

Choosing work wasn't new. It was how I'd always coped: Work hard, keep moving, keep your head down, don't stop long enough to feel too much. I had done it after the divorce. After I moved out on my eighteenth birthday. After the breakup with Kathleen. After everything bad that had ever happened to me. Grief scared me in a way that physical pain never could. So, I turned back to the one thing that had always made me feel in control.

But as I walked away from Ma that day, her broken heart clinging to the air behind me, I carried something new: a sense that I was leaving something sacred behind. I couldn't explain it other than to say the world was heavier than ever before.

George's cemetery plot was perfectly perched high on the hill, overlooking the town he had watched over for decades. As the preacher's voice droned on, I stopped listening. His words became distant, muffled by George's memory. I tilted my head back and stared at the sky, searching for something, anything, that might be him.

Was he up there, looking down on us? On me?

I can't believe you're gone. What am I supposed to do now?

The silence that followed washed over me like a wave, swallowing up the people, the prayers, even the wind. For a moment, nothing existed but the pale blue sky stretched out above me:

wide, empty, and still. Out of nowhere, two ducks flew in tandem from behind me, cutting through the quiet like the Blue Angels I had seen years ago with my dad. Their wings flapped just a few times before they stretched out and glided effortlessly overhead. I followed their path across the sky, watching as they moved in perfect sync, as if on a journey to a destination only they knew. For the first time in a week, a smile spread across my face and warmed my heart as the horizon gracefully swallowed their existence as quickly as they had appeared.

Zoe said, "You've mentioned a few times that you didn't go to George's visiting hours. Can I ask what pulled you toward Speedwell that day?"

It had been more than fifteen years since George died, and my body filled with different emotions as I sat in Zoe's office. Pride, honor, and gratitude now accompanied grief. I took a deep breath and said, "I couldn't do it. I couldn't see him like that."

"That makes a lot of sense, Jason. A lot of people feel that way, and there's nothing wrong with it. You wanted to hold on to the version of George that felt alive to you."

I nodded, thinking back to playing golf with him that last time. I couldn't remember anything but the sixth hole where he didn't feel good, but joy still found it's way into my heart as I knew we played golf together.

"I've learned to survive. To keep going when things fall apart."

Zoe nodded as if to say she understood and then said, "That kind of grief, the kind you hold down while you keep moving—it doesn't disappear. It waits. It's like water, Jason. You can dam it, freeze it, even reroute it. Eventually, it finds a way through. A song. A smell. Things that just seem random."

Two Ducks

I smiled and gave a little laugh. "Yeah. I remember smelling diesel and thinking he's still around the corner. Or I'd see a fuel delivery truck like Old Blue and it just punched me in the gut. Now, sometimes it just triggers memories of him."

Zoe gave a little smile and said, "That's grief trying to move. Not to hurt you, but to be acknowledged. To remind you that he mattered." She paused and said, "Can I ask . . . what would it be like to let yourself fall apart now? Just a little? Right here? What would happen if you stopped holding it all together?"

My throat tightened as my eyes slammed into the window, and the room became so loud I wanted to push my palms to my ears. "I don't know . . . I guess it's how I keep him alive inside me."

"It's normal to fear that if your grief eases, you might start forgetting him. Letting yourself grieve doesn't erase him. It helps you carry him in a way that feels less painful over time."

I nodded as my eyes became heavy.

"There are ways to remember him beyond the sadness. You've shared so many stories about the things he loved, the moments with him that you have told me changed who you have become. Those stay with you, long after the grief softens."

A smile warmed my face as I wiped away tears. I nodded.

16

THE WEB

As I hurried my way from pump to pump in the days following George's passing, Speedwell, as it was once known, had vanished in just four days. The building still stood, the pumps still faced the road, and Ma was still behind the scenes in her office, but the heart had gone silent. George's hand would never again grab a nozzle or wash a windshield, guiding them like he always had, like he had taught me to do. Old Blue would never idle by the tanks on a cold January night, headlights glowing through the snow while George stood atop the tank, preparing for a long night. I'd no longer be sitting in the passenger seat.

Without George, Speedwell became something else entirely, hollow and unfamiliar. It was like watching the shell of someone you loved walking around, but their spirit was missing. The laughter, the storytelling, the consistency of George's presence was gone. I didn't just lose a mentor and a father figure—I lost a place that had anchored me when everything else had felt uncertain.

The Web

As I worked, I was reminded of what George had told me: "I don't want people buying their fuel from Speedwell, I want them buying their fuel from me." It was evident he had succeeded, as the people entering Speedwell, car after car, truck after truck, were just as empty as their gas tanks. In George's effort to become Speedwell, Speedwell had become him. They were one and the same. And when he died, it felt like Speedwell had taken his place on the hospital bed. I couldn't help George get better, but maybe I could help Speedwell. Maybe I could help myself get better.

The disorientation ran deep. I had spent so much of my young adult life trying to figure out who I was, and for a time, I found myself through George, through Speedwell. When I ventured off to college both times in search of my purpose in life, Ma and George were in full support. Ma, George, and Speedwell had been my compass. Now, with George gone and Speedwell fading into something unrecognizable, I felt adrift again, just like I had after the divorce and when Kathleen and I broke up.

My train wasn't the only one to derail. Brian stepped away from his passion for farming and sold off his cows so he could help his mother manage Speedwell. Kathleen moved back home for a semester, enrolling at Lyndon State College, trying to be close while still holding on to her own future. Eventually, she returned to the University of Northern Colorado to finish her degree, but not without leaving a piece of herself behind.

Speedwell was now on life support.

The station still stood, but it no longer breathed the same way. The spark that had made it more than a place, more than a job, more than a stop for gas, was gone. We were all trying to hold it together, each of us carrying our grief in different ways, hoping routine would offer some kind of clarity. The conversations didn't flow the same. The regulars still came, but even their voices felt subdued, like we were all tiptoeing around a ghost we didn't know how to live with.

Speedwell had been diversified from the beginning, with George managing the front operations and Ma handling things in the back, their roles perfectly aligned, like two halves of a whole. After George passed, Brian and I stepped in to take on his responsibilities at the front, pumping gas and delivering fuel. At the same time, Ma began teaching Brian the ins and outs of her side of the business, passing down the knowledge she had carried for years.

My old routine, the one George had taught me, remained mostly unchanged. I sat in the diner every morning for breakfast and again at lunchtime, as if it could somehow summon his presence. I did everything I could to carry out what he had shown me, to uphold the standards he had left behind. George had prepared me to sit at the table, to make decisions, to be steady under pressure. But I had never truly believed he wouldn't be sitting beside me, guiding me with that calm wisdom I'd come to rely on.

Over the next twelve months, Ma called me into her office a handful of times to talk through a decision I'd made or a mistake I hadn't seen coming. She never raised her voice. Instead, she talked through the consequences, the ripple effect of one choice leading to another. She'd help me understand what to consider next time, what to do differently, what to see more clearly. It didn't happen often, but it was never good when she told me to shut the door. That door closing always brought a wave of tension, a reminder that I was still learning, still earning my place in a world that George had once made look easy.

I called myself to Ma's office in the fall of 1992 and closed the door behind me.

"You okay?" she asked, her voice soft but alert.

"I don't know, Ma."

"What's wrong?"

"I don't know how to say it," I said, lowering my head as I sank into the chair across from her.

The words jammed in my throat. How was I supposed to tell her that I wanted more from life than pumping gas and delivering fuel? After everything she and George had done for me, how could I sit here and say that Speedwell, this place that had become sacred to me, just wasn't enough for me anymore?

She waited, giving me space. One of Ma's superpowers was her ability to wait you out. She could sit in silence for hours if she knew you needed to be the first to speak. And she knew. "Just tell me," she said after a long silence.

After what felt like forever, I finally whispered, "I don't want to deliver fuel and pump gas for the rest of my life." The words tumbled out like a confession, and with them came the weight of guilt and shame. My hands pulled at my face, my head sinking into them as if trying to disappear under the pressure. I felt like I was betraying her, betraying George, betraying everything they had given me.

But there was a truth deep inside me. I needed to find out who I was beyond the Speedwell I had come to know.

"I'm glad you don't. I don't want you to do it for the rest of your life either."

My head snapped up. "You don't?" I asked.

"You can do so much more," she said without hesitation.

A rush of warmth ran through me as relief, thick and overwhelming, flooded my body. My shoulders, which had been locked in tension for days, maybe weeks, loosened. My lungs felt like they could finally fill with air. I hadn't even realized how tightly I'd been holding everything in.

"I don't know what to do," I admitted. "I don't want to be a carpenter, and I don't want to build bridges, either. I want to work for myself one day, like you and George. I want to own something."

And just like that, the weight came crashing back down. My head sank into my hands again.

Ma didn't rush in with answers. She just sat there patiently, letting me feel it, letting me say what I hadn't had the courage to say out loud until now.

"I'm lost, Ma."

"I know you are," she said gently. "It's okay. Let me think about it for a few days."

She opened her arms to me, and as I leaned in, not everything was figured out, but for the first time in a long time, I didn't feel trapped alone in my fear.

The following week, Ma and I walked through the front of the diner, passing the stools and tables where George and I used to sit. His absence still hung in the air, but the diner brought a strange kind of comfort. Ma led us to one of the quieter back booths, the ones she seemed to prefer.

"I've been thinking about adding a heating service business

to Speedwell," she said as we slid into our seats. "It makes sense for us to do it all."

My eyes lifted. "That's a great idea."

"What if we called it Speedwell Burner Service?" she added, watching me carefully.

"I like it," I said, already picturing the trucks and the logo.

Ma leaned her elbows on the table, her eyes steady. "Jason, I don't want you to leave."

"I don't wanna leave either," I said, the truth catching in my throat.

She gave a small nod. "I have a proposal for you. I want you to run Speedwell Burner Service. But you'll need to go to school first to learn how to install and repair heating equipment."

"Okay," I said, nodding slowly.

"After you finish school, I'll buy everything you need—the tools, a truck, whatever it takes—if you still want to do it. You'll be in charge of everything: marketing, billing, collections. You said you wanted to work for yourself one day. Well, here you go. It'll be yours to run."

The lump in my throat swelled. I reached across the table and took her hands in mine. "Thank you so much."

Ma looked at me with an expression on her face that meant she believed in me, a look I'd come to rely on. "When you work for yourself, you do the work. You understand what this means?"

"Yes," I said, nodding again. And I meant it.

In that moment, my life changed yet again. Grief, confusion, and feeling lost didn't disappear, but for the first time in a long time, it had competition: hope. Real hope. And it was Ma who handed it to me, not with pity, but with belief. Belief in who I was, and who I could still become.

"All the work. Every no-heat call is up to you. It means you're on call every night, every day, no days off. Working for yourself takes dedication. Are you willing to do all of this?"

"Yes, I understand," I said, as her words settled in. My mind flashed back to a moment with my dad, sitting with him in the truck. He asked me if I could stand shoulder to shoulder with the leaders of the varsity football team. That same question echoed in this one. Was I ready to lead? Was I ready to carry something bigger than myself?

"Where's the school?" I asked.

"Boston. It's called the New England Fuel Institute. It's a monthlong program that starts in two weeks, and I already enrolled you."

"You did?" I said, a smile breaking across my face.

"I did," Ma replied, her smile meeting mine.

Something about her confidence in me always made everything feel possible. Believing in someone had always been one of the greatest gifts Ma knew how to give. When she believed in me, it wasn't just words, it was something I could feel in my bones. Her belief trickled through me like water moving through brooks and streams, slowly building momentum. That encouragement turned into something larger, more powerful, confidence gathering like a river gaining speed and strength. Each moment she backed me, each time she trusted me to take the lead, added to the current. And before I knew it, I wasn't just drifting; I was moving forward, carried by something deeper than just my own will.

Two weeks later, I drove out of town, embarking on a new journey. As the miles slipped past and the road stretched out ahead of me, I glanced through the top of the windshield and whispered, "Did you have anything to do with this?" The sky didn't answer, but I kept talking anyway. "Can you believe it? You know what this means? I'm going to be one of the ones at the table, Speedwell Burner Service." I smiled, imagining George's voice in my head. *I know . . . I hear ya, family. I'm going to make you proud. I promise.*

The month flew by as quickly as it began. I did exactly as Ma had asked: I showed up. Every weekday, I sat in the classroom, soaking in everything I could learn about burners and boilers, wiring and diagnostics. Then, every Friday night, I made the three-hour drive home to work the weekend shift. Come Sunday afternoon around four, I hit the road again, heading back toward Boston with a tired body but a full heart. I wasn't just learning a trade; I was building something much bigger, piece by piece, from the ground up.

One afternoon, about a week after I completed my schooling, we got a call from Greg, a customer, who said he was out of fuel. I jumped in Old Blue, drove out to his place, and put a hundred gallons of warmth into his tank. Just like George had taught me, I bled the line and hit the reset button. The furnace kicked on, and I headed back to the station, delivering fuel on the way.

As I walked back into the office, Ma looked up from her desk and said, "Greg's furnace is off again. Looks like you've got your first service call."

I looked over at Zoe, and the look on her face said it all; she could feel how these past couple of sessions had beaten me up. As I looked at her, I wondered how she could do this every day. Client after client reliving the destruction of their life. I had no idea, but I was sure happy she was there in the room with me.

"How'd that make you feel, knocking on Greg's door?" Zoe asked.

I sat there on the couch rubbing my hands together, reliving that day. It was as if I could still feel the coldness of the metal door that seeped into my knuckles with every knock on Greg's front door. I could see myself standing there for a moment, the brisk air biting at my face, my breath visible in short puffs. I could see my new navy jacket with the words Speedwell Burner Service right above my name, both stitched in red thread. I remembered the jacket still had that new feel to it, stiff and proud, just like me.

I could see my blue service van in the driveway and pictured my toolbox, every wrench and gauge still shiny and new, untouched by grime or wear. I saw myself waiting for Greg to answer, and I saw myself look down at the lettering on my chest.

I made eye contact with Zoe and said, "I wasn't just a kid pumping gas anymore. I wasn't Kathleen's boyfriend, I wasn't George's helper, or Ma's project."

I paused and felt those words, verbalized for the first time. "I was there on my own merit, called to fix the furnace, trusted to bring warmth back into a home."

Speedwell Burner Service was the birth of something new: not just a business, but a piece of me taking shape. I had a title, a trade, and a truck. For the first time, I felt like I belonged to something of my own making, a version of Speedwell that carried George's legacy and my ambition.

Every aspect of Speedwell grew over the next few years. Ma retired in 1995, and Brian purchased the family business to keep his parents' dream alive. With that decision, Brian became the new face of Speedwell, while I was the face of Speedwell Burner Service. We had become brothers bonded in purpose as we carried on George and Ma's legacy.

I hadn't dreamed of this day. In fact, I didn't even know this mountain existed years ago. I had been wandering the foothills of life, unsure of where I was headed, unsure of where I wanted to go. I had spent years exploring paths in my mind and with my feet, only to abandon them, retreating back to the beginning. I had been walking roads that never quite felt like they were mine when I stopped to look around.

As I look back, I can see that purpose found me somewhere in the middle of buried grief through five dollars of gas, late night no-heat calls, and broken furnaces. My whole life was a web of moments, each decision standing alone, yet all intricately connected by an unconscious drive to achieve something bigger than myself. Kathleen returned alone a year after graduation, and the torch I'd been carrying since our breakup flickered back to life the moment I saw her. I had survived her years in Colorado. I was still single, still grounded in the place we both called home. My life was more together than it had ever been, and for the first time in years, I felt like I knew who I was.

She looked the same, only older in a way I couldn't quite explain. It was like time had shaped her but hadn't changed her.

I walked straight to her without thinking, heart pounding like it always used to. When we embraced, the familiar shape of her pressed against me like no time had passed at all. But her hug didn't linger like it used to. She let go a little too soon.

Ma had fixed up the basement into an apartment for me after George died, but Kathleen wasn't moving *home* home. That truth came tucked inside a conversation I hadn't expected. She had found a little apartment a couple miles down the road. I tried to nod like it didn't sting, but I felt the distance stretch between us.

A sharp pain pierced my body a couple of months later as the torch I had been carrying for so long plunged its way through my chest, searing the stitches in my heart. The torch smoldered with cold darkness as I watched the hand I used to hold in someone else's. In perfect stride, side by side. Kathleen walked down the street, away from me, toward her future with her fingers laced with someone else's.

For months I had sat on this couch trying to verbalize many of my emotions for the first time. Zoe asked me, "How did that make you feel?"

As I sat there searching for the words, I said, "I was heartbroken for the second time, but nothing like what happened after that."

17

COLD COFFEE

My alarm knifed through the darkness one morning in the summer of 1997, and I lay in bed, numb to the noise. I wasn't dreaming: This shit was real. Brian had decided to sell everything and return to farming. Kathleen had decided to buy the gas station, and Fred's Propane had acquired the fuel oil division, which included Speedwell Burner Service.

My life, as I had known it, was over. Speedwell, the company I had woven my identity into over the past decade, was being sold, and I hadn't even known it was for sale.

My identity was shattered into a million unrecognizable pieces. I stood empty as my life flashed before me in some gut-wrenching fragments of everything I had built. Everything I had poured myself into, sacrificed for, and believed in was gone.

How is this possible? Why is this happening? The questions looped through my mind, but no answers came, only silence and the pain of disappointment. Fear of the unknown pressed in from all sides, constricting me until I could barely breathe. I watched as purpose, the very thing I thought I had found, now evaporated from my body like steam from a boiling pot of water. This wasn't loss like before. It was as if I had been erased.

I had done nearly everything right. Sure, I had stumbled along the way. But I had come to see that life was really a collage of mistakes and setbacks, held together by threads of success that, over time, stitched themselves into something resembling a legacy. For a long time, I believed I was the one in control, that my fate rested securely in my own two hands. But I didn't realize, at least not until it was too late, that my fate also lived in the hands of others.

Spitting the nasty taste of cold coffee back into my cup, I looked up at the clock on the Miss Lyndonville Diner wall and realized I had lost time again. How long had I been sitting there? The diner buzzed as normal, only it all faded beneath the conversations in my head from my days sitting here with George.

Focusing my mind on any single thought for more than a few moments felt like trying to catch a fly with my bare hands. I could've had a job by lunchtime if I really wanted one, but just having a job wasn't enough. I needed more than that. I needed purpose and identity. And deep down, I knew I wasn't going to find that before lunch.

My mind raced backward, searching the past for answers, grasping at memories that had turned slippery as eels: there one moment, evaporating the next. Every time my mind paused, waiting for advice, the empty seat across from me never spoke. Surely, Fred would hire me—I'd known him for nearly a decade. It was the logical move. And then I thought about my jacket with Speedwell Burner Service embroidered

Cold Coffee

on the chest, and when I pictured the name Fred's Propane above my name, my stomach hurt. I thought about my dad in Oregon and our time that night on the porch after we disagreed about the roof. The longer those thoughts stayed in my mind, the more I shook my head.

Dad's voice broke into my thoughts with a message he had said countless times: "You can do and be anything you want in life if you want it bad enough."

The words dragged me back to a childhood memory that had never faded. I was maybe eight or nine, standing on a sun-baked tarmac with Dad's arm slung around my shoulder. We looked up as the Blue Angels roared just overhead, their formation impossibly tight, the jets screaming across the sky. He pointed upward as they climbed in perfect unison as if headed into outer space.

I was completely captivated. That day, the dream of flying fighter jets burned into my imagination. I still remember the surge of adrenaline, the awe that filled my chest, the certainty that one day, I'd be in that cockpit. On the ride home, I couldn't stop replaying the image of me climbing into the jet, pulling the canopy down, locking it in place, and feeling the wheels lift off the runway as I soared into the clouds.

At twenty-six, I'd long ago abandoned that dream. I no longer yearned to be a fighter pilot. It had been so long since I felt the rush of a dream through my body. So long I wondered how they even came to be.

After the divorce, Dad's advice was less about limitless potential and more about finding direction. "Find something you love to do," he told me one night on the phone, "and figure out how to make a living doing it." His voice had carried more than wisdom. He needed me to believe it too.

I had clung to that idea for years, quietly repeating it to myself as I built my life around Speedwell Burner Service. It had never been a job; it was the thing I had loved. I'd done exactly what he said.

Now, standing on the other side of its collapse, I questioned so much. The doubt was louder than it had ever been, but somewhere beneath it all, belief was still alive. Just because something hadn't worked before didn't mean it wouldn't work the next time. Maybe I hadn't found my purpose or the right version of myself yet. Maybe it had just taken falling apart to give birth to my calling.

I could hear my dad, as if he was sitting beside me, ask, "What did you love about what you did?" I loved the way running a business challenged my mind and how every day forced me to think, to solve, to adapt. I didn't exactly enjoy crawling under a trailer in thirty-below-zero weather at two in the morning to fix a heating system. But there was something deeply satisfying about being the one people called when everything had gone wrong. I took pride in that. I liked being relied upon, being the one to take something broken and make it work again.

Pumping gas hadn't thrilled me for the task itself. It was the people and the relationships George exposed me to. And farming—God, I loved farming. The dirt in my nails, the sweat on my back, the aching muscles and knowing that not everyone was cut out to be a farmer but I was. It was one of the hardest jobs out there, and I took pride in the fact that I'd chosen to do it anyway. There was nobility in that kind of work. And I loved it.

But I hadn't been in love with farming, and there was a difference. A big one.

"You okay?" one of the servers asked as she replaced yet another cold cup of coffee.

I nodded, offering a half smile, though the question lingered long after she walked away. *Was I okay?* I wasn't sure anymore.

What did I love to do more than anything? Golf. I loved golf more than anything else. I nodded to myself, as if some wiser, future version of me had known the answer all along and had just been waiting for me to catch up. *Yes*, I thought. *I love golf.*

As the truth settled in, my body eased into a calm I hadn't felt since that conversation with Brian. The turbulent waves of emotion that had been crashing relentlessly against the shores of my being began to soften, their force weakening with each breath. The storm, it seemed, was finally passing.

And now, it was time to untether my boat.

Purpose and passion are like twins: They look very similar, but there is an essential difference between them that you only recognize this after getting to know each one. Once you build a relationship with both, you'll never confuse one for the other. I pulled a wad of wrinkled one-dollar bills from my pocket, counted out ten, and placed them on the counter. I had figured it out; I knew which road to take, but I needed some help, and I knew just the guy.

18

THE QUESTION

Five minutes after leaving the diner, I found myself parked at the St. Johnsbury Country Club, staring up toward the sixth hole. It was the same spot where, seven years earlier, George told me he was okay. I remembered the way he smiled, brushing off the concern in my voice. But he hadn't been okay. Not even close.

The wind tugged at the branches lining the fairway. I leaned into the steering wheel, thoughts spinning faster than I could catch them.

George, is this crazy? I asked in silence, as if he might answer from somewhere just beyond the trees.

Am I even good enough?
What if I'm not?
What if I'm never good enough?
What if this doesn't work out?

The questions rolled in like distant thunder, each one rumbling louder and closer. But beneath the fear, buried deep and stubborn, belief had found another survivor: hope.

The Question

The brass doorknob of the golf shop felt strangely familiar, like the one in my mom's kitchen the morning I turned eighteen. Cold and filled with meaning I couldn't quite explain. I wrapped my hand around it, hesitated, then eased the door open.

Peering around the corner like a kid playing hide-and-seek, I glanced into Larry Kelley's office. A part of me hoped he wasn't there so I could just say I tried. But there he was, sitting behind his desk.

I stepped forward and knocked twice. The sound of my knuckles against the doorframe filled the room and settled in the question stirring in my gut.

"Slippery," he said with a grin. "Not fixing furnaces today?"

"Not today," I said, trying to steady my voice.

He turned in his chair to face me. "What can I do for you?"

I took a breath as I sat. The air burned a little as it filled my lungs, my heart beating somewhere in my throat.

"Larry . . ." I paused. "I want to be you. How do I be you?"

After a few minutes of questions and explaining my situation, Larry leaned back in his chair and said, "If you want to be me, you've got two options: Work as an apprentice for a PGA professional like me, or attend one of the four professional golf management programs in the country."

"I can do that," I said. "Will you hire me?"

"No," he said immediately, shaking his head.

I blinked. No one had ever said no to me before when I asked for a job. "Why not?"

"If you work for me, you'll never make it. Not in your hometown," he said in a tone grounded in truth and kindness. "If you want to be me, you need to go to college."

The thought of college again sucker-punched me in the gut. I didn't know what to expect walking into Larry's office, but going back to college for a third time was not on the list.

"How do I do that?" I asked, trying to hide the disappointment leaking into my voice.

"Here's the number for the PGA of America. Call them. Ask what you need to do."

My eyes dropped to the floor. Four more years. My Lyndon State College GPA flashed through my mind, dragging my SAT score along with it. I had done well at Vermont Technical College, but I wasn't sure if that counted enough to offset the mess of Lyndon State. I'd be thirty by the time I graduated, *if* I graduated.

No, I told myself. *If I'm going, I'm graduating.*

"Okay," I said, still staring at the carpet.

"Okay, what?" Larry asked.

"I'll call them," I said, lifting my eyes

Without a word, Larry took the phone on his desk, spun it around, and pushed it toward me. I stared at it, then back at him, then at the phone again. "Now? You want me to call them now?"

"If you want to be me, call them now," he said in a voice that left no room for doubt.

My heart pounded against my ribs, fighting like hell to escape the cage it was trapped in. The rest of my body froze, paralyzed by the fear I hadn't anticipated and the possibility of what I would learn.

I looked down at my arm resting on the chair, willing it to move. But it lay there like a log.

Summoning every ounce of strength I had, I forced my arm to lift. My fingers reached for the phone. When I reached the

The Question

last digit, I hesitated just like I had years ago when I tried to call Kathleen for the first time.

I took a breath, swallowed hard, and dialed the last number.

It's amazing what you can do when your back is pushed up against a wall. The fight inside me came roaring to life the moment I felt cornered by something beyond my control.

Why did it always surprise me? That sudden surge of will? That stubborn refusal to give up?

Our instinct to survive is buried deep, but it's always there, waiting. When everything felt like it was falling apart, that's when it showed up. I used to wonder: Where did that kind of courage hide during the ordinary days? Why did it only reveal itself when the stakes were high and failure loomed like a shadow?

"Well, what'd they say?" Larry asked as I hung up the phone.

"Same thing you told me," I said, exhaling reality. "I've gotta choose between the four accredited colleges in the country: Ferris State, Penn State, New Mexico State, and Mississippi State."

"Well?" he said, as if I should know already.

"I duno. Whaddya think I should do?" I asked, hoping he'd give me the answer I was too afraid to make for myself.

"You gotta figure that out," he said, leaning back in his chair.

And just like that, the ball was back in my court.

Life hit me as I sat in the St. Johnsbury Country Club parking lot before I left. It felt like all I was doing was figuring shit out. One decision led to another, each step forward revealing another fork in the path or a dead end. It was like being trapped in a maze, with hope lingering at every turn but offering only more questions. I'd picked myself up after falling off the proverbial horse more times than I could count, thinking each time this was the last hard choice. This was the turning point.

Maybe leaving Lyndonville was the best decision I could make for my future, and for my heart.

After all, Kathleen's boyfriend had gotten down on one knee and asked the love of my life to marry him. And she said yes. In a few months, she would stand in front of family and friends and say, "I do," but the words wouldn't be meant for me. Like the two birds in Gram's picture, it was time for me to fly away. I had to let Kathleen go, and I knew I couldn't do that in my hometown.

The next morning, the sun streamed through the porch windows, warming my legs as I sipped hot coffee across from Ma. The air smelled of fresh cut grass, lilacs, and something faintly sweet I didn't recognize. I hadn't shared my crazy plan with anyone yet. I mean, who goes back to college at twenty-six after failing the first time? But if there was anyone who'd tell me the truth, whether it was a good idea or not, it was Ma.

"I'm going back to college, Ma."

"You are?" she asked. "For what?"

"I want to be a golf professional. Like Larry Kelley."

She paused, and the corners of her eyes smiled at me. "That's wonderful."

We sat there for over an hour, talking through what came next. I told her about George, about Brian, about what Speedwell had meant to me. I told her what it felt like to lose it all. I even told her about Kathleen and how much it hurt to know she was marrying someone else. I wasn't ready to be happy for her, not yet. But maybe one day, I would be.

Ma listened with the lack of judgment she always did. And like always, in that moment of need, her belief in me made it all feel possible.

"Ma, how am I ever gonna repay you?"

She looked up from her coffee, a soft crease forming between her brows. "For what?"

"For taking me in. For letting me pump gas and deliver fuel. For Speedwell Burner Service. For the Airstream, the apartment in the basement. For never charging me rent. For feeding me. For loving me like a son. For teaching me. For listening. For encouraging me. For always believing in me . . . for everything. How am I ever gonna repay you?"

She didn't hesitate. Her eyes held steady on mine as she said, "Jason, you don't owe me anything."

I sat there, stunned. How could that be possible?

I wouldn't be who I was without her. From the moment I started dating Kathleen, everything I had, everything I was working toward, it all traced back to the Nichols family. How could I not owe her anything?

Tears fell as I held Ma close. "Thank you for everything, Ma. I love you so much."

"You're welcome. I love you too," she whispered. "You're going to make a great golf pro. I'll always be here for you. Let me know if you need anything, okay?"

I nodded, my chin resting on the top of her head.

"I'm proud of you," she said.

And in that moment, hope and belief stood above fear and doubt.

"How was that possible, Zoe? How was it possible I didn't owe her anything after everything she and the family had done for me?"

Zoe looked at me gently and said, "Why would you think you owed them something, Jason?"

Her question caught me off guard. I blinked, unsure how to respond. "What do you mean, why? How could I not?" I pressed with confusion. Somewhere in me, I knew I was supposed to feel grateful, not indebted, but the two had become so tangled over the years that I couldn't tell them apart.

"You told me they were like family and they treated you like a son," she said.

"Yeah." I nodded as memories rushed my thoughts.

Zoe nodded too. "How did you feel when your mom used to lay with you, or when your dad helped you with baseball and football? Did you feel like you owed them something?"

I stared at the floor. My mind drifted back to the warmth of my mom's arms, the sound of my dad's voice guiding me from the dugout fence. I had felt supported. Loved.

"No . . . not that I remember," I said quietly, almost afraid of the realization forming behind the words.

"What about now? Do you feel like you owe them something now?"

"No," I said. "I was grateful then, and I still am." The difference between owing and appreciating was suddenly becoming clear, like the view through my windshield after a thunderstorm passed.

Zoe leaned in slightly. "Why do you think your mom and dad did those things for you?"

I leaned back on the couch, laced my fingers behind my head, and exhaled a long, heavy sigh. I could feel something uncoiling inside me as years of pressure, guilt, maybe even shame loosened their grip. "Because I was their son and they loved me. That's what parents do."

Zoe tilted her head. "What do you mean, 'That's what they do'?"

"They help you," I said, the words barely above a whisper. As I spoke them, I realized that love didn't have to be earned and repaid. She smiled softly.

A wave of emotion rose from deep within me. My throat tightened, and tears I didn't know I'd been holding began to spill. I pressed the pads of my fingers to my eyes, cupped my face in my hands, and wept with appreciation and an understanding that *real* love is given, not traded.

19

THE MAZE

A week later, I sat on the edge of the bed, elbows on my knees, staring at the concrete floor like the answer might crawl up out of the cracks.

Papers were scattered across the kitchen table, pages of notes from Ferris State and Mississippi State, tuition estimates, loan estimates, to-do lists, all of it blurring together like a bad hand of cards. I rubbed my face and fell backward on the bed.

This was the bed Mom used to talk about, the one I'd have to lie in after making my choices. It wasn't a metaphor anymore but a very real mattress, and I wasn't sure if I could lie in it without sinking straight through.

My so-called "stellar" academic achievements had barely gotten me a foot in the door at Penn State's Pre-Professional Golf Management Program. It wasn't a full acceptance but more like a tryout.

New Mexico State was off the list. I just couldn't see myself there. That left Ferris State and Mississippi State. Both had good programs, but neither came cheap. I figured I'd need over fifty grand to make it through: tuition, housing, meals, everything. All I had was a thousand dollars and a mountain of college debt from the first two attempts at finding myself.

I glanced at the rotary phone next to the bed. One call to Ma, and she'd help me, no questions asked. She always did. She'd tell me not to worry about the money, that I could pay her back after graduation. She'd say, "Your dream matters more than the money." But I couldn't do it. She'd already given me more than anyone had a right to ask for. If I was going to make this leap, I needed to find a way to jump without her this time.

My mom had two children in her second marriage, Margaret and Patrick, and the two of them seemed to tighten the soil beneath all of us, making it easier for Mom and me to find steady ground. Our relationship was still rocky, but we were trying. She kept Coors Light in the refrigerator for me.

Every time I opened the door and saw that familiar silver can sitting on the shelf, I knew it was her way of saying, "I see you. I haven't forgotten you." It was a small gesture, but one I appreciated more than I ever let on.

I hadn't tucked my tail between my legs, but it wasn't wagging either as I sat at the bar in Mom's kitchen. I explained how lost I had been the past couple of weeks. As I spoke, I saw her face change. Her eyes filled with sorrow and sadness that was hard to look at.

My mom, the mom I knew as a kid, sat across from me at that moment. I hadn't seen this mom in a long time. She wasn't the mom that I fought with at every turn from my teenage years. She wasn't the one who had seemed so far away when I needed her most. No, this was the mom I remembered from way back, the one who whispered encouragement at bedtime. The mom I had wanted so badly to show up when I turned eighteen, when I packed my things and walked out the door like I had it all figured out. She hadn't been there then. But she was here now, sitting across from me.

I had worked hard trying to turn myself from a boy into a man who was strong and self-sufficient. I had convinced myself as I walked out the door at eighteen that I was doing this on my own, but the truth was that even though I was working hard and was proud, I wasn't doing it alone. Leaving home gave me strength, but it also cost me. I'd learned to figure out many things on my own, but that strength came with a price of silent nights and unspoken fears. Independence had become both my armor and my burden.

Sitting in that kitchen, I felt both of those truths pressing down on me. I wanted to make it on my own. I needed to, but the only way forward was to ask for help because I couldn't do it alone.

Mom agreed to help under one condition. The money she would loan me must be paid back in ten years. I had no idea how I would repay her on top of all the loans the school was giving me and the school debt I had already amassed. But it didn't matter; it was a decade from now. I would figure it out. Mom was helping me, and for the first time in a long time, I felt like her son as I walked out the door. Not because she gave me money. Ma would have done that for me, and it would have been much easier to ask for her help. I felt like her son for the first time in years because she chose me at that moment and believed in me.

The Maze

On the morning of June 20, I filled up the tank of my Jeep Wrangler, tossed a couple of duffel bags in the back, and slid the crisp US atlas onto the passenger seat. This wasn't a road trip; it was a journey toward something. As I looked at the glossy cover of the Atlas, I thought about Gram and all her adventures cataloged on the walls of her apartment. I wondered if she felt the same way I did: a blend of excitement and hope stirred with a little fear and doubt.

Two days later, I rolled onto the Mississippi State University campus for a visit. The humidity hit my skin like a wall the same way the vast campus hit my eyes. I wiped the sweat from my forehead as I made my way across campus to meet Dr. Jones, the director of the Professional Golf Management (PGM) Program, and Scott Maynard from the Co-op office. Both men were polite and professional, and their Southern warmth radiated through button-down shirts and firm handshakes. They talked me through the Professional Golf Management Program—its rigor, the expectations, the internship requirements, and the job placement statistics.

The next day, I found myself in a packed auditorium. I hadn't seen this many people in one place since the church for George's funeral service. The irony of this memory put a sad smile on my face. I slid into a seat somewhere near the back, hiding and listening as an alum stood at the front, lit by five hundred pairs of eyes. He talked about his journey and how Mississippi State changed his life.

As I listened, something stirred in me. Maybe it was hope. Maybe it was desperation masked as belief. But there was something about the way he spoke: there was a certainty in his voice, an ease in his posture as he traveled the stage. It made me wonder: *If this place changed his life, maybe it could change mine, too.*

Influence is like that: It sneaks up on you without your knowledge. One person's story can plant a seed and make you imagine a version of yourself you haven't met yet. And while we're not always aware of how deeply those words embed themselves, we feel the emotional gravity of possibility.

I walked out of that auditorium with what I needed: a nudge forward, not from family or a loved one, but from a stranger, from someone with nothing to gain or lose by my decision or my journey through life. And yet, the whole time he spoke, it was as if I was the person he came to talk to. The one person he hoped to reach was me. He would travel the stage, peering into the crowd, but every time he turned back toward me, it was as if his eyes looked through the people between us and directly into mine.

"Scott, can I talk to you for a minute?" I asked, standing in the doorway of the PGM office. Scott gestured for me to come in.

"This is where I want to go," I said, meeting his eyes without flinching. "What do I do now?"

There was no hesitation in my voice, no wavering in my tone. I knew exactly what I wanted. For the first time, I wasn't following someone else's idea of success. I was about to become a college freshman for the third time in my life, but this time, it wasn't about proving anything to anyone else. It was about chasing something that belonged wholly to me.

In less than two months, I'd be leaving Lyndonville behind, tying up the final threads of a life that had shaped me but no longer held me. The seed George had planted in me years ago had finally broken through the surface with purpose.

I wasn't just going to college. I was chasing a dream. My dream: a dream of becoming a PGA professional.

The weeks after returning home from Mississippi State University were eye-opening. As I shared my plan with friends and family, most offered smiles, nods, and words of support. But beneath the surface, I could sense the doubt. Some didn't even try to hide it.

"You're crazy."

"You're too old to go back to school."

"Why not just start your own heating company?"

That last one came from a friend who genuinely meant well. And truthfully, I had explored that idea with Uncle Tom not long after Brian told me Speedwell was being sold. But I didn't have the money, and there was no way a bank would loan what I needed. Truth be told, the idea of starting out on my own was my way of grasping for a branch as I fell out of the tree. I was chasing something different now. Something mine.

When I finally called Uncle Tom, Dad's older brother and the person I always looked to for major life advice, there was a long pause on the other end of the line.

"You're going to be what?" he said.

"A golf professional," I replied.

Another pause.

Then, finally, he said, "Good for you, Jas. Good for you."

Those words, "Good for you," meant one thing: This dream of mine was lofty, and leaving my hometown was a good thing. Those words meant, "I believe in you." And that was powerful.

I learned quickly that when you're lucky enough to find your dream, your four-leaf clover, you have to protect it. You have to hold it like a newborn, shield it from the cold breath of doubt, and nurture it before the world has the chance to harden it. Negativity can be loud or subtle, and sometimes even well-intentioned, but it has power.

It's funny how people think they're talking about you when they say, "You can't do that. That's impossible. That'll never work." They're telling you about themselves. They don't believe they could do it. My friend who encouraged me to start a heating company said, "So, your goal is to be a golf professional? Well, if it doesn't work out you can always come back and fix furnaces again."

I thought about what he said, and none of it settled well. This wasn't a goal. I didn't even like goals; they never seemed to work for me. Becoming a golf professional wasn't a goal. It was my dream. I remembered that emptiness during high school graduation when I realized the field was missing the green rope that once kept me off the football field. I remembered realizing I hadn't had a dream in so long I couldn't remember how they came to be. This wasn't a goal. Becoming a PGA professional had become my dream, and I was willing to do whatever it took to climb that mountain. Returning back home if it didn't work out, having a plan B—nope, no thank you. I was the one climbing this mountain. Not going to make it? Get the hell out of the way and watch me.

My sunglasses fogged over like a bathroom mirror after a hot shower the moment I stepped out of my air-conditioned apartment into Mississippi's suffocating August heat. "Damn, it's hot," I muttered, pulling the glasses off my face and blinking as the sun pinched my eyelids shut. *You have got to be kidding me.*

The short walk to the grocery store felt like swimming through a pool of humidity hanging low over the parking lot. My shirt clung to my back, and the air felt thick enough to chew. After nearly a hundred yards of slogging through that invisible swamp, the automatic doors opened, and I was rescued by a blast of cool, dry air.

I wandered through the aisles, grabbing what I needed without much thought. Just as I was about to toss a cereal box into the cart, something on the back caught my eye. A child's maze. A little grey cartoon mouse with whiskers sat at the top, arrows pointing to pathways into the labyrinth. At the bottom of the box, tucked away behind one narrow opening, was a wedge of cheese.

I paused for a moment, my eyes tracing the maze, before tossing the box into the cart. Then, a few minutes later, in the middle of the store, I tugged my cart to a stop.

"No way," I said out loud, pulling the box from the cart and studying it again. I'd solved the puzzle, but not the way they intended. I had started at the cheese and worked backward, finding the mouse with ease.

I stared at the path I'd traced, and Grandpa's voice echoed in my head like he was sitting in his aluminum throne right there beside me. "If you walk the track forward, you aren't preparing for what will happen. All you know is where you've been, not where you're going."

He had taught me that when I was thirteen after I had gotten lost after my first ever hole shot in motocross, not knowing which way to turn. I hadn't thought about it in years.

Why do memories disappear from time to time?

It was strange how something so small could unearth a lesson buried so deep. As if parts of our past, even the ones we need most, tuck themselves away like a bear settling in before winter, waiting for the right moment to wake again. That lesson Grandpa taught me, planning backward, hadn't vanished, not really. It had just been in hibernation.

Maybe I was too young back then to understand. Grandpa had been talking about the racetrack that day. But standing in the grocery store, I realized he wasn't just talking about the track. He never was.

How had I forgotten that?

Maybe life just gets loud—too loud. And in the noise of loss, change, fear, and distraction, the truths and lessons go silent. But here it was again, rising like breath on a cold day. Start with the cheese. Work your way back to the mouse.

I stared down at the maze one last time and smiled. I wasn't lost. I just needed to remember how to find my way.

"We need a plan," I announced as I stepped into my advisor's office the following day at Mississippi State.

She looked up from her desk, eyebrows slightly raised. "We already planned your schedule," she said.

"Not for this semester," I said, closing the door behind me. "For my entire college career."

Her pen froze in midair. "All four years?"

"Yup," I said, settling into the chair across from her. "We need to figure out what classes I need to take each semester, starting with my senior year and working backward."

The Maze

She leaned back in her chair, studying me for a moment, as if trying to decide whether I was ambitious or just plain crazy. This look reminded me of so many back home when I told people about my plans.

A smirk tugged at the corner of her mouth. "That's . . . not how most students do it."

I shrugged my shoulders and said, "I'm not most students."

Shaking her head and rolling her eyes with a half smile, she pulled out the course catalog and we got to work, mapping out every semester as if the current schedule of classes would remain the same for the next four years. It was hypothetical, but exactly what I needed. As we laid it out, I realized something: If I wanted to graduate in four years and still complete the internships required by the PGM Program, I'd need to take a heavy course load every single semester.

"How many hours can I take?" I asked, scanning the long list of course codes and prerequisites.

I listened intently as she told me that students normally take twelve to fifteen hours. *She did it again*, I thought. *She just stuffed me into another normal box.*

"I'm gonna be here forever if I take the normal hours," I said. "Can I take twenty-one?"

She gave a little huff. "You haven't been in school for a long time. How about we ease into this a little?" I could sense she was a little annoyed and even a little protective, and rightly so: She had seen my stellar academic performance when she looked at my records. That bed Mom warned me about—well, I was tucked under the covers, as only one of my classes transferred from Lyndon State College.

She was right, but that wasn't me now. The person sitting across from her now was on a mission. "I don't have time or money to ease into anything," I said, firm and with a little laugh. "Can I at least try it the first semester?"

"Not without permission from the academic dean," she said, and I knew what that answer would be.

"Okay, I can take eighteen, right?" I said.

Yes," she nodded, slowly.

"Okay. Let's move it around to get me to eighteen for now. We'll bump it up next semester."

She gave me a long look, as if trying to measure my determination, but she didn't argue. We manipulated the schedule like two gamblers trying to stack the odds in our favor, pushing courses around like poker chips on a crowded table. When we finally stepped back and looked at the plan, it was tight. Unforgiving, really. No room for missteps. No room for slipping up or slacking off. I walked out of that office with a plan in hand, a road map that would get me to a bachelor's degree of business administration in marketing, alongside my PGA of America accreditation, in exactly four years.

The pressure wrapped itself around me like a vise. I wasn't eighteen anymore. I didn't have the luxury of aimless semesters or discovering myself in elective classes as I tried to figure out what I wanted to do with my life. I had already traveled down that needed road. I wasn't here for the college experience. I was here to transform my life.

Whether it was crawling under a trailer in subzero temperatures to fix a furnace, pumping gas at dawn, or running Speedwell Burner Service on grit and long hours, I'd spent my life proving I could outwork whatever was thrown at me. And now, with the clock ticking louder every day, I knew this wasn't going to be any different.

And for the first time since my last dirt bike race, the path ahead didn't feel like fresh, untouched snow. I had been here before. Planning backward from graduation day, I began walking through each of my class schedules like checkpoints on a track I was finally learning how to read.

20

LUCKY #7

The past few weeks blurred through my mind like a movie on fast-forward one morning as I sat alone on a bench outside McCool Hall on campus. I had come here chasing a dream, but it was becoming clear that chasing it wasn't enough. If I wanted to graduate in four years, I first had to survive, and that meant staying enrolled. To stay enrolled, I needed two things: grades good enough to register each semester, and money to pay for the right to keep showing up.

Ironically, I didn't need great, or even good, grades to stay in college. All I had to do was pass. But money? That was a different story. Money had to come from somewhere, and I didn't have enough. Staying in school had less to do with academic performance and more to do with financial survival.

I did the math more times than I cared to admit, hoping the numbers would magically work. But they never did. I had underestimated the cost of college.

Getting a job was urgent. It wasn't about extra spending

cash or filling time between classes. It was about keeping my dream alive.

The university's golf course had already told me they weren't hiring when I called after arriving in town. A quick reminder that I wasn't in Lyndonville, Vermont, anymore.

Chatter among the three PGM students in the office about the recent football win over Memphis and their concerns about having Kentucky in town that weekend highlighted the distance between them and me. The PGM office walls were covered in plaques, photographs of famous golf holes, and glossy brochures promising careers in golf. It all felt just slightly out of reach, like I was looking through glass at a world I hadn't quite earned the right to step into.

Scott Maynard sat behind his desk, tapping away at his keyboard before swiveling his chair to face me. He was the only person I had in this unfamiliar place who might be able to open a door for me.

"Scott, I need a job," I said, trying to keep my desperation hidden. "You know anyone looking for help?"

He leaned back slightly. "What kind of job are you looking for?"

"In a perfect world, one at a golf course would be great. I called the university course, but they told me they weren't hiring." Quickly, I added, "But I'm willing to do anything."

He didn't hesitate. "Okay. Let me make some phone calls."

The following day, Scott told me that a friend of his, Felicia, managed a convenience store in town and had a part-time job waiting for me.

It didn't take long to learn an unspoken rule: If you're willing to do someone else's work, they'll gladly let you. I jumped in without being asked. Stocking shelves, cleaning the bathrooms, mopping the floors after closing. Within a week, I was doing more than just my share. And no one was stopping me.

Still, guilt followed me through each shift. I wasn't in Mississippi to run a cash register or sweep sticky tiles at midnight. This job was a stepping stone. I explained that to Felicia early on. As soon as something opened up at a golf course, I'd have to take it.

"I understand," she said, nodding. "Scott told me you were in PGM."

I thanked her and told her I'd be the hardest-working employee she'd ever had. If I showed up and gave everything I had, maybe she'd be sad when I left, but she wouldn't be disappointed in me. That mattered more than I could explain.

I arrived at my apartment one afternoon in late October and found two thick books wrapped in plastic sitting at my door. I didn't need to see the covers to know what they were. A book of White Pages stacked on top of another filled with yellow.

The White Pages listed personal phone numbers in alphabetical order, names of strangers I hadn't yet met in a town I was still learning to navigate. The Yellow Pages, though, that was where opportunity lived. Before I left home, Mom told me, "Keep a copy of the Yellow Pages in your Jeep. You never know when you might need to look up a phone number." Now, flipping through the ads, I was glad I listened.

A third of the way through, under "golf courses," a full-page ad stopped me cold. A sweeping image of a grand Southern clubhouse, draped with a waving banner that read, *"Old Waverly,*

Golf Club, 'Host to the 1999 U.S. Women's Open.'"

The following day, ammonia tickled my nose soon after I turned off Old Highway 82 on my way to Old Waverly Golf Club. I figured a farm had to be nearby, but not a dairy farm. This smell was sharper, but it still reminded me of what I had left behind. The aroma of home grew stronger as my eyes scanned for a familiar-looking red barn. The smell I'd mistaken for cows and silage wasn't from a farm at all. I was smelling Bryan Foods, a slaughterhouse tucked alongside the road.

Two stop signs later, the old country road began to float gently through the rolling terrain. Large homes dotted the landscape, each framed by edged bushes and long, curving driveways that cut through the hills like ribbons. The grass, a lighter shade of green than back home, perfectly manicured, stood in the warm fall sun.

A white-railed fence emerging from a grove of trees ran alongside me to the crest of the hill and guided me into the entrance of Old Waverly Golf Club. A tall man stepped out from the guardhouse, which sat on an island in the center of the drive. Everything about him was, well, perfect. Not a strand of his thick gray hair was out of place. A rich black tuxedo clung to his slender frame with precision, complementing his upright posture and confident authority. I had never seen someone dressed so well. He looked like he belonged to another world. A world I wasn't sure I had any business stepping into.

"How may I help you, sir?" he said, stepping forward.

"This Old Waverly Golf Club?" I asked, leaning slightly out the window.

"Yes sir, it is."

Being called "sir" was a first for me. This place had to be fancy. "Yes, um, I'm Jason Prendergast. I'm a PGM student at Mississippi State, and I'm here for a job."

"Is anyone expecting you, Mr. Prendergast?"

No one had ever called me Mr. Prendergast before either. "Nope. I saw the advertisement in the Yellow Pages," I said, pointing to the thick book on the passenger seat. "I need a job, so I drove here to get one."

"Hold on a minute, Mr. Prendergast," he said before disappearing into the white building behind him.

A couple minutes later, he returned. "We're not hiring, Mr. Prendergast."

"You're not hiring?"

"No sir. You'll have to drive around the building," he said in a polite voice as he pointed the way with a stiff hand.

And just like that, I was being turned away before I even had the chance to step inside.

As I drove away from Old Waverly, the air carried the pungent sting of ammonia again as I passed Bryan Foods.

It was strange how something as foul as the scent of a slaughterhouse could trigger something so tender as the memories back home, whole chapters of my life rising like dust off an old barn floor.

I hadn't thought much about Vermont lately. I'd been too focused on surviving here. But now, the smell drifting through my Jeep pulled me backward. I missed it. God, I missed it. I missed the farm, the early mornings, and the way my clothes smelled like cow shit and diesel by midday. I missed drinking too many beers with Brian while the milkers pulsated in the barn, and the feeling of wind against my face while throwing hay under the July sun.

Brian should've been by my side when Kathleen walked down the aisle. He should've been there to elbow me when I froze, to make me laugh, to remind me who I was. And George, those cold nights with him and Old Blue and wisdom shared in silence. Oscar's, the diner, the worn stools, and the strong coffee.

That life was gone. Long gone.

I didn't like being called "Sir" or "Mr. Prendergast." It felt stiff and meant for someone else. I liked Jason, Jasper, and all the other nicknames people used when they actually knew me. Those names held history.

Here in Mississippi, no one knew me well enough to call me anything but what they saw on a piece of paper.

George had taught me how to have the kind of relationships rooted in trust, loyalty, and time. But how do you build those when you're a thousand miles from everything you know? What do you do when the ground beneath your feet isn't familiar and it's hard to get people to look beyond who you appear to be?

The smell of death from the slaughterhouse faded behind me as I approached Highway 82. Earlier, on the way to Old Waverly, my eyes had scanned the horizon with anticipation. Now, they were locked on the road just a few feet in front of my Jeep.

"What did it feel like being shown how to leave Old Waverly?" Zoe asked.

I paused, staring down at my shoes. "I was just another guy looking for a job. No one knew what I'd done. What I'd been through. It's like . . . I didn't exist unless I proved myself all over again."

"That's a hard place to be," she said.

"It is. It's like everything I thought I was was actually just how others saw me. I've never really figured out who I am."

Zoe didn't respond.

For the first time in a long time, I didn't try to disrupt the silence. I was starting to see that I had built my identity like scaffolding, one piece tied to George, another to Ma, to Kathleen, another to Brian, another to Speedwell. All solid. All real. But none of it was mine alone. And now, in this small office, miles from stability, I was left standing in the center of myself.

My eyes left the plant I had been staring at when she said, "What happened after you left Old Waverly?"

"Let me tell you."

I felt as if I had imploded as I sat alone in my apartment. I felt every part of my body collapse as I slumped further into the rented chair, staring at the wall like it might give me answers I hadn't found anywhere else.

I had plans. Good plans. I didn't come all this way to stock shelves or rent U-Hauls from behind the counter of a convenience store. I didn't drive halfway across the country for just any job. I didn't leave Vermont for normal or average. I came to Mississippi to chase a dream and become a golf professional.

But how the hell was I supposed to become a golf pro if no one gave me a chance?

I leaned back, eyes scanning the ceiling like it might offer up some wisdom the floor and the walls didn't seem to have. And then, just like that, I was back in time, hearing Uncle Tom's voice as I sat next to him under the arbor on the back porch of his home in Maine.

"No one is going to give you anything in life, Jas," he had said. "If you want something bad enough, you have to go get it." That memory triggered the story of when he returned from the Vietnam War. He was without a job, lost just like me, and he walked into the kitchen and made a list of all the food companies on the boxes and cans resting on the shelves. He then started calling each company, and Campbell's Soup gave him an opportunity.

His words landed differently now. Back then, they had been motivation and inspiration. Now, they held the keys. Opportunity didn't know where I lived and wasn't going to come knocking. I had to go bang on the door myself.

No way. Springing forward, I smacked my forehead with my palm. *What an idiot.* I never even told him what kind of job I wanted.

The next day, I was more prepared. As I pulled into Old Waverly for the second time, I had only one thought circling my brain: *I'm getting a job today.*

The same man stepped out of the guardhouse, clipboard in hand, as my Jeep rolled to a stop. "Mr. Pen-de-grass?" he said, raising an eyebrow.

"Yeah, Pren-der-gast. But, close enough," I said, surprised he remembered my name.

"What can I help you with, Mr. Prendergast?" he asked, his tone as measured and formal as his appearance.

"I'm here for a job on the golf staff," I said, sitting up straighter in my seat.

"I told you yesterday we weren't hiring."

"Yeah, I know, Mr. White," I replied, spotting his name tag

for the first time. "But I never told you what kind of job I was looking for."

Mr. White didn't move. He just stared, his eyes boring into mine, trying to figure out if I was serious or just too stubborn to take a hint.

"Would you ask them if they're hiring in the golf shop?" I said.

He paused for a long moment, then turned and disappeared into the guardhouse.

When he emerged, he straightened his jacket and said, "Mr. Prendergast, we are not hiring in the golf shop."

His hand gestured toward the exit.

"You can drive around the guardhouse on your way out."

The following day, I drove back to Old Waverly, bound and determined to get hired. The person Mr. White kept calling each time I showed up, whoever they were, held the ticket to the table I wanted to sit at. But in order to get to that table, I had to get past Mr. White first.

He met me on the drive again, just like before. "Mr. Prendergast, I told you yesterday, we aren't hiring."

I heard the same thing on days four, five, and six.

"We. Aren't. Hiring."

Each time, I nodded respectfully, thanked him, and drove away.

On day seven, I made the thirty-five-minute drive again. The sun was already high, and heat radiated off the pavement as I pulled to a stop in front of the guardhouse.

"How are you today, Mr. White?" I asked, keeping my tone upbeat.

"I am fine, Mr. Prendergast, thank you," he said with a

slight sigh. "But Mr. Prendergast, I have told you every day this week—"

"Okay, Mr. White," I said, interrupting him. "I'll see you tomorrow."

"Tomorrow?" he asked in disbelief.

"Yes, tomorrow. I'm coming back every day until I get hired. From what I understand, this is the best golf club around, and this is where I want to work. So, I'll see you tomorrow."

For the first time all week, he didn't respond. He just looked at me as I started to drive around the guard house.

"Mr. Prendergast, wait."

I stopped, my heart thudding as I glanced back toward him. "Yes, sir?" I said, trying to be calm.

He let out a long breath and looked at me. The kind of glare that that could mean more than one thing. "I believe you," he said, shaking his head with something that might have been the beginning of a smile. "Here's what I want you to do."

He lifted his arm and pointed down the drive. "The golf shop is to the left of the clubhouse. You want to talk to Richard Taylor. He's the head golf professional. He's the person you have to talk to if you want a job."

I sat motionless in my jeep. After seven days of rejection, this was my one shot.

"Thank you, Mr. White."

He nodded and added, "If he asks how you got through the guardhouse, you tell him there wasn't anyone there. Good luck, Mr. Prendergast."

For the first time since leaving Vermont, I felt my old self inside me. The young oak trees lining the drive reminded me of the mature maple tree canopy that covered one of my dad's favorite roads on Darling Hill back in Vermont.

That memory tugged at me as the road into Old Waverly dipped slightly and then rose, revealing a grand Southern-style clubhouse. It was the same one I had seen in the Yellow Pages. It stood proudly as it pierced the sky. It was one of the most impressive things I had ever seen.

I parked and stepped out, trying to smooth the wrinkles from my shirt as I walked inside. My heart pounded. I was used to walking into barns and milking parlors, not places like this.

"Is Richard Taylor here?" I asked as I entered the golf shop.

A dark-haired man in a golf shirt stepped forward. "I'm Richard Taylor," he said. "Can I help you?"

"My name is Jason Prendergast," I said, extending my hand. "I'm a PGM student at Mississippi State. Are you hiring?"

He looked at me, confused. "Did Mr. White let you in?"

I hesitated. "No, sir. I didn't see anyone at the guardhouse, so I just drove on in. I've been here every day this week looking for a job. And every day, I was told you weren't hiring. Are you hiring today?"

"You've been here every day for a week?" he asked.

I nodded. "Yup. Every day. Except Monday—you were closed."

Richard picked up the phone and dialed. "Mr. White, this is Richard Taylor. I have a Jason Prendergast here looking for a job. He says he's been here every day this week."

There was a pause while he listened, then he said, "Okay," and hung up.

Before he had the chance to tell me no, I said, "If you're not hiring today, I'll be back tomorrow. This is the best golf club in Mississippi. I'm putting myself through college, and I need a job. I'll work this week for free. If you don't want to hire me after that, I'll leave and never come back."

His silence stretched long enough to tighten my stomach. I swallowed.

"All I want is an opportunity to prove how hard I can work."

Richard nodded, as if weighing something deeper than just my words. "Okay, you can work this week. Wear khakis and a golf shirt."

Relief hit me like cold water. "Thank you, Mr. Taylor. I'll see you tomorrow after class."

Mr. White was standing outside the guardhouse as I approached, his posture as straight as ever, arms folded across his chest. The late afternoon sun cast a golden hue across the manicured drive, and for the first time all week, I felt its warmth settle into more than just my skin.

"Well, did you get a job?" he asked.

"I did," I said, unable to hide my smile. "Thank you so much. I'll see you tomorrow."

Something in his eyes acknowledged me in a way that went deeper than words. "That's great. Congratulations, Mr. Prendergast. I'll see you tomorrow."

I stopped at the stop sign in front of Bryan Foods and looked across the parking lot, thinking about Uncle Tom going through the kitchen cabinets. I reached up, pulled the rearview mirror toward me, smiled, nodded, and looked myself in the eye the way Dad had taught me as a young boy. I smiled again.

21

MOSS IN THE COURTYARD

Richard Taylor hired me, and I received a paycheck for my first week of work. Felicia was sad to see me leave. I wouldn't miss stocking shelves, bagging ice, and mopping the floor. But I would miss Felicia, and I thanked her for the job.

A slow day at Old Waverly the following week found me pacing the brick courtyard outside the golf shop in khakis, a little wrinkled from class, and a new logo on my shirt with the words "Old Waverly." I thought back to my days at the gas pumps as I looked at the lined-up golf cars. In a weird way it felt like a version of home, which was comforting given nothing else around me resembled my hometown in the least. Everything about this place whispered of money and excellence.

I had played several public golf courses in the Northeast but had never stepped foot on the grounds of a private country club, and Old Waverly's clubhouse perched on a knoll like a king's throne. This place belonged in a magazine, not the Yellow Pages.

The dark bark mulch, kept in place by perfectly edged grass, hosted a variety of plants. Multiple shades of green provided a soft canvas for blossoms in the spring with enough color to fill a crayon box. The strategically placed landscaping gave life and personality to the perfectly white columns and veranda, softening the grand architecture with the hum of nature's finer details. Even the breeze seemed curated, whispering through the hydrangeas as if to say, "Welcome." But I wondered if I belonged here.

So that question lingered.

A lone, dark green weed growing up against the brick wall outside the golf shop stood out as much as I did in that courtyard that day. Both of us had been blown here from somewhere else. Uninvited, unplanned, and out of place.

I stared at that weed longer than I should have, and the more I looked at it, the more I saw myself in it. It wasn't supposed to be there. It hadn't been planted or pruned or fertilized. It didn't match the manicured perfection around it. And neither did I. The uniforms, the Southern drawls, the polished names, none of it belonged to me. I was the kid from Vermont in off-brand khakis, with too many miles between who I had been and who I was trying to become.

Being "blown here" didn't feel romantic. It felt disorienting. My feet shuffled on the bricks like they hadn't earned the right to stand still. My voice was quieter here, unsure if it had permission to speak, like the days of Oscar's all over again. That weed, for all its bold green defiance, looked like it could be plucked at any second. And in that moment, I felt the same way.

I realized just how fragile my identity really was, how much of it had been shaped by people who knew my name, who had seen me work, who had trusted me. Without that context, I wasn't connected to anything. And yet, that weed had taken root anyway. That image stayed with me because, deep down, I hoped I could do the same. Take root where I wasn't expected and, someday, belong because I endured.

And even after all that unease, after staring at the weed like it was my reflection, I reached down and uprooted it from its home. Its thin roots tore away from the soil with little resistance, and I stood there holding it, unsure if I had just erased something I needed to see. But then I looked around and realized I wasn't the only one still out of place.

I had been pacing that courtyard for a week and was just now noticing the moss and small weeds living quietly among the village of bricks. They had found their way into the cracks, growing stubbornly between the perfectly laid pattern like misfits who didn't know they weren't supposed to belong.

Failing to pull some of them by hand, I went into the cart barn and came back with a butter knife I had found on a shelf. I pressed the dull blade into the tight joints between bricks. It was as snug as a bug in a rug, but it worked. I pushed and pried and twisted, working the knife through the perpendicular seams, uprooting the imposters one by one.

Each tiny plant came out, sometimes leaving just enough behind to grow again. I realized then that being out of place didn't always mean being unwelcome. It just meant no one had planned for you. And maybe, like the weeds, I didn't need permission to grow here. I just needed to find the cracks.

An hour had passed when, from behind me, I heard, "Excuse me, what are you doing?"

Startled, I stood up quickly, brushing dirt from my hands. "I'm sorry, I didn't see you drive in," I said, glancing past him at the sleek gray BMW 7 Series parked behind him. "Are you playing golf today?"

In a soft, composed voice, the man replied, "No, I'm not playing. What's your name?"

"I'm Jason Prendergast," I replied, wiping my palm as clean as I could on my khakis before extending it toward him.

"Nice to meet you, Jason."

His fingertips met the back of my hand, and immediately my grip relaxed to match the feathery lightness of his confident handshake.

I had only felt a handshake like that a few times before, usually at the Miss Lyndonville Diner. Back then, it always made me feel like I didn't quite measure up. Standing there in the courtyard at Old Waverly, I felt the same flicker of insecurity.

"You must be new?" he said.

"Yeah, I started last week."

"What are you doing here?" he asked again.

Maybe this wasn't such a good idea after all, I thought, suddenly feeling the butter knife heavy in my hand. "I'm digging up all the weeds," I said, my voice quieter than before.

His eyes narrowed slightly before drifting from mine, slowly examining the courtyard like he was seeing it for the first time. "Who told you to do this?" he asked.

"Nnn-nobody," I stammered. "It didn't look so good. I tried pullin' 'em out with my fingers, but it didn't work, so I'm using this," I said, lifting the butter knife in my hand, suddenly aware of how ridiculous it looked.

The man paused. His eyes moved side to side once more across the courtyard.

He nodded. "Welcome to Old Waverly, Jason."

"Thank you," I replied, as he walked past me and disappeared into the golf shop.

I stood there for a moment, unsure of what had just happened. He hadn't told me to stop. He hadn't laughed. He hadn't questioned my place. He'd just . . . welcomed me. And somehow, that felt bigger than it should have. I could hear my dad's voice reminding me to never judge a person by their appearance, but this time it was difficult.

Sometimes, you just know you are in the presence of someone important. Everything about them feels unique. Their posture is perfect, yet every muscle in their body seems relaxed. Their tone holds a pitch that your ears have seldom, if ever, heard. They have a presence that effortlessly draws you in as if you were gliding on ice. These individuals are rare, like unicorns, and all you want to do is be around them as much as possible.

A short while later, Jon, one of the assistant golf professionals, called me over the PA system.

"Do you know who that was?"

"No. Who is he?"

"That's George Bryan."

I blinked. The name meant nothing to me. "Who is George Bryan?"

"Mr. Bryan owns this place."

Moss in the Courtyard

"What?" I said, nearly laughing. "You mean, one guy owns this whole place?" I circled my finger in the air to emphasize everything around us.

George Bryan became a name I wouldn't forget.

22

A NEW TABLE

I looked at my grades after the first semester ended. I had both survived at Mississippi State University and had earned the best grades I had ever earned in my life. I had never realized the power of receiving A's. They weren't telling me how smart I was; they validated the hard work and the possibility of realizing my dream. I thought back to how seeing my SAT score had made me feel more incapable and dumb. I pondered the difference as I sat in my Mississippi apartment and realized only one thing was different: my purpose.

Richard called me into the golf shop one Saturday morning and said, "Mr. Bryan would like for you to caddie for him and his guests today."

I froze. For a moment, I couldn't speak. Mr. Bryan wanted me to caddie for him? I stood there nodding, trying to act cool, but inside I felt validation, something I hadn't felt in a long time. And better yet, it was the kind you earn, step by sweaty step.

This wasn't a favor. This was a request. His request.

A New Table

Weeks earlier, I was caught digging weeds out of the brick courtyard with a butter knife. Now, I was being asked by the man who saw me, the man who owned the place, to caddie for him. I had seen caddies on TV before, but this was different. Richard explained that my job was to position myself in the fairway on each hole to help locate golf balls after the tee shots, provide yardages to the green, clean clubs, rake bunkers, and assist in reading putts when needed.

After Mr. Bryan introduced me to his guests on the first tee, I took off sprinting two hundred and fifty yards down the fairway. My heart thudded in my chest, not just from the run but from the pressure of doing this job well. After each ball soared through the air, I darted across the pristine fairway, tracking its bounce and roll like a bloodhound on a trail. When the ball came to rest, I pulled out the handheld laser and measured the distance to the green, writing the yardage on a scorecard to be ready when they arrived.

As the golfers hit their next shots, I cleaned their clubs. Then I sprinted to the green ahead of them. I took pride in reaching the green via the shoe leather express before they arrived, hearing Dad's voice echoing in my head, "Show 'em how hard you can work, son." Each hole was its own small battle of staying one step ahead. And even though I was far from home, soaked in sweat beneath a Southern sun, part of me felt exactly where I belonged.

The days of hustling through snowbanks and crisp, cold Vermont air to find the fuel pipe on the side of a house felt like another lifetime, back before George's voice echoed, "Okay, she's ready!" Now, those days had been replaced by manicured fairways stretched beneath the Mississippi sun, the air thick with humidity and magnolia blooms. I stood on a course polished to perfection, the kind of place that had once existed in magazines I read while teaching myself how to play golf or on Sunday afternoon TV as George and I ate popcorn and watched the PGA Tour.

This wasn't just any course; it would soon host the US Women's Open. Every blade of grass had a purpose. Every brick was laid with intention.

But what surprised me most was the pride. Every weed I pulled from the bricks, every grain of sand raked back into the bunkers, every "Yes sir" and "No ma'am" became bricks in a new foundation I was laying beneath my feet.

The sadness of what used to be hadn't disappeared. I still missed everything about home. But slowly, that sadness became something else. It became gratitude. Those years were preparation. The lessons from Vermont started to make sense in ways they never had before.

Hope fueled belief. I wasn't just here; I was becoming part of it. I showed up every day and earned my place. The cold was gone, but the discipline remained. And with it, a kind of happiness I hadn't expected: the feeling that maybe, just maybe, I wasn't like that weed in the courtyard after all.

I dashed onto the fairway of the next hole right after the last putt dropped, cutting through the woods whenever it looked faster. For eighteen holes, more than four miles over the course of four hours, my mission was clear: Create an unforgettable experience for Mr. Bryan and his guests. I could hear Kathleen's father saying, "I don't want them buying fuel

A New Table

from Speedwell, I want them to buy it from me." Every sprint, every raked bunker, every cleaned club was part of the story I was writing. If they remembered me, they would remember the round.

By the time we gathered in the courtyard after the eighteenth hole, my legs were trembling with fatigue. I hadn't sprinted that much since football practice in high school, and the cotton caddie jumpsuit I wore clung to my skin.

Mr. Bryan turned to me, handing me some folded bills. "I want you to go with us tomorrow. We play at eleven."

His words landed like a medal on my chest. I nodded, holding back a smile that stretched behind my sunburnt cheeks. *You've got to be kidding me*, I thought as I walked toward the golf shop. *Eighty bucks? It takes me three days to make eighty dollars.* There was only one problem.

"Richard," I said, walking into the golf shop. "Mr. Bryan just asked me to go with him tomorrow, but I work in the bag room tomorrow. What am I supposed to do?"

"If Mr. Bryan wants you to go with him, that's what you do," he said. "I'll find someone to cover your shift."

Mr. Bryan asked me to caddie for him the following week, as he had more guests in town to play. Three more days chasing golf balls around Old Waverly would pay my rent.

On Wednesday, I informed each of my instructors that I would be missing Friday's class and let them know I was working for Mr. Bryan. I explained that I was returning to school at twenty-six years old to pursue my dream of becoming a PGA professional. I wasn't some eighteen-year-old who had partied too much the night before or slept through an alarm. I let them know I understood that missing class might affect my grades, and I hoped they would understand. To my relief, my professors respected the honesty. They asked me to keep them updated about future absences and were always willing to work with me on due dates and exams.

After that second weekend, I became Mr. Bryan's personal forecaddie. Often, I'd be working in the bag room when he'd arrive and say, "Get suited up; I'm going to play." Without hesitation, I'd change out of my work clothes and into the jumpsuit, load his bag onto a cart, and wait for him in the courtyard where we had first met.

Unlike the weed I had pulled from the bricks that day, Mr. Bryan didn't treat me like something out of place. He fed and watered me in his own way. He was cultivating someone my parents and the Nichols family had planted many years before. My parents had taught me how to be kind and to work hard. George had taught me how to connect with people. And now, Mr. Bryan was teaching me how to carry myself in the company of society's elite, not by changing who I was, but by showing me how far who I was could take me.

My elbows were now rubbing against those belonging to musicians, Super Bowl champions, major winners on the PGA Tour, NBA players, and multiple executives of companies worth tens or even hundreds of millions of dollars. And yet, to my surprise, the conversations weren't all that different from those at the diner or Oscar's years ago.

I had learned to listen when I was with George, to pay attention, to hear what was said between the words, and I did the same on the golf course with Mr. Bryan and his guests.

A New Table

That skill, born from nights in the cab of a truck or stools at the diner back home, became my quiet advantage. I didn't have the titles or the money, but I had the presence. And in rooms (and fairways) where people often just waited for their turn to talk, listening taught me in ways textbooks and classrooms were unable to do.

Twenty-three years later, in 2021, I received a phone call from a good friend, E. B., back in Vermont. His voice was heavy, and the news he delivered hit even harder: Our friend Johnny had been diagnosed with a deadly illness. There was a pause on the line, the kind that carries more than words, before E. B. asked if I could help make a dream come true for Johnny.

Johnny had a hero, someone larger than life in his eyes. As fate would have it, I had met that very man two decades earlier at Old Waverly. I had caddied for him several times, running beside his cart in the Mississippi heat. He was more than an athlete: He was a presence. And now, I was reaching out to him not as a caddie but as a friend asking for something deeply personal.

Through the help of friends in Mississippi, I was able to get a message to him. And then, incredibly, he sent a video for Johnny. In it, he said he was sorry. He said he was thinking about him. He told him to dig in and fight with everything he had. To keep the faith in the old man upstairs, saying, "That's where it all begins and ends."

When Johnny watched the video, he called me. The moment I heard his voice, overwhelmed, full of disbelief and gratitude, I thought of how Zoe made me understand I didn't owe Ma anything.

Johnny was dying, and in that moment a part of him was happier than he had ever been. I felt something rise up in me that words could barely touch. It brought me back to the first time I met that man on the course, how my own heart had pounded in my chest, how the moment had seemed unreal. But hearing Johnny's voice, knowing I had helped bridge the gap between hope and reality for someone I cared about—that feeling was deeper. It wasn't just admiration anymore. It was a full-circle moment that reminded me how important relationships mattered in life.

23
WHO'S THE BEST?

Zoe sat across from me, legs crossed, her notebook resting on her lap. She hadn't written anything in several minutes. I'd been talking about the first time I walked into the PGM auditorium at Mississippi State University, how packed it was, how young everyone looked, how small I had felt.

Therapy was no longer just a place to talk; it had become the place where I figured out how all the pieces of my story fit together. Each session with Zoe was like returning to a map of my life, only this time, the lighting was better, and I wasn't navigating alone. She was in the passenger seat, gently pointing out turns I hadn't seen the first time through, showing me how even the detours held meaning. It was where I stopped running from the past and started examining it, choice by choice, belief by belief.

It didn't always feel good. Some days, it felt like peeling sunburned skin—raw, sensitive, and uncomfortable. But for the first time, it also felt honest. Necessary. I began to see not just what had happened but how I had responded to it.

I realized that the choices I made were not necessarily right or wrong; they were made so I could survive. Those decisions were actually symptoms of the lens through which I viewed the world at the time. What Zoe revealed to me wasn't just the power to make different choices, but something deeper: the power to choose a different lens entirely.

"You said something just now," she finally said. "You said, 'If I am going to make it, I need to be better than everyone else. All I need is a chance. There isn't anyone here willing to do what I am willing to do. Nobody in this room wants to be a PGA professional more than I do.' Where do you think that need comes from?"

I looked past her, out the familiar window that always led down the path of light toward understanding more of life. I took a breath.

"I think it's always been there," I said. "Back home, you earned your place. Nobody handed you anything. My dad always told me the hardest worker on the crew would never be without a job. So I learned early on to prove my worth by working harder than everyone else. That's how opportunities present themselves."

Zoe nodded, her brow softening. "And when you walked into that room full of students at Mississippi State, what did it feel like?"

"Like I didn't belong. Their hands didn't have calluses. I assumed they were all better at golf than me, I could tell just by looking at them. So I told myself, if you can't beat them with talent, you better outwork every damn one of them."

Zoe leaned forward slightly. "What does it cost you to live like that? To always feel like you have to earn your worth?"

That question sat heavy in the air.

"I don't know," I said quietly. "Some days it feels like pride. Like I'm doing something nobody else would. But other days . . ." I looked back at her. "It feels like I'm running on fumes, chasing something I'm not even sure I'll recognize when I get there. Like I'm trying to prove I belong in a room that no one else is questioning whether I should be in except me."

Zoe nodded again. "That's a lot of pressure to carry, Jason. And it makes sense, given your story. But maybe belonging doesn't always come from proving. Sometimes it comes from being."

I sat with that. The idea of being instead of proving.

"Zoe, my ambitions have always been high. My dad used to tell me never to think I was better than anyone else, and he assured me I wasn't. Proving myself and being better than everyone else has always been a measuring stick for my own effort, my own growth." I paused. "This drive I have, it comes across sometimes the wrong way from the outside looking in. It's why I don't share it often."

Zoe nodded but remained quiet, and I could tell she was listening. I hadn't explained this to many people, if any at all for that matter.

"Zoe, I am trying to reach my full potential in life, and it comes at a cost that I am willing to pay."

"And what cost is that?" Zoe asked.

My body tensed, causing me to pause a moment, and I said, "Discomfort."

I took a breath and tried to exhale my anticipation of Zoe's reaction to what I was about to say. "Feeling uncomfortable is hard and exhausting sometimes. But being uncomfortable is important. It means I am growing. Getting better. Still chasing my dream."

"And comfortable? What does that mean?" Zoe asked.

"Comfortable is a dangerous place for me. It's complacency. It is hard to explain," I said as my eyes hit the floor. I looked back up after piecing the words together. "I've never had to explain this before, but . . . I'm happy and proud of what I have accomplished every day, but I'm not satisfied. Regardless of the effort put forth to get to today, I am here. Still standing with desire still inside me. There's more waiting for me, and I want to experience what awaits. Always."

"And the idea of being instead of proving?" Zoe asked.

"I accept who I am, how I am wired, flaws and all. I believe in myself more so than any other person on the planet because I know the limits to my willingness to make something happen. I believe in myself even when I am faced with doubt. It's why I don't quit. Let me tell you a story about what I mean."

I sat in Scott's office the morning after he greeted all of us by saying, "Welcome to the Professional Golf Management Program. Interview days are in October, so start thinking about where you want to go." I was determined to figure out my internship. Becoming Larry Kelley wasn't going to happen by accident. It would take intention, strategy, and more than just any internship. "Scott, my pro back home told me to accomplish three things while in school," I said. "Work for a PGA Master Professional, work at a club with a name every golfer would recognize, and work for someone who will actually teach me."

Scott nodded. "That's good advice."

"So, I was thinking, why not try to get all three of those

things in one internship? Who's the best pro in the country to work for?"

He didn't hesitate. "There are a lot of good ones, but Bob Ford at Oakmont is probably the best."

"Who's Bob Ford? And where's Oakmont?" I asked.

"Bob is the head pro," Scott said, "and Oakmont is in Pennsylvania. It's one of the most prestigious clubs in the world."

"Is he coming to the interview days?

"No, he won't be here."

I had never heard of Oakmont, and I certainly hadn't heard of Bob Ford. If this was the place I needed to work, it wouldn't be as simple as signing up for an interview on campus. Pennsylvania was too far away to just show up at like I did at Old Waverly. The method that had worked before, just keep showing up until someone says yes, wasn't going to work this time.

"Bob Ford is one of the best PGA professionals in the country," Scott said. "And Oakmont is ranked in the top ten golf courses in the world."

"Seriously?" I asked, trying to process what I was hearing.

"Getting this internship isn't going to be easy," Scott added. "Everyone would like to work for Bob at Oakmont."

His words landed hard, but not in a discouraging way. They stirred something. An opportunity to reach for something I hadn't known to exist.

Frozen to the chair, I felt the same heaviness I'd once felt in Larry's office, that mix of uncertainty and resolve twisting deep in my gut. I had been afraid of things before in my life, but I had never been afraid of something just because it was hard. In my mind, hard simply meant most people weren't cut out for it.

Okay, everyone wanted to be at Oakmont. But did they really? Was that statement like the one I made so many years ago when I threatened to move out of my house? Everyone might wish they could be at Oakmont, but wanting it and wishing for it were two very different things. I wanted to be at Oakmont. I wanted to work for the best.

I couldn't stop at the question of what I needed to do. I had to push deeper, lean into the corner like I did in motocross, throttle twisted, no backing off. The real question wasn't what, it was how.

"I need to work for someone who knows Bob," I said, the words coming out slow but certain. "Who knows Bob Ford?"

"A lot of people know Bob," Scott said, folding his hands on the desk. "What would be better is working for someone Bob knows."

I had heard that saying before. "It's not what you know, it's who you know." But I had never thought much of it, only nodding and agreeing. Scott was right, though. It wasn't about who knew Bob Ford. It was about who Bob Ford knew. And if I was going to earn that kind of recognition, I had to find my way into his circle.

Scott helped me coordinate nine interviews over the two days employers would be on campus, each one with someone he believed Bob Ford either knew personally or would recognize by name. It felt like a golden opportunity, but as fast as the interviews began, I realized something painful: I wasn't good at interviewing. Hell, I sucked.

And why would I be any good at it? I had never done a real interview before. Sure, I had shaken hands in a hardware store once and at Speedwell more than a few times, but sitting across from someone in a blazer asking questions as polished as my new dress shoes? That was new terrain.

My thirty-minute time slots were filled with basic questions and rambling, unfocused answers. I talked too much in some moments, not enough in others. After the third or fourth person leaned back and asked, "So, what have you been doing since high school?" I started to understand the uphill battle I was fighting.

Being a twenty-six-year-old freshman had more disadvantages than I'd anticipated. I wasn't prepared to explain the world I'd come from, not in a way that made sense in a golf operations context. I couldn't figure out how to make milking cows, pumping gas, or pounding nails sound like preparation for anything in this polished world of golf. The fact that I had run a business, worked on a farm, and installed heating systems didn't seem to matter as much as I thought it would.

The hay fields turned into Barton Golf Club and the cracked cart paths at St. Johnsbury Country Club might've shaped me, but they didn't stamp me with prestige. Not like the magazine-worthy clubs these people were representing. They proved one thing: I was a greenhorn, as green as a gourd.

I didn't belong at a place like Oakmont. Not yet, anyway.

I was offered three internships at the end of interview week, and Nemacolin Woodlands Resort and Spa in Farmington, Pennsylvania, was one of them. Scott's advice was to take it.

"Bob Ford will know the pro," he said. "They're both in the Tri-State Section of the PGA."

That was good enough for me.

The internship would run through the summer, ending just

before school resumed in the fall. It wasn't at a high-end private club like Oakmont, but rather a high-end resort. My duties revolved around the outside services operation, golf carts, practice facility setup and breakdown, cleaning clubs, and greeting guests as they arrived. I was a neck-down once again.

There were no official sounding titles, and the only key I would be given was to the cart barn, not the golf shop. Just sweat, repetition, and standing tall with a smile when people pulled up with their golf bags. And yet, somewhere inside me, I knew this was part of it. This was the start of earning my way. My eyes were set on Oakmont, and this was a necessary mile marker on the road there.

24

A WHITE LIE

The sun had just started to dip behind the hills of Western Pennsylvania, casting long shadows across the cart staging area at Nemacolin Woodlands Resort and Spa. The hum of the final golf carts being plugged in echoed faintly through the cart barn.

With the last of my duties finished, I walked toward the clubhouse. Doug's office, located above the golf shop, had the faint scent of leather chairs. A wall of framed photos and tournament memorabilia filled the space with accomplishment and authority. Doug, the head golf professional, was leaning back in his chair, the sleeves of his polo pushed slightly up, his forearms tan from years of sun.

"Hey Doug," I said, knocking gently on the open door. "Got a minute?"

He looked up from his computer and waved me in. "Sure, what's up?"

I stepped inside, closing the door behind me.

"I wanted to talk to you about my internship," I said, taking a seat across from him.

"I know this internship is about learning the business," I said, sitting forward, elbows on my knees. "And I'm going to do everything you ask, be on time, keep the carts clean, set the range right, smile for every guest. I'll do it all."

Doug looked suspicious. "But?"

I shook my head. "No but. Just . . . I have one particular goal that matters more than the rest."

"Oh, really?" he said, a half smile forming. "What's that?"

I looked him in the eye and said, "I accepted this internship because I want to go to Oakmont. I figured my best chance to get an interview with Bob Ford is by working for someone he knows. My hope is that you will call him for me before I leave."

"Really? That's a pretty big ask," Doug said.

"Yes, it is."

"So, you're here to get an interview with Mr. Ford?"

"That's the hope. I realize that kind of phone call will have to be earned. That's why I'm telling you this now. I want you to know, right up front, what I'm working toward and why I'm here."

Doug nodded, his expression unreadable. "I can't guarantee I'm going to call Mr. Ford."

"I understand," I said. "But I can guarantee you something."

"What's that?"

"I'll work any shift. As many hours as you need me to. I'll do anything you ask. By the time my internship is over, I'll have been the hardest-working employee you've ever had."

Doug leaned back in his chair, the leather creaking as he laced his fingers together and rested his hands on his lap.

"That's a big guarantee," he said, his voice low and deliberate.

"I know," I said. "But it's one I intend to keep. I can't guarantee you will call Mr. Ford for me, but I am willing to do whatever it takes to earn that chance. No questions asked."

My heart raced with every step as I left Doug's office. Dad had told me long ago that striving to be my best was important. Had I gone too far? Had my confidence crossed into arrogance?

Still, how would Doug ever notice me if I didn't put my intentions out in the open? This wasn't a time to blend in or be camouflaged into my surroundings. Playing it safe had never opened doors before, so why would it now?

But doubt pressed in. *What if he doesn't call? What if I never get to Oakmont?*

I had seen the competition I was up against back at school. If Mississippi State was anything like the other three PGM universities, there were hundreds of students who were more golf prepared than me. Some were in the program because being a golf pro seemed fun or glamorous. I wasn't. I didn't have the luxury of figuring things out as I went. I was already years behind most of them.

I had made it a habit to put myself in Doug's office every week, asking questions and soaking up any advice he had about my career. As my internship neared its end, Doug called me into his office.

"You have an interview with Mr. Ford on Monday at one o'clock," he said.

"Really? Awesome. Thank you so much."

"You're welcome. You earned it. Just like you said you would."

"Thank you," I replied, as a rush of pride filled me.

"This is a bigger opportunity than you realize," Doug continued. "Your interview will probably last twenty minutes, thirty max. I've put my name on the line for you. Make sure you show up early, wear a coat and tie, and bring a copy of your resume."

"Of course," I said with a nod. As if I would do anything at this point to jeopardize my chances of getting to Oakmont. "Any advice?"

"Be yourself. You're interviewing for an internship, not an assistant's position. He's not going to expect you to know how to do everything. What he's going to want is someone he can trust to communicate well with members and guests. Someone who's passionate about golf and willing to work hard."

Being myself was hard during interview week. I wanted the job so badly I could taste it, and the last thing I wanted was to screw it up. Depending on who I spoke with, I had anywhere from a few seconds to a couple of minutes before someone formed a first impression, one that was nearly impossible to overcome. I had worked countless hours and sacrificed more than anyone knew for the opportunity of a lifetime, and it all came down to one play. The best play in my playbook.

After I ran that first play, I would spend the rest of the interview either trying to convince someone to change their opinion of me or reassuring them that their first impression had been right.

That Monday, behind the driver's seat hung a perfectly pressed white shirt and creased khakis, accompanied by my blue JCPenney blazer that was a little too big for me. The solid red tie looped around the hanger was no accident. I had attended a seminar on dressing for success during my first semester of college, where I learned that a red tie symbolized strength, passion, and confidence. My blue jeans and T-shirt would absorb the wrinkles during the seventy-five-mile journey north from Nemacolin Woodlands Resort and Spa to Oakmont Country Club. The fastest route to Oakmont had been highlighted on my Pennsylvania state map, much like the ones thumbtacked to Gram's wall back home, to help guide me along the way.

Reality slowly forced its way into my mind as I sped down the Pennsylvania Turnpike, watching the mile markers fly by through the passenger window. What was Bob like? Was he going to offer me a job? Was I good enough? What if he didn't hire me? What would that mean? This was my chance. My only chance. Thirty minutes to convince him to hire me. I wonder what makes him so good?

Oh *shit*. My hands strangled the steering wheel. I muttered, watching the exit blur through the window.

"Seriously? You've got to be kidding me." Panic surged as I scanned for the next exit. *How far is it?* My eyelids fluttered faster than my heart as the rush of 70 mph wind seemed to thump inside the cab. *This exit needs to hurry the hell up. How the hell did I miss the turn? What an idiot.* I slammed myself back into the seat, arms locked on the wheel. *If I don't get this job because I missed the damn exit . . .*

The annoying clicking of the blinker replaced the thumping wind in my truck as I finally approached an exit. My eyes locked on to the green paint of the sign, almost melting it with my stare as I pulled off the turnpike. My gaze darted frantically in and out of parking lots, searching for a pay phone like my life depended on it.

I stood at the first pay phone I found, more nervous than ever. My heart pounded in my throat with every beat. I had gotten up between four and five every morning to study when I was in school, too exhausted to open a book after long days of class and working at Old Waverly. I had done everything right, everything except something as simple as getting off at the correct exit.

Maybe I didn't belong at Oakmont. Maybe missing this turn was a sign that I wasn't ready.

"God, I hope I haven't ruined my chances," I whispered, as I began to dial the number for Oakmont Country Club.

I crossed Hulton Bridge shortly after exiting the turnpike for the second time and pulled into the gas station a mile before Oakmont Country Club. My perfectly pressed outfit had done its job hanging behind the seat, but I had failed at mine. I was late, but there was nothing I could do about it now. Nothing but own it.

"You got a bathroom?" I asked the cashier as I walked through the convenience store, hangers in hand.

"Right there," he said, pointing to the corner of the store.

The blood in my veins flowed fast, like the rapids of the Colorado River, with every step as Oakmont awakened. The walkway between the golf shop and clubhouse meandered slightly before depositing me at the foot of the historic Oakmont Country Club clubhouse overlooking the eighteenth hole.

The eighteenth green had seamlessly appeared in the rising fairway like a cougar crouching in the wide open, ready to pounce on her next unsuspecting victim. Beyond the eighteenth green stood a quaint snack shack nestled under the large canopy of a small oak grove. The dozen or so oak trees had stood guard since 1903, protecting Henry C. Fownes's masterpiece.

As I stood on the path, a warmth settled in my body. It was as if the game's greats were walking through me on their way to the first tee box, depositing their footsteps of history inside me. *So, this is what one of the world's greatest golf courses looks like*, I thought.

The old wooden floor of the golf shop's porch creaked beneath my feet as I approached the door. My stomach tightened, and my chest expanded as my fingers wrapped around yet another doorknob. My eyes rose and fell over clothing fixtures and golf clubs, searching for something, anything that might bring comfort as I stepped inside the shop.

I was here. I was at Oakmont.

Where's Mr. Ford? What does he even look like? Is he going to be upset? I found myself squeezing the fabric inside my pocket, trying to stay calm.

A man over six feet tall stood near the front counter. The sleeves of his crisp white golf shirt were creased perfectly from shoulder to elbow. A brown belt looped through a pair of sharply pressed khakis, stopping just above a pair of polished brown golf shoes. His left hand, almost clutched, looked as if an invisible golf club was resting in his fingers. *That has got to be him*, I thought.

"You must be Jason. I'm Bob Ford," he said, extending his

hand. "Welcome to Oakmont."

My hand met Bob's, and for the first time in a long while, mine wasn't the biggest. It was the first time I had felt at home in a handshake since leaving Vermont, the way his fingers wrapped around mine.

"Yes, I am. Thank you. I'm sorry I'm late," I said, looking into Bob's eyes.

"It's okay; it happens sometimes," he said as his grip softened. "Come on back," he added, leading me through a break in the front counter and down a short hallway lined with signed sports memorabilia.

Bob sat down at an antique roll-top desk cluttered with paperwork. In the corner rested a vintage leather golf bag, and memorabilia from the hallway spilled into his office, covering nearly every inch of the walls.

"So, tell me a little about yourself," he said.

I gave him the rundown I had practiced over and over again on the turnpike: short, sweet, and to the point.

"Why do you want to be a golf professional?" he asked.

"I love golf and everything about it," I replied. "I love to play and teach others to play. I had the chance to caddie for John Daly at Old Waverly, and that was a lot of fun."

"I bet it was. John's a good guy, isn't he?"

"He's great," I said. "My dad always told me to find something I loved and try to make a living doing it. I love everything about golf."

"Why do you want to work at Oakmont?" Bob asked.

"My pro back home told me to work for a Master Professional at a recognizable club, and for someone who would teach me. I asked Scott Maynard who the best person to work for was, and he told me you."

Bob leaned back in his chair, his fingers forming a steeple against his chest. *Oh man, he's made up his mind already. Damn it. I can't believe I missed the turn. After all the hard work and sacrifice to get here, Bob has already decided.*

We talked about Oakmont, about me, and about the game of golf for the next twenty minutes or so. The interview officially lasted half an hour, but Doug had been wrong. It was over in less than five.

"When are you available?" he asked.

"January first. I need to do a twelve-month internship"

"I don't make decisions until the fall," he said. "So stay in touch. I'll let you know the first of November."

Pride, hope, and anticipation had traveled the northbound lane of the turnpike earlier that day. Now, doubt, disappointment, and uncertainty rode with me in the southbound lane as I headed back to Nemacolin Woodlands Resort and Spa. What was I going to tell Doug? He was going to be so disappointed in me for being late.

Walking into Doug's office reminded me of the times Ma had summoned me to hers, being unsure of what was coming.

"How'd it go?" Doug asked.

"I don't know," I said. "I was late. I missed the exit on the turnpike. I pulled over and called him from a pay phone, explained what had happened, but . . . I don't know. I just don't know. I'm so sorry."

"What did he ask you?"

I filled Doug in on Bob's questions and added, "He made up

his mind in less than five minutes. I could tell. His whole body language changed."

"How did it end?"

"He asked me my time frame."

"Well, that's good," Doug said.

I felt like I was sitting in Dad's truck again, wondering if I would make the team.

"What do you think? Do I have a chance?" I asked.

"I don't know. I guess we'll find out in November," Doug said.

I had a couple of weeks left to fulfill my promise to Doug. Regardless of the outcome that day, or whether Bob would hire me in November, I had promised Doug that I would be the hardest worker he had ever had, and I was determined to keep that promise.

I can't believe I missed the damn turn. I can't believe I was late. I had no idea how slowly the next few months would crawl by.

25

THE TURNPIKE

I sat in the auditorium during my sophomore year, arms crossed loosely over my chest, watching the new freshman class file in. Their faces were wide-eyed and eager, just like mine had been the year before. Some of them wore polos a little too tucked in, while others draped over their belts. I couldn't tell if it was confidence or ignorance; I only remembered that the previous year, those two things battled inside me for weeks.

Scott Maynard stepped onto the stage with the same message I remembered. His voice carried throughout the auditorium, as he welcomed the new class to the PGA Golf Management Program. He talked about the expectations, the opportunities, and the level of professionalism that would be required of them from day one. It was almost word for word what he had said the first time I heard him, but this time, something was different.

This time, I was different.

A year ago, I had sat in one of those same seats, pretending to belong, hoping no one would see through me. I had doubted whether I was good enough to make it, good enough to even deserve a seat in that room. I remembered how I kept my head down, afraid to ask questions, afraid my small-town background or late start in golf would expose me.

But now, after a year and one unforgettable interview with Bob Ford, I sat taller, even though my future at Oakmont was undetermined. I knew what it felt like to walk through the front door of one of the most prestigious clubs in the world. I knew what it meant to earn an invite to that table, not because someone handed it to me, but because I had earned it and someone believed in me.

I wasn't pretending anymore. I belonged in that auditorium, and yet those same worries were now about a new room I was now wanting to belong to. A room big enough for only a few. So as Scott spoke, I watched the freshmen the way a big brother might, knowing the road ahead of them would be tough, but also knowing that if I could get through it, they could too. I caught myself nodding at Scott's words, not in nervous agreement like before, but in recognition. Confidence had taken root. And for the first time, I realized I wasn't chasing a dream anymore. I was living it.

A couple days after arriving back at school, I made the familiar drive out to Old Waverly. As I turned onto One Magnolia Lane, the sun filtered through the trees. My tires slowed as I pulled in, and there he was: Mr. White, standing at his usual post in the guardhouse, just like always.

"Well, look who it is," he said with a grin as his hand reached toward mine, extended through the window.

The Turnpike

"Hey, Mr. White," I said, smiling back. "Good to see you."

"Glad you made it back," he said.

As strange as it might have sounded, that short drive down One Magnolia Lane, past the planted oak trees and toward the clubhouse, felt like coming home. A smile came across my face as I thought about my journey to get here and how I wouldn't be here without Mr. White.

My brain had racked up the miles traveling the Pennsylvania Turnpike, both north and south, and the traffic was always the same as the first time: hope going north toward Oakmont, and doubt traveling south back to Nemacolin. It became more than just a stretch of highway. It was a map of my emotional landscape, a corridor where my internal battle between belief and fear played out every mile.

The first trip north, toward Oakmont, had been filled with anticipation. But the drive south told a different story. That's when doubt crept in, gripping the steering wheel with the same panic I'd felt when I missed the turn. It asked questions that had no answers: *Did Bob Ford already make up his mind? Did being late cost me the opportunity? Was I even good enough, or had I just been fooling people this whole time?*

That stretch of road became a space of second-guessing, of silence louder than any radio station could cover up.

I often traveled south in the weeks that followed, and the ride became longer each time. Every day that passed without a call from Oakmont, the further south I drifted emotionally.

But even in those darker moments, I held on to something. Maybe it was pride. Maybe it was faith. Or maybe it was the stubborn belief that I had done everything I could. Even if the outcome didn't go my way, I believed I had stood in that room with one of the best golf professionals in the country and told the truth about who I was and why I loved the game of golf.

That was the hope I clung to: not just the hope of getting the job, but the hope that everything I had done to get there actually meant something. That the hard work, the growth, the risk of showing up late and still walking through the door—all of it mattered.

The next couple of months would stretch out longer than I could have imagined, and November couldn't come soon enough. But as the leaves began to turn and the seasons shifted, I realized that the turnpike had given me more than just a path to Oakmont; it had traced the road between who I had been and who I was becoming.

Many careers hinge on pivotal moments that test whether you're good enough. For aspiring PGA professionals, that moment was the Player Ability Test (PAT), our version of the bar exam. The PGA of America required every candidate to pass it: two eighteen-hole rounds with a set target score. At Mississippi State's course, the number was 155.

Playing casually with friends was one thing. But with those thirty-six holes, each shot carried the weight of a career and, in my case, a dream. The pressure felt just like the turnpike all over again: relentless, personal, and unforgiving. Thirty-six holes, pass or fail. This was one of the keys on the key ring I would need to become a PGA professional.

My first attempt at the PAT had been an eye-opener. I realized I wasn't as good at golf as I had thought. Rumor had it that within the PGM Program, only about 20 percent of those who attempted passed. Failing that first attempt was disappointing, but I knew I still had time to pass it before graduation.

Right then, the most important thing wasn't the PAT—it was getting to Oakmont.

Interview days arrived in mid-October. But unlike the year before, I didn't sign up for a single one. I was waiting to hear back from Bob.

The responsible thing would have been to interview. I had no guarantee Bob was going to hire me, but I resisted the temptation. While I wasn't particularly superstitious, something about interviewing for a job I didn't want felt laced with bad karma. If Bob didn't hire me, I wanted to work for the next best golf professional in the country, and the truth was, I had no idea who that was.

What I had learned so far was that getting those kinds of jobs was harder than it looked. I wasn't just looking for an internship: I needed a mentor, someone who could shape me into the kind of professional I wanted to become.

I woke up early for work on Sunday, November 1, the way a kid wakes up on Christmas morning. The room was still dark, I sat up in bed, heart already racing as questions hummed beneath my skin like a second heartbeat.

What time is Bob going to call?

I wish I could afford a cell phone.

What if he calls and doesn't leave a message?

What if my roommates forget to tell me he called?

I can't believe I have to work today.

I stared at the answering machine as if it could give me answers, but it just sat there, silent and still. I got dressed, forced down some breakfast, and headed to Old Waverly with a knot in my stomach.

When I returned home that afternoon, I rushed through the door, already scanning the machine's tiny screen for a blinking light. Nothing. No message. No call.

Maybe Bob will call tomorrow, I told myself. After all, it's Sunday.

But Monday came and went. Still no message. Still no call from Mr. Ford. The silence had me traveling south down the turnpike.

"Damn it, what's going on?" I muttered, hovering over my answering machine Tuesday afternoon. "Is this thing even working?" I stabbed at the buttons, replaying the nothingness just to be sure.

The hell with it. I couldn't wait any longer. I grabbed the phone, my heart pounding faster with every ring. Impatience boiled over until finally I heard a voice on the other end.

"Scott, I haven't heard from Mr. Ford yet. Should I call him?"

"When did he say he would contact you?" Scott asked calmly.

"The first of November," I said.

Scott laughed. "It's only November third. You have to be patient. If Bob said he'd call, he'll call."

"Okay," I replied, deflated.

I walked away from the phone. I didn't like this one bit. Sitting around waiting. It wasn't in my nature. Uncle Tom's voice rang in my head. "If you want something bad enough, you have to go after it."

Maybe being patient was a part of going after it. Maybe restraint took as much strength as action. But damn, it didn't feel that way. Nobody got anything in life just sitting on their hands, hoping and wishing.

Still, Scott had been right. I had done everything I could. Now, it was out of my hands.

I had barely made it to the kitchen when the phone rang, slicing through the room like a lightning bolt. I froze.

Maybe it's Scott, I thought. Maybe he changed his mind.

"Is this Jason?" a man's voice asked.

I swallowed. "Yeah, this is Jason."

"Jason, it's Bob Ford. Are you still interested in working at Oakmont next year?"

My legs locked beneath me. For a second, I forgot how to breathe. "Yes, sir." *Who's he kidding? Hell yeah, I'm interested.*

"Great. I have a spot for you, but it isn't the position you interviewed for."

"Is it in the golf operation?" I asked, trying to keep my voice steady.

"Yes, it is."

"Okay, I'll take it," I said without hesitation.

There was a pause on the other end. "You don't want to know what it is first?"

"No, sir. It doesn't matter."

Another pause. "Do you want to know what it pays before you decide?"

"No, sir," I said. "That doesn't matter either."

As I hung up the phone a few minutes later, a wave of pride surged through me. The anxiety that had consumed me for days cracked and crumbled under the weight of what had just happened. Bob Ford had called me. I was going to Oakmont.

Maybe not in the role I expected, but I had earned a place. And that meant everything.

The great news was that I was headed to Oakmont. The bad news was that I couldn't start until May. I would need to find somewhere to intern from January through April, but it didn't matter. I was going to work for Bob Ford. I was going to work for the best.

How would I tell Scott Maynard in the PGM office that the internship Bob offered, and that I had already accepted, was a level one position, not the level two I needed? What would I do if he told me I couldn't go? Surely, he was going to let me go.

Just when I thought I'd figured things out, something new showed up to challenge me. Doubt never disappeared, just changed shape. One worry faded, another took its place. I started to realize that this was the rhythm of life: Solve one problem, face the next. The pressure never really let up, it just shifted.

Sometimes I wondered if these challenges were as big as they felt, or if my mind gave them mass just so I had something solid to push against. Maybe that's how we cope: with monsters we can name, even if they're not real.

"Scott, Bob just called me. I'm going to Oakmont," I said.

"Congratulations," he said, calm as ever.

"Here's the thing. I . . . um . . . he wants me to work in the bag room, on the range, and with the caddie master. Sounds like a level one internship. That okay?"

"If you have the chance to work for Mr. Ford," Scott said without hesitation, "you take it, regardless of what you'll be doing. Yes, it is more than okay."

Northern clubs shut down in the winter, and finding an

The Turnpike

internship from January through April turned out to be more challenging than I had expected. My options were limited, so we focused on clubs in Florida, Texas, Arizona, and Southern California.

Scott handed me a brochure from a place in Scottsdale, Arizona, called Desert Mountain Golf Club. It was one of the top private clubs in the country. The place looked incredible. I flipped through the pages, each one showcasing rustic clubhouses perched against the Arizona mountainside. There were four golf courses already built and a fifth under construction, each one a deep, lush green that looked completely out of place on the brown desert floor.

The thought of five Old Waverly Golf Clubs tucked behind one guardhouse blew me away. How is that even possible?

"This place looks awesome. Would this be good?" I asked.

"Yes, it would be great," Scott said. "Dick Hyland is the director of golf and would be a great guy to work for. Dick is regarded as the Bob Ford of the West Coast. The number's on the back. Give him a call."

I took the brochure, dialed the number, and introduced myself. I explained who I was and that I was looking for an internship from January through April.

"This is a short internship," Dick said. "Why so short?"

"I start May first at Oakmont," I replied.

"Ahhh, you're working for Bobby?" he asked.

"If Bobby is Mr. Ford, then yes, sir, I am."

"Yes, Bob's a good friend. You're lucky to be working for him."

"Yes, sir."

"Well," he said, "if Bobby is willing to hire you, so am I."

At that moment, I began to understand the impact of working for Mr. Ford. My interview with Dick Hyland, if you could even call it that, reminded me of the kind of small-town trust I grew up with back in Lyndonville. The call lasted five minutes. Bob Ford had already put his name next to mine, and that was enough to convince Dick Hyland to do the same at Desert Mountain.

I was following Larry Kelley's advice, and Doug had been right all along. I was being hired for my passion for golf, not for what I knew about being a golf professional, which was minimal.

My passion, strong work ethic, and a growing network of respected individuals in the golf industry continued to open doors for me. I knew a time would come when hard work alone wouldn't be enough, but that time hadn't arrived yet. One day, people would hire me for the skills and knowledge I had, not just the potential they saw. And I knew it was time to start carving those skills, to begin whittling the wood for the arrows I'd eventually need in my quiver.

26

LIFE ON THE PORCH

"I've been thinking a lot this week," I said, eyes drifting to the window. "About the road from Lyndonville to Oakmont."

Zoe's expression softened, the way it always did when she sensed I was circling something important.

"I went into the PGM Program to chase a dream, but also to find myself, my purpose in life. Every moment felt like a test: Old Waverly, Nemacolin, even just walking across campus. Like I was waiting for someone to point out that I didn't deserve to be there."

I paused.

"But something changed that year. My meeting with Bob didn't go perfectly, but I was the best version of Jason I had ever been in an interview. I started to believe I deserved to be in that room because Doug believed in who I could become, and I'd earned that."

Zoe's voice was low and steady. "You stopped chasing permission."

I nodded. "Yeah, I guess you could say that."

"Bob's offer was a big moment," I continued. "Not just because he said yes, but because his yes validated my belief in who I was and wanted to become. I had that belief when Mr. Bryan took me under his wing at Old Waverly, but when I sat across from the person regarded as the best in the country, that was a whole new level. I believed I was worthy of the opportunity, but I honestly didn't know what it took to belong at one of the best clubs in the world."

She smiled. "That sounds like a shift from validation to self-belief."

"It is. I used to think confidence came from other people choosing you. But now I think it comes from choosing yourself. Over and over, even when the shit hits the fan. I think in order for someone to choose you, you have to first choose yourself," I said. "Does that even make sense?" I asked

Zoe nodded. "Yes, it does."

I paused again, then added, "I still had doubts. I have them today. They don't ever go away. But they didn't own me anymore. That voice inside, the one that used to whisper I wasn't enough—it wasn't so loud. Then another voice started to take its place. One that said: Keep moving forward. Ya gotta believe it's gonna happen." I sat silent again, then said, "It's kinda like my old self was arguing with my future self, and my current self was always stuck in the middle."

Zoe looked at me for a long moment, then said, "Sometimes growth doesn't feel like we think it should. Sometimes it feels like finally exhaling."

I smiled. "Yeah. I can relate to that," I said. "I guess so. Proving myself to others hasn't stopped, but I started to see myself, well my future self, as a golf professional. I truly believed it was gonna happen."

Zoe sat quiet and I said, "But I had a long way to go, let me tell ya."

My time at Desert Mountain exceeded my expectations. Jason Walters, the head professional I reported to, involved me deeply in the operation. Every week, I tagged along with him to check progress on the new golf course under construction, gaining insight into the planning and vision behind it. But my primary role was with the outside service team and taking on a new responsibility: valet.

It took nearly fifteen minutes to drive up the meandering road from the guardhouse to the clubhouse. The absence of streetlights draped the desert in a thick darkness, not unlike the woods during deer season when I'd sit perched in a tree, waiting for Mother Nature to wake up. That darkness felt familiar.

I enjoyed working valet and found myself assigned to that team often. I wasn't any better at it than anyone else, but I couldn't understand why more of them didn't sprint to the parking lot. I was chasing the same cars I'd once thumbtacked to my bedroom wall as a kid. Lamborghinis, Porsches, Ferraris. To me, it wasn't just parking cars; it was stepping into a dream.

Most guys jogged, some ran, but a few of us sprinted. For me, it felt like running down the fairways of Old Waverly or charging up the hills during football practice back home. The effort wasn't about making anyone else look bad; it was more about earning respect. I wanted control over what people judged me on, and sprinting gave me that control. I couldn't dictate everything, but I could dictate how hard I worked.

Soon after arriving at Desert Mountain in January of 1999, Jason Walters introduced me to Jim Flick, the PGA of America's Teacher of the Year in 1988. Jim had a teaching academy on one of the courses, and he agreed to let me help set up and clean up before and after his clinics whenever I wasn't on the clock. I spent over a hundred hours with him, sitting in a chair watching and listening as he coached everyone from weekend amateurs to PGA Tour players.

The only rule was simple: Don't speak during the lessons. I could ask him anything I wanted after, but while he was teaching, I was to observe and listen.

Bright green grass stood out sharply against the dull, dusty tones of the desert. At over half a mile above sea level, the air felt crisp, like the stillness after a fresh snowfall back in Vermont. I sat there under the bluest sky I had ever seen, with a pen, a notebook, and one of the greatest teaching professionals in the world just a few feet away.

My time at Desert Mountain came to an end on April 28. It was time to pack up once again. This time, I was heading east, on my way to Oakmont.

After more than thirty hours of driving across 2,100 miles and sleeping in my truck at rest areas, I was finally getting close. The butterflies hatched in my stomach as I crossed the Hulton Bridge and fidgeted behind the wheel on my way up the hill. I wasn't late this time.

Before I left Desert Mountain, Bob had told me he had a room for me and that I didn't need to rent an apartment. That was great news. My studio in Arizona had eaten up most of my income, and I'd only managed to save a little during the last four months.

Life on the Porch

I stood on the path above Oakmont's eighteenth green, the same spot I had stood almost a year earlier. The fairways stretched out before me like a dream I was finally awake inside of. A smile crept across my face as I remembered the guy who pulled up next to me on the interstate the day before, waving his arms, trying to get my attention.

At first, I didn't understand what he was saying. Then it clicked. Something had flown out of the back of my truck.

I made a U-turn at the next emergency crossover and drove back. That's when I saw it: A garbage bag I had packed full of clothes had burst open on the highway. My jeans and shirts, most of them from Vermont, were now scattered across the pavement like confetti after a parade. I sat in the breakdown lane, helpless, watching cars whip past, driving over pieces of the life I used to wear. I thought about jumping out and trying to retrieve it all, but there was no safe way. And the longer I watched, the less I wanted to.

I let out a quiet chuckle and shook my head. Then I nodded toward the clothes, like I was tipping my hat. I watched for a moment, then eased back onto the interstate.

Walking through Oakmont's golf professional shop, I introduced myself to the assistant golf professionals behind the front counter. It felt surreal. Of all the assistant pros in the country, these were the ones who had made it to Oakmont. I couldn't help but wonder how they got here. Had their path been anything like mine?

Part of me wanted to say, "Hey guys, I made it too." But I didn't need to. It was already evident. I was here.

When I entered his office, Bob welcomed me back with a

smile and the same firm handshake as before. Only this time, the inside of my pocket wasn't soaked in nervous sweat. I asked Bob where my room was, and he said, "You'll be in the clubhouse."

"In the clubhouse?" I asked, a little surprised.

"We have some rooms up on the third floor for our assistants; one is for you."

"Awesome, thank you."

"Jason, there are two rules," he said, his voice suddenly flat and serious. "No girls upstairs. No alcohol."

The shift in tone was unmistakable. It reminded me of my dad when he needed to make something perfectly clear: calm, direct, and final. Bob didn't need to raise his voice or offer a second warning. The message was as vivid as the Arizona sky I had been sitting under just a few days earlier.

In just two years, I had worked at some of the most spectacular clubs in the country, and I was proud of that. Old Waverly Golf Club, where it all started, was ranked among the top 100 best private clubs in America by *Golf Digest* and was preparing to host the US Women's Open. Nemacolin Woodlands Resort and Spa, where I spent a summer grinding and learning, would go on to host the PGA Tour's 84 Lumber Classic. At Desert Mountain, I worked alongside some of the best in the game while the club hosted The Tradition, a major on the Senior PGA Tour.

And now, I was at Oakmont.

At that time, Oakmont had already hosted seven US Opens, three PGA Championships, a US Women's Open, and four US Amateurs. Oakmont wasn't just historic, it was legendary. It was impossible for me to find the words that aligned with how I felt about being a part of its history.

The porch of the golf shop stretched wide, its wooden railing framing a perfect view of Oakmont's daunting eighteenth hole. From there, I could see the towering oaks standing sentinel around it, their shadows stretching long in the late afternoon sun. The air smelled of fresh cut grass and a scent I'd sworn I'd never smelled before. Bob had just introduced me to Jon Migely—Migs, as everyone called him—who was the caddie master I'd be reporting to every day.

As I stood leaning on the railing, Migs' voice cut through the awe of Oakmont. "Ever caddied before?" he asked.

I shook my head. "I've forecaddied, but I've never carried a bag for someone else."

Migs gave a half smile. "You'll be fine. I'll pair you with one of the veterans. They'll show you the ropes, the Oakmont way."

The sun dipped lower, casting a golden glow over the green as I watched a group finish their final putts, remove their hats, and shake hands. I felt a mixture of nerves and excitement settle in. My first loop would happen in the morning, and with it, my true introduction to the traditions of this revered place.

"I'll get you out in one of the first groups, so be here at 7 a.m.," Migs said.

Bob chimed in and said, "You can pull around the back and take your stuff up the fire escape. One of the guys behind the counter will help you get moved in."

The following morning, I walked down the stairs inside Oakmont's clubhouse in awe and stopped to look at all the memorabilia gathered over nearly a century. Every step was more surreal than the previous one. I walked through the doors onto the porch of the clubhouse for the first time and looked over the dew-covered grass as my heart raced with disbelief. It was the most beautiful place I had ever seen. A perfect piece of Mother Nature, manicured in understated elegance. I thought about how I would describe what was in front of me and inside of me at that moment to someone, and there was nothing I could say to do either justice.

Oakmont was open Tuesday through Sunday for member play, and sometimes on Mondays for "Member Mondays," when a member could sponsor a group of multiple guests. My schedule quickly settled into one of the best routines of my life. I would caddie almost every morning, sometimes carrying two bags. Afterward, I'd grab a quick lunch and report to work on the porch by one o'clock, staying until the last guest or caddie finished around dark.

It was rare that I ever asked for a day off. Why would I? I was working at one of the best private golf clubs in the world.

One morning a couple of weeks after I'd started, I was standing on the porch, sipping coffee and organizing the bags for the day, when the first assistant stepped out of the golf shop and walked toward me. He leaned on the railing beside me, eyes scanning the eighteenth green as if he were just making conversation.

"Hey," he said casually, "one of the members can't get away from work this morning. He's got a few guests going out and needs someone from the staff to play with them."

I turned to face him, hoping this was going where I thought it was.

"You wanna play today?" he asked.

My eyes widened before I could control them. "Yeah, of course," I said, trying to sound nonchalant, though a rush of adrenaline shot through me like a jolt of electricity.

He nodded and pointed toward the cart path. "You're off in twenty. Go grab your clubs."

As I made my way into the bag room, the nerves became more intense than I had ever felt before. This wasn't just a casual round. I was stepping onto the first tee not as a guest, not even as just a staff member, but as a representative of Oakmont who was standing in for the member himself. My swing, my attitude, my words, even the way I carried myself reflected back on Bob and on Oakmont.

By the time I reached the first tee, my heart pounded as I shook hands with the guests. I tried to breathe without anyone noticing, but it was impossible.

This was Oakmont. And today, I was playing in its name.

The morning mist was just starting to lift as I walked off the first tee, the fairway grass cut so tight it didn't look or feel real under my feet. The sun peeked through the overhanging oaks as if to say, "Good morning, Jason," the way I had done at Speedwell every morning. I glanced back at the imposing clubhouse behind me.

Was this even real?

Two years ago, I had been sitting in a small-town diner in Vermont, nursing a coffee and wondering what came next. I had no idea this kind of life existed. This luxury, the history underfoot, the caliber of people I was surrounded by. None of it had seemed even remotely possible back then. And yet, here

I was. Walking the same fairways where legends had won and lost major championships. I wasn't just working at one of the most storied golf clubs in the world. I was representing it.

I wasn't special. I was just a hardworking kid from Lyndonville, a speck on the map in Northeast Vermont. But I'd said yes to everything I could. I showed up early, stayed late, and believed that maybe, just maybe, effort could carve a path to my dream. And now, I had seen more in two short years than most people I knew would see in a lifetime.

Dad used to say, "There's a big world out there, son. Don't be afraid to explore it. You can always come home." His voice rang in my mind as if he were walking beside me now. He used to say things like, "Anything is possible," or, "You can become anything you want." But the picture was always vague. He never described what that world looked like, what it felt like. I don't think he knew this world existed either. Not Oakmont. Not this level of excellence. This sacred ground.

And still, he had been right.

I didn't want to go home, not in the literal sense or any sense for that matter. I missed the routine of my old life, but I didn't long for it. I was born again, maybe for the third time. Everything felt new. Even the simple things I had once overlooked now felt fresh. The smell of the air after it rained. The way people smiled and meant it when they said good morning to me on the porch. Those small things grounded me here as much as the legacy of Bob and Oakmont.

But not everything was perfect. I missed the Vermont fall.

I had never expected to miss the colors of home until I didn't see them for the first time as a freshman at Mississippi

State. No burning reds. No fire orange. Just green fading to brown. I hadn't realized how much the autumn colors meant to me until they weren't there. Then one day, a box arrived.

It was featherlight. Mom had collected leaves from the big maple in her yard—orange, red, yellow—and mailed them to me. As I opened the package, a sweet, earthy scent rose from the cardboard. It smelled like home. Like a sugarhouse boiling sap in March. Like the woods behind our house after the first frost. Like Vermont.

I closed my eyes and breathed it in.

As I walked the back nine at Oakmont, my thoughts drifted to Kathleen.

She was pregnant now, and for the first time, I felt peace. Things were different, so different from the ache I had carried for so long. I was genuinely happy for her. Somewhere along the way, life had stitched up what had been torn. The love of life itself had done what time alone couldn't. My heart, once broken in ways I didn't know how to name, had finally healed. The sutures had dissolved. The scar remained, sure. It always would. A wound like that doesn't disappear; it stays forever. But it no longer throbbed with pain. It simply marked a part of my story.

I didn't know what the future held. I didn't know if Kathleen or her baby would stay in my life in any real way. But I hoped so. Only time would tell.

For now, I looked around at where I was. The fairways at Oakmont were so much more than grass. They were proof. Proof that belief, dedication, pain, and forgiveness could walk hand in hand and somehow lead you to a place like this.

27

A NEW BRIDGE

Twenty golf carts were squeezed beneath Oakmont's professional shop, tucked into an area barely big enough to hold them. One slow and uneventful afternoon, I found myself pacing around, restless, like the day I first met Mr. Bryan back in Mississippi.

I hosed the carts down every night as part of my regular routine, but washing carts was different from really cleaning them. That day, I decided they needed a deep scrub.

I filled a bucket with soap and water, grabbed some brushes, and got to work. As I scrubbed around the tires, I noticed dark, grimy water running off the wheels. Curious, I grabbed a screwdriver and popped a hubcap off. Underneath showed months, maybe years, of caked mud buildup. I scrubbed until the white returned, then snapped the hubcap back into place. One by one, I worked my way through the carts, my hands turning black.

I looked down and chuckled at my dirty hands, stained just like they used to be after cleaning the barn back home. I smiled as I remembered the time Ma made me scrub my hands with bleach because they were so filthy with cow shit and diesel fuel.

About halfway through the carts, I heard Bob's voice behind me.

"Jas, what are you doing?"

I turned around. "I was bored, so I'm cleaning carts. Do you need me to do something for you?"

"No," he said, walking a little closer. "Why do you have the hubcaps off?"

"I'm cleaning the wheels too. Look how nasty they are."

I would never forget the look on Bob's face. It reflected the same look that George Bryan had as he scanned the courtyard.

And truthfully, popping those hubcaps off was a first for me, too. I had simply never thought to look that closely before.

Over the course of my internship at Oakmont, I had the chance to caddie for Bob several times during casual rounds with members and in Tri-State Section PGA events. The summer flew by, and before I knew it, the time had come to head back to school.

Throughout the past few months, I'd spoken with Bob about my next internship and, like Larry Kelley, Bob offered me advice that stuck: "Go somewhere you can learn."

My truck was packed and ready. I stepped into the professional shop to say goodbye to the staff.

"Anyone know where Bob is?" I asked.

"He's out playing golf," one of the assistants replied. "You missed him."

"Thanks," I said, heading out onto the porch.

Bob might've been on the golf course, but I hadn't missed

him. There was no way in hell I was leaving Oakmont without saying goodbye.

I found Bob's group on the fourteenth tee. After they all hit, I drove down the fairway and waited. When Bob approached, I stepped out of the cart and walked alongside him.

I thanked him for the opportunity to work at Oakmont and reminded him about helping me find an internship for the following year. He nodded and said he'd work on it.

"Do you care where you go or what you do?" he asked.

"No, sir. I'll go wherever you tell me to go."

"Okay," he said with a small nod. "I'll be in touch. Thanks for the hard work, Jas. Good luck in school."

"Yes, sir," I said. "You're welcome."

For the last time, I idled my way out of Oakmont Country Club and onto Hulton Road. The butterflies that had once stirred in my gut months earlier were gone and left me something I hadn't expected: grief.

Not sadness about leaving Oakmont, though it was that, but a more dense emotion. It was like saying goodbye to a part of myself I had just gotten to know.

When I arrived at Oakmont, I still believed I was chasing a dream of becoming a PGA professional like I had first seen through the lens of Larry Kelley, the man who had first shown me what being a golf professional looked like. I wanted to be just like him.

And then I met Bob, and everything changed.

Bob Ford wasn't just excellent at what he did. He was exceptional. I had never met anyone like him. He was polished beyond measure, with a calm command that made people lean

A New Bridge

in when he spoke, not because they had to but because they didn't want to miss a single word. His team moved with a kind of unspoken language, like trust was baked into the Oakmont way. When Bob entered a room, the atmosphere changed. Respect was simply there.

Watching him became my new classroom. On the fairways of Oakmont, with his bag on my shoulder and his voice in my ear, I studied every detail. How he greeted members. How he carried himself with humility and poise. How he remembered the small things. I paid attention after rounds to how he shook hands, the way he made every person feel important. I had been exposed to this before with George at Speedwell and Mr. Bryan at Old Waverly, and I took mental notes like my future depended on it.

Because in many ways, it did.

I realized as I made my way away from Oakmont that I had been chasing others my whole life; Kathleen's brother Brian, her father George, Ma, wanting to be like them. When I arrived at Oakmont, I wanted to be Bob just as I had wanted to be Larry Kelley. It was as if I was trying to climb in their shadow somehow. But somewhere along the way, I realized I wasn't chasing them or even the dream of being a golf professional. My eyes had locked on to something bigger. Something hard to name and more intangible than ever before.

I was now chasing what I saw. I was chasing greatness.

The kind of greatness that doesn't come with a title or a paycheck. The kind that feels like flying wide open down a dirt track on a motocross bike, an impossible feeling to explain to someone who's never felt it. Greatness that comes from being deeply, unapologetically excellent, and making people around you better because of it.

But that realization came with a cost.

Letting go of the dream to become a PGA professional wasn't easy. That dream had anchored me through the uncertainty of Mississippi and the newness of Old Waverly. It had gotten me this far. But standing at Oakmont, shoulder to shoulder with Bob Ford, I knew I had to let it go. The grief was real. But so was the pull of something larger, something that no longer lived in someone else's shadow.

Two years ago, I wanted to be a PGA professional. Now, I wanted to be one of the best PGA professionals in the country.

And I knew, for the first time, that it was possible because I was willing to want it.

The bridge I had built between my desire to become a PGA professional and the life I thought I wanted had served me well. But now, staring into the vastness between where I stood and where I knew I needed to go, that bridge no longer spanned the gap. It wasn't built for the weight of this new dream.

It was time to build a new bridge, completely reengineered.

It was time to become dream driven.

Roughly eight hours after leaving Pennsylvania for the last time, I crossed into Tennessee, and it hit me again: My time at Oakmont was over. My time with Bob was over. The most incredible experience of my life had come to an end, and I felt a hollow inside and that emotion was confusing.

I gripped the wheel tighter and stared straight ahead, my thoughts louder than the tires humming beneath me. I sure hoped I'd learned enough. The truth was, I had never aspired to be great at anything. Not school, motocross, skiing, or football. I liked to win, sure. I loved to compete. I like to push myself to become better. But greatness? That was something reserved for someone else. Someone born with it. Someone chosen.

I had been good at a lot of things. But I wasn't great at anything. Well, that's not entirely true. I was great at working hard. But working hard doesn't take skill, it takes grit, commitment, willingness, and a decision you make every single day. That part came naturally to me. Being great at anything wasn't something I'd avoided; it was a concept I didn't even know existed, and it's hard to chase something you've never seen.

Still, I wondered, was that enough? Could effort and desire alone carry me to the kind of greatness I'd witnessed in Bob Ford? That question settled in my gut, pushing me forward even as the road stretched on into the night.

At that moment, I realized I hadn't been planning for this day. I had been so focused on reaching Oakmont that I hadn't considered what came next, who else I should work for or where else I might go. The plan had been so singular, so consuming, that everything beyond it had disappeared into a fog. The question I should have asked Scott Maynard as a freshman wasn't just, "How do I get to Oakmont?" but, "Who else should I work for in addition to Bob Ford?"

I knew I needed three internship terms, but I hadn't even thought about the third one. I was so locked in on reaching the pinnacle that I forgot to map out what came after. Reverse engineering a career, it turned out, was more complicated than working backward through a cereal box maze.

And right then, behind the wheel on that long Tennessee

stretch, I felt both pressing in on me. I had reached the summit of something I'd only ever dreamed of, and in the same breath, I was staring down the uncertainty of what came next.

A couple of weeks passed, and the phone rang in my apartment. It was Bob. After a few minutes of catching up, he said, "I found you a job."

"That's great," I said, my heart kicking up a beat. "Where is it?"

"You said you don't care where you go or what you do, right?"

"No, sir. I'll go wherever you tell me to go."

"That's great. Your job is here at Oakmont. I want you to come back and work on the porch again. How's that sound?"

For a moment, I couldn't speak. Blinded by the shock of it, I stood motionless. I hadn't even considered that going back was an option.

"Wow . . . that's awesome. I would love to come back, but I have to intern at different places," I said, the words filled with disappointment.

"You can come back, Jas. You just let Scott Maynard know I want you back at Oakmont. He'll understand."

"Yes, sir. I'll let him know today," I said. "Bob, we've come a long way, haven't we? Just a couple of years ago, I was doing everything in my power to find my way to Oakmont, and now . . . you want me back."

"Yes we have, Jas."

As I hung up, I stood still for a moment, the receiver still warm in my hand. The impact of what had just happened consumed me. I wasn't asking Bob to hire me; he was asking me to return.

A New Bridge

I'd been transported back to the Pennsylvania Turnpike, driving south through the fog of doubt and fear all over again. The purpose behind spreading out our internships had always made sense: It was about broadening our experiences, seeing different operations, and learning from a variety of professionals. But now, I needed to convince Scott that going back to Oakmont was the right move. He'd already made one exception for me, allowing a level one position for my second internship. Would he bend the rules again?

Bob had said Scott would understand, but I wasn't so sure. Scott always emphasized how critical it was to have diverse experiences before interview days. Oakmont was extraordinary, but would Scott see the value in returning there?

That afternoon, I walked into Scott's office. He looked up from his desk as I stepped in.

"I have an offer for my final internship," I said.

"That's great," he replied. "Where is it?"

"Oakmont," I said, grinning. "Bob asked me to come back and work the porch again. But . . . I know the rule about different places."

He leaned back in his chair. "Yes, that's the rule. But this is Bob Ford. If Bob asks you back, you go back. Plain and simple."

Relief hit me like a warm wind. "That's good," I said with a laugh. "I already told him yes." I smiled. "Hard to believe it wasn't that long ago I was trying to figure out how to get to Oakmont."

"I remember," he said. "You've worked hard. I'm happy for you. Plenty of people across the country would kill for the opportunity Bob's giving you. You're one of a few who get to learn from one of the best."

I nodded. "Thanks for all your help."

"You're welcome," he said. "But I haven't done much. You've done this on your own. You're the one who found your way to Oakmont, twice. You're the one who worked hard. Not me."

As I pushed through the heavy doors and stepped into the sunlight outside McCool Hall, I couldn't hold it in any longer.

"Hell yeah! I'm going back to Oakmont!" I shouted, not caring who heard as I strode across the campus.

The first time around, Oakmont had towered over me with its history, its prestige, and Bob himself. It had taken me months just to find my footing. But now? Now, I had traction. The power of Oakmont wouldn't shake me this time. I wasn't showing up to prove I belonged. I had already done that.

When Bob first called to offer me the job again, I was thrilled. But walking across campus now, I felt something deeper. Returning meant I'd earned Bob's respect. I wasn't just an intern anymore; I was someone he wanted in his orbit and someone he believed in.

A gust of wind swept across the quad, rustling the trees and sending a few golden leaves spinning across my path. I smiled, slowing for a moment as it hit me.

Bob Ford didn't offer returning positions lightly. He had picked me, again. A second seat at his table, one of the most coveted tables in the golf business. And that could only mean one thing: He wasn't done with me yet.

28

TRASH GODS

I pulled into the parking lot behind Oakmont in May of 2000, my truck still carrying traces of the Mississippi Yazoo clay. As I stepped out and looked up at the familiar clubhouse, a wide smile stretched across my face. I was back. The grief that once consumed the butterflies was now replaced with appreciation and pride.

"Jack!" Migs called out, a nickname I had been given last year, as my loafers hit the Oakmont porch.

"Look who's back!" one of the assistants chimed in as he walked out of the pro shop.

I was met with a round of handshakes and hugs, their grins matching mine. It felt like a reunion. Bob had wanted me back. That mattered. And they knew it.

Later that week, I met PGA member Sean Farren for the first time. He carried himself like someone who'd been shaped by the same places I had. Turns out, he had. Sean was a Mississippi State grad and one of the rare few who had played on the golf team while in the PGM Program. He had worked at Oakmont years earlier and had recently moved back to Pittsburgh for a new job.

Sean had the kind of energy that filled a room and was someone you wanted to be around. He asked if I'd caddie for him in a couple of weeks during a Tri-State Section PGA event, and of course, I said yes.

But things didn't start well. By the third hole, he was over par. I had already caddied for him a few times at Oakmont by then and was learning that Sean played with an edge and every swing carried emotion.

Sean teed off on a par-five with a fairway that sloped drastically from right to left. I waited at the top of the hill, ready for him to come down toward me. He had just missed the fairway with another poor shot. Frustration was etched across his face as he marched forward. When he reached me, I looked him square in the eye and said, "Seriously, Sean? You need to get your head out of your ass and start playing golf. Come on, we need a birdie on this hole."

Sean dropped his driver to the ground, grabbed me by the front of my shirt, and pushed me back a step with both hands. "That's what I'm talking about!" he shouted, his eyes suddenly alive.

The clubs in his bag, slung across my back, clanged together as I hurried to keep up with him down the fairway. His stride had doubled in speed, and mine had to match it. Speeding up your tempo on the golf course isn't always a good thing. But for Sean, getting into gear was exactly what he needed. He was back. Focused. Fired up. And for the first time that round, I saw a glimmer of the player that he was.

I had spent most of my time at Oakmont (and in the internships before) absorbing, listening, and learning. I had watched people like Larry Kelley, Dick Hyland, and Bob Ford command rooms and navigate conversations with authority and grace. But I had never seen myself as someone who could push others, who could use my voice to pull the best out of someone in real time.

But when I told Sean to get his head out of his ass, it was instinct. And it worked. His whole energy flipped, and he fed off it. Watching him march down the fairway, I realized I had a voice that could move someone, not from a position of authority but from conviction.

That moment taught me leadership didn't always wear a blazer. I didn't need to be the most experienced to lead. I just needed the courage to speak up when it mattered and to know the personality of the person in front of me. A year earlier, I would've stayed silent. Now, I was learning the shape of my own authority.

Sean made three birdies finishing up the front nine, and we turned to the back nine under par for the first time all day. Walking down the tenth hole, he veered off toward the tree line. I paused, confused, and watched him go as I made my way toward his ball.

A few moments later, he returned with an old water bottle dangling from his fingers. "Throw this away for me," he said, handing it over.

As Sean bent to pick up a candy wrapper and tucked it into my caddie bib, he said, "If you take care of the Trash Gods, they'll take care of you." I laughed in the moment, not thinking much of it beyond a quirky superstition.

But I would come to learn, in the years that followed, that the Trash Gods weren't just about litter. They were about the little things, the unnoticed, thankless acts of care and attention that shaped the bigger picture of yourself. They were about respect. Discipline. Integrity when no one was watching.

I didn't know it yet, but the Trash Gods were going to show up again and again in my life, sometimes in wrappers and Styrofoam cups, sometimes in moments where I'd have to choose between cutting corners or doing the right thing. And each time, I'd remember that line in a fairway near Pittsburgh, Pennsylvania. A strange sort of gospel handed down not in a boardroom or a classroom, but on the back nine of a Monday morning round of golf.

As great as Oakmont was, there were still challenging days. I would call back home to my pro, Larry Kelley, with frustration from time to time, wanting more from the experience. Every day that passed was one less day I'd work for Bob, one less day at the world-renowned Oakmont. I knew I could do more if given the opportunity, and I badly wanted to be in the pro shop. After all, the professional shop was where all the magic happened.

During one conversation that summer, after venting about not learning enough, Larry cut me off.

"So, you're not learning enough, huh?" he asked.

"No," I said. "I need to get into the pro shop. I'm gonna graduate without ever working inside."

"Tell me what you've learned so far," Larry said.

So I launched into a rant, five solid minutes of explaining how to clean a golf cart, set up a range, pick and wash balls, clean clubs, and pay the caddies.

He let me go on, then interrupted again.

"That's great," he said, "but you knew how to do all that before you got there the first time. What have you learned from Bob? Have you been watching him?"

"Of course," I said.

"Well?"

I told him about watching how Bob glided when he walked. Never in a rush, never passing anyone without saying hello. He was always clean-shaven, and his hair never looked out of place, always "high and tight." He dressed like he was on TV every day. His pants were perfectly pressed, with the fingers of a golf glove casually hanging out of his back pocket. His shirts looked brand-new, like the tags had just been pulled off. During every club event, he wore an Oakmont-crested blazer, and he always took his hat off indoors, saying, "You only need one roof over your head."

I told Larry how I watched Bob interact with his peers. How he'd sit down to eat lunch with them before and after golf, never too big for the table. I paid attention to how he spoke to Oakmont members, asking about their families, their children's schooling, and how their businesses were doing.

I described how he'd say, "How's your game?" to a member, and if they responded with "Not good," he'd follow with, "Let me help you sometime." I told Larry how Bob listened more than he talked. How he'd walk up to someone on the range struggling with their swing, watch them hit a few balls, then offer a simple piece of advice and give them that Bob Ford wink of approval after a good shot.

I remembered how he asked his assistants, "What do you think?" before offering his own direction. And how, when an assistant crossed a line, he didn't shy away from the tough conversation. He stood firm, calmly explaining that Oakmont's standards were high for a reason.

Larry let me finish, then cut in with a knowing tone: "Not learning anything, huh?"

"Yeah, I hear ya."

"What do you think happens in the pro shop anyway?" Larry said.

"I mean, I dunno. That's where the assistants are."

"He's got plenty of assistants. Your job is to study Bob, every step he takes, every word he says. Watch and listen. That's your job. You want to be like him one day, don't ya?"

"Yeah."

"He's teaching you how to do that," Larry said. "That's what'll separate you from everyone else. Working in the pro shop is easy. You can learn that later."

"You're right," I said.

"You're damn right I'm right. You have no idea how lucky you are."

"Yeah, I do."

"No. No, you don't. But one day, you will."

Later that night, back in my small third-floor room in the Oakmont clubhouse, I sat in silence. Larry's words rang like church bells in a quiet town. The space wasn't fancy—just a bed, a lamp, a dresser, and my clothes hanging from exposed water pipes in the ceiling. In that stillness, I saw it clearly: I needed to learn how to chase the greatness I was chasing. I needed patience just like when looking for four-leaf clovers.

I lay there in my bed, staring at the ceiling through the pipes, and remembered a round of golf Bob played while I was on his bag. I remembered him saying, "There's always room for an all-star," when we talked about where I would go after Oakmont, and that line stayed with me. He explained that every job falls into one of three categories—a sinking ship, a well-oiled machine, or something in-between. An all-star has value in each.

He said, "If you rescue a failing club, your stock rises. If you join a great one like Oakmont, you'd better be great too, or you'll be exposed."

It reminded me of Dad's old advice about hard work and never being without a job. But Bob's version had more depth. At Oakmont, excellence wasn't optional; it was oxygen. The best clubs attracted the best people. "All-stars find all-stars," Bob told me that day. And if I wanted to belong to this tier of club, I had to become one.

The Suburban hummed quietly beneath us as we pulled away from the club hosting that Monday's section event. I sat in the passenger seat, tired from the long day, staring out the window as the Pennsylvania countryside rolled by in a blur of green.

I turned to Bob and asked the question that had been sitting with me all summer: "Where do you think I should go after college?"

Without missing a beat, he asked, "Have you passed the PAT yet?"

I paused. "Not yet," I admitted, staring out the passenger window. At Oakmont, the assistants were top-tier players. Playing well was expected. And here I was, still trying to clear the first hurdle.

Bob glanced at me, then back at the road. "Ever thought about becoming a locker room attendant?"

His question hit me out of nowhere.

The words didn't register at first. It was like he was speaking a foreign language. "A locker room attendant?" I echoed, stunned.

"Yes," he said calmly. "A good locker room attendant can make six figures if they're at the right club."

I blinked. "No, I've never thought about it."

"Well, think about it, Jas." That was all he said. An unspoken reality.

But deep down, I knew what was really happening. His words pressed on the softest bruise: I hadn't passed the PAT. I wasn't good enough yet, and maybe I never would be. The truth was, Bob wasn't trying to take my dream away. The plane was running low on fuel, and he was handing me a parachute.

29

LIFE'S CANVAS

I sprinted through the downpour across the parking lot outside Zoe's office, my steps splashing in puddles, getting wet in both directions. I reached cover and grabbed my breath, looking into the parking lot, and I laughed as I remembered being in the barn one afternoon during chores when Katleen's brother, Brian, looked outside and said, "Damn, it's raining like a cow pissin' on a flat rock," his hands on his hips.

I made my way up the stairs and into Zoe's office. The sound of the rain bounced off the window and filled the room.

"So, talk to me about this newly formed dream."

I hadn't shared this dream often, trying to protect myself from external judgment, and I was uneasy in the moment. "Yeah. It wasn't just about becoming a golf professional any more. I wanted to become one of the best. I wanted to be great."

Zoe's expression, unlike so many others, never wavered, and she asked, "What did 'greatness' mean to you back then?"

"It was about respect. About climbing a mountain. A steep one.

Like Bob said, "You'd better be great too, or you'll be exposed."

She scribbled something in her notebook, then looked up. "And when Bob suggested you become a locker room attendant . . . how'd that make you feel?"

I swallowed hard. "Honestly? I didn't like it. I felt like a sailboat at sea without sails. Like maybe he didn't believe in me. I was busting my ass for this dream, and suddenly I was being told to consider . . . that." I paused for a long minute. "Zoe, it sounds bad, but it isn't."

"What sounds bad?" she asked.

"Being a locker room attendant. Dad always told me never to think I was better than anyone else."

"I remember," she said.

"It wasn't about that. I have shoveled more cow shit than any locker attendant has polished shoes," I said, struggling to make sure she understood. "This was about my dream of becoming one of the best golf professionals in the country. Not a locker room attendant or anything else."

Zoe nodded. "That sounds painful. How did you feel in that moment with Bob beside you on the way home?"

"I had so many emotions, and at first I couldn't believe he would say that. Then I realized, he was protecting me, the way a parent does." I gathered myself and said, "He was pushing me just like I had pushed Sean that day. I needed a wakeup call." I looked at Zoe, and her presence in the chair softened me somehow. "I realized that day that my dream might not want me as much as I wanted it."

"The tension between protecting your dream and protecting your ego—did you notice how it affected you?"

I frowned. "I realized how big my new dream was. I realized I had no chance if I couldn't pass."

Zoe let me sit silent for a moment and said, "What about the Trash Gods? What do you think that meant for you?"

I sat up straight and said, "That was about respect. Discipline. Doing the right thing, even when no one's watching."

"Exactly," Zoe said. "And those little moments? They teach us about our own worth before the world even recognizes it."

She paused, then added, "You learned to carry your standards like armor. But I'm curious, what did that armor cost you?

I looked down. "A lot of doubt. A fear of disappointing myself and everyone who believed in me."

Zoe nodded. "That's a heavy burden for anyone to carry. But it's also the beginning of leadership, learning to stand in your worth, even in uncertainty."

I breathed out slowly. "Maybe I was trying to pass that test too. I don't know. I believed in myself, and I told myself every day I did. Maybe I didn't believe it as much as I thought I did."

Zoe smiled. "Maybe. And that belief? It's the foundation for everything that follows."

I agreed.

"What happened after that ride home?" she asked.

My time at Oakmont was over for the second time in my life. I sat in Bob's office, glued to the chair, thanking him for everything. As I shook his hand before walking out, he thanked me for the hard work and wished me good luck in school and with the PAT.

The drive down Hulton Road felt different this time. I was sad to be leaving and had learned so much. My internships were over, and the next time I returned to Oakmont, I would be doing so for fun and a round of golf, not to work. My mind was on a treadmill as I drove out of town, and my legs were weighted down by the greatest experience of my life and the worst feeling I had had since this journey started.

I made my way through Ohio, and when I saw the sign for Columbus, the town where Jack Nicklaus, the greatest golfer of all time, was born, that sickening feeling hit me again as I heard Bob's voice say, "Think about it, Jas."

In the dim glow of the dashboard, I sat alone in my truck, parked at a gas station. The silence seemed to be swallowing me whole. My hands were still wrapped around the steering wheel even though I'd been parked for ten minutes. I hadn't moved. I didn't want to. I couldn't.

I was like a boxer lying on life's canvas, gasping for air. Only there was no bell, no corner man yelling for me to get up. Just me.

For the first time in this new world, someone had stripped me down to face reality. I was just a hardworking kid full of passion and a dream, but I was also a kid who hadn't passed the PAT. The dream I'd built, this perfect vision of being one of the best PGA professionals in the country, took a hit I hadn't seen coming.

My future self, the version of me that had been cheering me on and giving me all this hope, met my current self that day. And he didn't like what he saw.

It was a moment of collapse. The belief I'd held until now, that I was destined for greatness simply because I wanted it badly enough, cracked right down the middle. That belief was dying in that truck, and something would rise to take its place.

Bob wasn't wrong. Not really. But I wasn't angry at him.

I was angry at myself for letting the dream get that far ahead without laying down the path to get there. Angry that I thought belief alone would be enough.

I realized then: This wasn't about proving Bob wrong, or the world, or any of the assistants who'd breezed through the PAT and cruised through Oakmont.

No, this was about proving my future self right.

Up until now, he had been quiet. Just a shadow up ahead, walking steadily, waiting for me to catch up.

But now, he looked back. And for the first time, I saw him hesitate.

My current self clenched the wheel harder, pressing my palms into the leather. I wasn't going to let him walk away.

Not like this.

I hadn't told anyone what Bob said that afternoon on the way home. How could I? Everyone cheering for me only knew the highlight reel, the polished version I'd chosen to share. From the outside looking in, my journey looked bulletproof, as certain as the diploma I would soon receive.

Was Bob my corner man? Was that his version of throwing me a towel or, was this way of telling me to get up and not quit?

I sat with those questions, unsure of where to take them. How would I tell someone I might need a plan B when all I've ever done is sell them on plan A? Who do I confide in?

My mom, who was loaning me money and believing in every step like it was already written? Uncle Tom, who thought I had so much potential? Ma, who was the first to support my idea?

Dad, who'd raised me to believe I could outwork doubt and become anything I wanted in life? Larry? What would I even say to him? "Hey, I wanted to be you, but I'm not good enough." The words tasted like rust before they ever left my mouth.

So I kept it to myself. Let it sit like a lead ball in my gut. And I drove on, trying to convince myself it was just a moment, not the end.

I returned to school and graduation wasn't creeping in—it was charging full speed, barreling toward me like a linebacker on a blitz. I was supposed to graduate in August, and suddenly life had broken through my front line. I was staring it down, face-to-face, and I knew sometimes you had to call an audible just to avoid a sack. Maybe becoming a PGA professional, say nothing about becoming great, wasn't in the cards for me.

I had poured tens of thousands of dollars into a marketing degree I had no desire to use once I walked across the stage. That was a Grand Canyon–sized crack in the plan.

"Walk the track backward, boys," and "Find something you love, son." Those mantras sounded great. Inspirational, even. But they all assumed one thing: that I was good enough to pass the PAT.

So, it was back to the drawing board. I needed a plan B. The next best thing? Maybe a stockbroker. I was good at math, and I could see myself on the floor of the New York Stock Exchange. I envisioned myself on the floor with my tie slightly loosened, sleeves rolled up to the elbows. I could see myself thriving under the pressure. *Yeah, maybe a stockbroker*, I thought.

"I need a plan B if I don't get past this damn PAT," I said, sitting across from my advisor. "Can I add economics as a major. That possible?"

"We can certainly do that," she said, scanning my transcript. "Why economics?"

"I think I'd enjoy being a stockbroker if golf doesn't work out."

"Well, if that's the case, you don't want economics; you want a finance degree."

"Okay, works for me," I said, having no idea what the real difference was. Honestly, I didn't care what the fancy calligraphy on the degree eventually read. I was going to be either a PGA professional or a stockbroker. One way or another, I wasn't going into marketing, and I wasn't going to be a locker room attendant.

"This even possible? I mean, with my schedule?" I asked.

"We can make it work. All you need is six additional classes."

"That's doable," I said. "Can we add them to my remaining semesters?"

"Add them?" she raised her eyebrows. "You're already taking a heavy load. There isn't room."

No sooner had I dragged myself off life's canvas before the count of ten than life hit me again, a right hook knocking me into the ropes and down to the mat. Everything had a price, and plan B's was an extra semester to wrap it all up. More money I didn't have. More time. More sacrifice.

I pushed graduation from August to December of 2001. But there was an upside buried in the frustration, a shadow of opportunity. More time. More chances. More shots at passing the PAT.

30

EYE ON THE PRIZE

During the spring semester of 2001, my final semester on campus, I sat in my truck in the Mississippi State golf course parking lot. I hadn't told a soul I was playing in the PAT again. I couldn't bear another round of phone calls explaining why I'd come up short. Not this time.

Three tries. Three failures. Only one of them close. And now, with another attempt looming, I couldn't shake the truth I'd been avoiding: *What if I'm just not good enough?*

The PGA didn't care how well I managed a staff, handled a budget, or communicated with members. If I couldn't shoot a number, I didn't belong. Pass or fail, that hard truth about life was that simple. You are either good enough or you're not. I struggled to get my breathing under control. I'd traded nearly everything for this dream, I moved across the country, worked more hours than I slept, survived on chicken, rice, and PB&Js. But maybe I'd built my bridge too high. Maybe all I'd done was create a longer fall. Was thinking about becoming a

Eye on the Prize

stockbroker jumping mountains too soon? Or admitting I was never built for this one? Had I misunderstood what prize I was supposed to keep my eyes on, as Dad had always said?

I stared out at the gray sky above the course, the fairways barely visible beyond the tree line, and I asked the question I hadn't dared say out loud: *What if all those people back home were right?*

I closed my eyes to focus on my breathing, and I remembered teaching myself how to play. I subscribed to three golf magazines; *Golf Digest*, *Golf Tips*, and *Golf Magazine* and devoured every issue like a textbook. I remembered laying the magazines open on the floor and copying what I saw in two mirrors, one in front of me and one to my right. I could see myself immersed in those magazines and cutting out the best instructional pieces, sliding them into plastic sleeves, organizing them into thick three-ring binders. I remembered spending hours flipping through those pages, analyzing golf swings, trying to understand how the body moved to make the club work.

I posted my best PAT opening round ever, 40 on the front, even par 36 on the back for a 76. Through 27 holes, and a second even par 36, I stood at +4 and well under the +11 pass/fail line. But then came bogeys at 10, 11, and 13. The voice in my head pushed harder, demanding answers I didn't have. On the fourteenth tee, out-of-bounds stakes stared me down. Somehow, I saved par with a nervy six-foot putt, but bogeyed hole fifteen— leaving me only three strokes to spare over the final three holes.

At hole sixteen, my nerves got the better of me. I topped the ball, laid up, missed the green, and made double. Now I needed to play the last two holes in ten strokes or fewer.

On seventeen, my hand trembled. I topped my drive again toward the water and screamed, "Stop!" The ball barely cleared the pond on my second shot, and I scrambled for another bogey.

Eighteen was a long par five, and I needed a par to pass. The drive had to thread a needle of pine trees. I heard Dad's voice in my head: "You gotta talk to yourself out there. You want the ball, son?" I clenched my fist, pulled a club, and said, "I want the ball, Dad."

I hit a high draw, but when I got to where it should've been, I couldn't find the ball. My heart plunged through my body. Five minutes to find it. Just as time was expiring, I spotted it far down the cart path, still in play. I let out the breath I'd been holding for four years.

My ball had traveled nearly three hundred yards, bouncing down the cart path before coming to rest in the light rough just short of a grove of trees. It still sat almost two hundred and fifty yards from the green. I looked at the ball, up at the grove of trees, tracing the line to the top of the branches. That was option one, going over the trees. Option two was safer: Pitch the ball slightly forward but sideways, back into the fairway.

My eyes moved back to the sky above the treetops, then to the right, scanning the fairway. I had stood in a moment like this before, years ago with George at St. Johnsbury Country Club. Going over the trees would leave me with an easy shot into the green, a short club, provided I could launch the ball high enough to clear the treetops and far enough to find the fairway. But if the ball hit the trees, I would most likely fail the PAT.

Pitching sideways into the fairway was the safer play, but it would leave me needing a 3 wood to reach the green. The chances of landing on the green with that club were slim, meaning I'd likely have to chip on and one-putt to pass.

My eyes lifted to the sky as I drew a deep, slow breath. *I know, George, but I can't make a six this time. Gotta make five.* I looked again to the top of the trees. *I'm good enough now.*

I grabbed an 8 iron and opened the face slightly, adding loft. I took one last look to the sky above the trees, then back down at the ball.

Don't get ahead of yourself, I told myself. *One shot at a time. Just make a good swing.*

I swung. By the time I looked up, the ball was already climbing, sailing over the treetops with room to spare. Relief washed over me. "Told ya I was good enough," I said. "I'm passing this time."

The flag was in the front left corner of the green, guarded by bunkers short and right. I stepped off the yardage twice; it was a perfect 9 iron distance. After taking a deep breath and one last look at the flag, I swung. The ball soared high into the air, landing safely in the middle of the green.

Hell yeah! Two putts and I would pass.

Sitting in the golf cart next to the green, I counted my scorecard again. The math added up just like it did on the tee. I was twenty-five feet and two putts away from becoming a PGA professional.

Come on, Jason. Just do it one more time, I thought as I walked toward the green and realized that I had had several "just one more time" moments in my life. My mind tried to rush forward, and each time I reminded myself of what Bob Rotella, a world-renowned sports psychologist, had written about staying in the present moment and accepting the results, whatever they were.

I hit the first putt and glanced up a little too early, hoping to see the ball drop. Instead, I watched it stop three and a half feet short. *Seriously? No way.* My head flopped back, then dropped to my chest. I took deep breaths, trying to slow myself down one last time. It all came down to this moment. This shot. Pass or fail.

As I marked the ball, my lungs expanded larger than I could ever remember. Placing the ball back on the green, I squatted down to read the putt before taking a couple of practice strokes.

Come on, Jason. Take a deep breath, align the putter, take one look at the hole, let your eyes come to rest on the ball, make the stroke, and hold the finish before you move your eyes. It was either going to go in or it wasn't.

My eyes settled as I finished my routine, and the stroke began, smooth, automatic, like it had bypassed my brain entirely. A surge of heat pulsed through my chest, where fear had been sitting like a stone all day. My hands buzzed and my body froze, no longer from nerves but from the release of them as I held the finish. I looked up just in time to see the ball disappear into the center of the hole.

"Hell yeah!" I shouted, knocking the wind out of the air with my fist. Years of belief, doubt, fear, and sacrifice were released in that one exhale.

I practically yelled into the phone the second I got back to the apartment.

"Bob, I passed!"

"Congratulations, Jas. Well done," he said, as if he had no doubts.

"You know what this means, don't ya?" I said, still catching my breath.

"What's that?"

"I am not going to be a locker room attendant."

Bob laughed.

"No. No, you're not. Great playing. I'm proud of ya, Jas."

I leaned back against the wall, phone still in my hand, and felt something deep inside me finally let go. It was like my dream of greatness had just taken its first real breath, and graduation would be its second.

In 1999, I made it clear to Steve Archer, Bob's first assistant at Oakmont, that I planned to work for him after graduation.

"Arch, I'm going to work for you after I graduate," I said on the Oakmont porch.

"Oh really?" he replied.

"Yup. Save me a spot."

I reminded him more than once. By the time I returned in 2000, Arch had become a head professional in New Jersey. As graduation approached, I called to follow up, and he had a spot waiting for me. We'd even started talking about apartments when, out of the blue in October 2001, Arch called.

"What do you think about Florida?" he asked.

"Florida? Why?"

"I just accepted the head professional job at a brand-new club in Vero Beach. Quail Valley Golf Club. Want to come?"

"If you're going, I'm going. I'm all in."

Graduation was on the horizon, and so was Florida.

My head shook as I finished reading over the answers to my Financial Markets comprehensive final exam a few months later, in December. Only one question remained on the first page, in the top right-hand corner, with the words "Final Exam Wager" and a blank line staring back at me.

With only three tests and a final exam for the semester, Financial Markets and I had married and divorced multiple times over the past several months. Our first divorce came after I scored a 40 percent on the first test. After long hours in the professor's office, I took her back, only to divorce again after a 60 percent on the next exam. I had never experienced a class this hard before. I eventually rekindled the flame with Financial Markets, caving under the constant pleading to give her one more chance, and I scored an 82 on the third test.

On the last day of class, the professor announced that we could wager a percentage of our total grade on the final exam, ranging from 25 percent to 100 percent. I had spent countless hours meeting with him outside of class, performing CPR on my grade. Just the day before, he had encouraged me to bet everything on the final. "You know this material," he had said. "Your exam scores are improving."

I had long since abandoned the idea of becoming a stockbroker the moment the final putt fell during the PAT. My finance degree no longer mattered, except that I needed an A in the class to graduate cum laude. The only person other than me, my reflection in the mirror—a future version of myself—who gave a rat's ass about my grades would have to keep yet another secret.

Financial Markets had beaten me up all semester, and

there we were again in one last battle. I felt I had done well on the final and wrote "70 percent" in the top right corner. It was just too risky. Sure, I had been getting better, but there was no way in hell I would risk failing the class just to pat myself on the back and graduate cum laude.

"Scott, I'm outta here," I said, shaking his hand in the PGM office. "Can't thank you enough."

"See you at graduation?" he asked.

"Nope. I'm headed south."

"You're not walking?"

"Nah. I don't need to walk. They'll mail it to me," I said, laughing.

My speedometer barely stayed alive as I drove off campus, glancing one last time at McCool Hall.

You did it, ole boy, two degrees, the PAT, and just a few months away from being elected into the PGA of America. And you did it in four and a half years. Well done.

The effort, or lack of it, that I put forth during my first trip to college at Lyndon State still haunted me from time to time. That ghost would only leave me alone if I gave everything I had, right up to the end, this time at Mississippi State. I had never earned a 4.0 in a semester, and as I left campus, I knew that aspiration would go unrealized.

But my Financial Markets professor, the one I had spent countless hours with outside of class, had changed my wager from 70 percent to 100 percent after I made an A on the final exam. So much for the SAT saying anything about my academic potential. I graduated from Mississippi State cum laude. I was outta there.

See ya later, Mississippi. I'm headed to Quail Valley Golf Club.

Tests measured your knowledge at a specific time, on a specific subject, based on specific questions and how they were framed. They were the best tools we had to predict potential success in college, but they overlooked one crucial factor: willingness. That deep desire for something was hard to quantify.

Zoe smiled at me from her chair and let my story settle into the room and into myself. It took a moment for me to realize what she was doing, and when a smile broke free on my face, Zoe said, "So . . . you didn't tell anyone about the PAT this time."

I shook my head. "Nope. Didn't want to make those phone calls again. I'd failed three times already. I couldn't bear to hear, 'You'll get 'em next time,' or, 'It's going to be okay.' Not again."

"Because that sounded like maybe you're not good enough?" she said.

"Yeah. There was so much internal pressure."

"And what made this PAT different?" Zoe asked. "You sat in that truck with the same fear, same pressure. What changed?"

"I remembered who I used to be. The kid in the mirrors with golf magazines on the floor. The one who studied swing mechanics like scripture. I thought, *That guy was all in.* I owed it to him."

"Owed what?" Zoe asked.

"To not play scared. To not be afraid of failing again."

Zoe gave a soft smile and said, "You didn't try to believe in yourself. You just acted like someone who did. And the belief followed. That's powerful."

I nodded. "Yeah, I guess it is." I paused. "The fear never left. It got scary on the last nine holes."

"Fear doesn't need to go away to stop influencing you," Zoe

said. "Can we talk about that last putt for a moment?"

I laughed softly. "Yeah. Felt like the entire universe was sitting on that ball."

"You described your lungs expanding more than they ever had. Was it anxiety . . . or something else?"

My eyes moved up to the ceiling for a moment and then back to Zoe's. "Maybe. I don't know what I'd call it. Everything just released. Years of grinding. All the sacrifice. Years of hope. It all came down to one putt from three and a half feet, and I knew I couldn't will it in. I had to let it happen."

"That's presence, Jason. That's trust. Not in the outcome, but in yourself."

"It wasn't easy, that's for sure," I said.

"Can I ask something about graduation?"

I nodded. "Sure."

"Why didn't you walk?"

I could feel Zoe's question, and I knew she was trying to get to a spot deep inside me. A string left untied. A circle not closed.

"I didn't need to walk for closure. I had it."

In retrospect, walking would have felt good. That sense of accomplishment on display. But I had been celebrating my wins as they happened. I had "walked across a stage" when I signed my scorecard after passing the PAT, and my score was posted for the world to see.

Maybe I should have walked for those who supported me. For my mom and dad. For Ma, Uncle Tom, my family, my teachers, and Scott Maynard. I never thought about that at the time, and I hate I took that opportunity for joy away from them all. That would have been worth walking across the stage for.

31

DON'T WE ALL?

When I arrived at Quail Valley in December 2001, it was weeks away from opening. Kevin Given, the general manager and operations partner, along with developer Steve Mulvey, shared their vision of the club with me in my first few days and months ahead of the completion of the Shinnecock Hills–inspired clubhouse.

The first time I stood on the back veranda, I took everything in. The views of pristine fairways, dotted with white bunkers, cradled large bodies of blue water that sat in the salt-touched air. I felt a quietness come over me, the kind of hush you get near the coast when the wind takes a deep breath. I looked to the sky, smiled, and gave George a nod.

Arch pushed me hard at Quail Valley. Every time I figured out one layer of the job, he had another waiting. I could feel it. A bigger responsibility, a higher standard, some unspoken next level that I hadn't earned yet. And that was the part that drove me the most, knowing there was more but not being ready yet.

I appreciated it. I really did. It lit a fire inside me that was hard to contain. I wanted it all now. I didn't want to wait for my shot. I wanted to be ready. Wanted to be recognized as ready. I was learning fast, but my mind kept drifting forward as my future self called to me every day.

I'd remember Larry Kelley's voice, calm and measured like a metronome: "Be patient, Slippery. Your time will come. Learn everything you can now. This is the foundation."

I knew he was right. Larry always played the long game. But I wasn't wired for patience. Patience felt too much like inaction, and I couldn't afford that. Not when I saw the clock the way I did.

I kept doing the math. Retiring at sixty-five gave only thirty-five years. Thirty-five years to chase what some of my peers would have nearly an additional decade to pursue. If most assistants stayed three to four years at each club, as Arch said, and if head pro gigs averaged another five to seven, then even if I did everything right, my dream job wouldn't appear until my late forties. Maybe fifty. I didn't want to spend the first half of my career just getting into position.

That impatience churned inside me. No one saw it, but it was always there, clawing at the edges of my focus. The thought that if I wasn't accelerating, I was falling behind.

But the day-by-day job itself it was reshaping me. I walked in knowing how to work, but Kevin Given and Arch taught me how to lead. How to anticipate. How to interact with a member, perfectly mixing formality and familiarity to create an experience. I learned how to run a tournament that left nothing to chance, how to watch a member's face for what they weren't saying, how to handle a complaint without flinching or folding.

I was learning how to move with intention, speak with clarity, and own a space without making it about me.

And somewhere in the middle of all that, I changed. My instincts sharpened. My delivery softened. My hands stopped shaking when I spoke in meetings. I didn't even notice it at first.

One early morning, I found myself standing alone in the pro shop, straightening up the merchandise. The sky was still gray-blue, and dew covered the course in a damp blanket. I paused, staring out at the eighteenth fairway, and just for a moment, I was back at Oakmont, walking beside Bob with his bag on my shoulder, his gait smooth, his mind focused on the shot at hand, and yet he found room to get to know me.

"Most guys take two, three clubs before they find the one," he had said, casually, as if we were talking about a golf shot and not a career. "Takes time. Every stop matters. Don't skip steps."

I hadn't forgotten, but standing there, I realized how badly I had wanted to jump ahead because I was afraid. Afraid that time would run out before I arrived. Afraid that all this work would leave me short of the summit if I didn't push hard enough, fast enough, or find the quickest way from point A to point B.

But the truth was that every late night and early morning, every tough conversation, every shift that taught me something, was the long game. The only one that really mattered. I remembered George at Speedwell talking about focusing on the relationships and the value a customer brought over a lifetime, not just the interaction at hand.

I looked down at the shirts I was handling, perfectly folded and ready to invite a member's eyes and hands. My dreams hadn't changed. I still wanted the big job, the big stage. But for the first time, I understood that chasing greatness wasn't about speed. I remembered being a little kid with Aunt Deb, standing over a bed of clovers looking for a lucky one hiding. It took a long time for me to learn how to focus only on what I wanted to see.

As I looked at the table display, a wonderful blend of props and merchandise layered in levels ready to take members' eyes on a shopping journey, I realized something: My decisions came faster. My voice held weight with the team. I wasn't the same guy who arrived here two years ago, wide-eyed and trying to impress. I was growing into someone better, right now. The patience I lacked internally was being built into me from the outside, one interaction, one success, one mistake, one long day at a time.

Arch would push again. I knew it. That was what I had asked of him. And when he did, I'd be a little more ready because I was learning how to earn the moments and to let the journey unfold.

Even if I still hated waiting.

I had agreed to a three- to four-year stint at Quail Valley when Arch brought me on board, and by the spring of 2004, it was time to start looking for my next job.

The last time I interviewed for anything, I'd blown right past the exit on the Pennsylvania Turnpike doing seventy, heart racing, map be damned. I showed up late. That interview had been for an internship and lasted all of five minutes. Now, I was staring down my first shot at a head professional position that reported directly to the top. Stakes were higher. The margin for error, thinner. I needed help. A lot of it.

Arch had started forwarding job leads my way that spring. Most weren't what I was looking for—smaller clubs, places that didn't align with my reverse engineered career. After I passed on another one, Arch sat me down and leveled with me.

"You know," he said, "most guys take a few head professional jobs before they find the one, it's normal." He gave me a look I'd come to recognize: part mentor, part realist. I sat in the chair across from his desk, dumbfounded.

Most guys? Normal? Did he know me?

I could hear Dad's voice in my mind, as if shouting at me to ensure I heard him. "You can be anything you want be, son, if you put your mind to it."

I looked up at Arch, my voice firmer than I expected.

"Arch, I want a private club. Something like Quail Valley or Oakmont."

He smirked. "Don't we all?"

The big world my dad used to talk about, the one that stretched far beyond our dirt roads, had sucked me into its current. I was ready for the long haul, willing to go wherever the road led, as long as it led to greatness.

I couldn't tell Arch I was chasing greatness. Hell, I hadn't even told Bob.

I mean, what was I supposed to say? *I want to be great. Can you tell me how to do it?* Or worse, *I want to be one of the best in the country. Will you show me the way?*

There was something sacred about ambition at that level, something that felt too fragile to say out loud. Once spoken, it risked sounding ridiculous. Naïve. Arrogant, maybe. So I kept it to myself. Always.

Only one person in the world knew the whole truth, and that was the guy staring back at me each morning as I dragged a razor across my jaw and again each night when I washed the day from my face. I trusted him with everything because I had to. No one else could carry the weight of that dream the way he could. No one else was close enough to see how much it mattered.

But it wasn't always easy.

Sometimes, I hated him. I resented the pressure he put on me, the relentless internal monologue that never let up. I couldn't understand how the same guy who could outwork everyone in the room during the day could still doubt himself at night. How he could be so smart, so locked in, and then turn around and say something so reckless, like the time I said, "Hey, Mulvey," to the man who owned Quail Valley in front of several members. Sometimes I would be confused as to who I saw in the mirror.

But he also knew how to keep a secret. He never slipped. Not once.

And that secrecy protected me. It gave me a private world where the dream stayed safe, untouched by other people's doubts, their ceilings or casual dismissals. As long as I kept it inside, it couldn't be mocked or misunderstood. I could chase it without explaining it. I could protect the fine china inside of me that believed.

But that kind of solitude was expensive.

It got lonely in there sometimes, lonely carrying something that big and heavy alone. I couldn't celebrate out loud. Couldn't grieve losses with anyone who really knew what was on the line. I had to smile when I wanted to scream, nod when I wanted to ask, "Why not me?" and pretend I was fine when I was quietly unraveling inside.

Still, every morning, that guy in the mirror showed up. He splashed cold water on his face and said, "Let's go. No excuses. No shortcuts. Just get back to work. We have a dream to chase today."

And so I did.

I leaned forward, elbows on my knees, looking at Arch.

"The job needs to at least lead there. Ya know what I'm saying?"

He nodded, more thoughtful this time.

"Yeah, I get it."

Arch got it—well, to the depth I allowed him to swim in it—but he didn't *really* get it, and that wasn't his fault. It was mine alone.

"Well, that's what I'm looking for," I said.

Arch pointed me toward three head professional openings he thought aligned with my desire to end up at a Quail Valley or Oakmont. The first was in Southwest Florida, but I bombed the phone interview and never heard back. The second didn't progress beyond the résumé stage.

The third was in Missouri. That interview went well, so well they invited me back for a second. The salary was nearly triple anything I'd made, and the club seemed solid. Still, something in my gut churned. It wasn't Quail Valley. It wasn't Oakmont. But how many places were?

After the first interview, I sat in the rental car and stared out at the frozen ground. It reminded me of Vermont. One question from the panel kept repeating in my head: "How long do you see yourself here?"

"As long as I'm challenged." I'd replied honestly, but maybe not wisely.

I rubbed my eyebrows and picked up the phone.

"Bob, they asked me back for a second interview in Missouri."

"That's great, Jas."

"Yeah, but I don't know. "

"You sure you don't know?"

The shine of a bigger paycheck and a new role had caught my eye like a lure in murky water. But I needed to spit the hook before it dragged me somewhere I didn't want to be.

"It's not for me," I said. "What do I do now?"

"You exit professionally," Bob replied.

The ride back to the hotel had me second-guessing everything. What if Arch was right? Maybe this should be my first head professional job. The offer was strong. The club was good. It checked a lot of boxes.

But I'd learned over the years that emotion, any emotion, could derail sound judgment. Most bad decisions were born from feelings, not facts. And ironically, excitement could be just as dangerous as fear. Both clouded your vision. The best choices came when emotion was stripped from the equation, and yet it might be the hardest thing there is to do in life.

By morning, the answer was clear. I called the committee, thanked them sincerely, and told them they had a wonderful club, but it didn't align with the path I was pursuing. I wished them the best of luck in their search and thanked them again.

It wasn't an easy no, but it was the right one. I felt a wave of pride that night as I looked in the mirror.

One evening in mid-July of 2004, my cell phone began to vibrate on the table.

"Is this Jason Prendergast?" the voice said.

"This is Jason."

"Jason, this is Mike Taylor."

Mike Tayor? Who is Mike? "Wha . . . what can I do for you, Mike?"

"I am a member at the Country Club of Jackson in Mississippi. Billy Anderson gave me your number."

"Ohhhh . . . how's Billy doing?"

"He's good. I played in a member-guest at his club this past weekend."

"Billy's in a great spot up there in North Carolina," I said.

"He is. I told Billy we lost our pro and wanted one just like him. He said, 'I know just the guy. He works for a buddy in Florida, and we all worked at Oakmont. You should call him.'"

"Yeah, we all worked for Bob," I said.

Mississippi? I never thought I might go back. Mike talked about the Country Club of Jackson, explaining that they wanted a pro who could teach and someone passionate about junior golf. I knew little about the Country Club of Jackson and had never heard of Mike Taylor. But Billy had given him my name, which was good enough for me.

After hanging up, I called Billy. He repeated everything Mike had told me and assured me the Country Club of Jackson was a great opportunity and that I should definitely interview.

Over the course of the week, Mike called a few more times

Don't We All?

with questions about my work history and my experience under Bob. But one question kept coming up, every single time: "Can you teach?"

And each time, my answer was the same: "Yes, Mike. I can teach."

The interview process would involve a committee of country club members, along with the general manager. Kevin and Arch helped prepare me, walking me through what to expect. During one of our meetings, Kevin asked, "Have you called the golf course superintendent yet?"

"The superintendent?" I replied.

"He's the most important person on the team," Kevin said. "You're going to be working with him every day. The sooner you get to know him, the better."

Mr. Bryan at Old Waverly had already filled me in on what he knew about the Country Club of Jackson, and I'd reached out to a couple of PGM guys still in Mississippi. But I hadn't even thought about calling the superintendent.

Later that day, I got on the phone with Stanley Reedy, the golf course superintendent. We spoke for over thirty minutes about the club's vision, challenges, and how the 1,100 members treated him. Before we hung up, he said something that stuck with me: "It's the best job in the state."

That was all I needed to hear.

The best job in the state was right up my alley. As I traced my path backward through the maze of possibilities, I figured my dream job likely lived at a private club ranked in *Golf Digest*'s top 100—or better yet, the top 25.

It sounded ridiculous, but the math was what it was: Only a

hundred jobs in the entire country made that list. Getting one wouldn't be easy. First, the job had to become available. Then I had to hear about it. Then I had to be invited to interview and survive a stacked field of elite candidates.

The next best thing? Land the best job in a state. Some of those overlapped with the top 100, but even still, it left me aiming for maybe 75 dream jobs out of roughly 16,000 clubs nationwide. A long shot, sure, but not impossible.

I started digging up everything I could find about the Country Club of Jackson. I printed every article I came across, though my digital shovel was pretty small given this was still the early Internet days. One piece caught my eye: something about harsh winters at the Country Club of Jackson.

Harsh winters? In Mississippi? What does Mississippi know about harsh winters?

Then I flipped the page and froze.

Oh, shit. This is about the Country Club of Jackson in Michigan.

I laughed to myself and shook my head. *Damn. Are all of these articles about Michigan?*

32

A SLEEPY CLUBHOUSE

I had left Mississippi in December of 2001, never expecting to return. Yet, there I was in July 2004, boarding a plane bound for Jackson for an interview.

Less than an hour after landing, I pulled into a parking lot and glanced around. *Is this it?* It didn't look like a clubhouse. My head tilted and weaved inside the rental car as I crept past a brick wall with the words *The Country Club of Jackson* etched into it.

A long, white, one-story building sat behind a few scattered trees, playing a quiet game of hide-and-seek. The flat roof didn't stretch into the sky like most clubhouses I'd seen. No exterior grand entrance. No towering columns. Just understated simplicity.

That sleepy clubhouse turned out to be a facade. The real structure was a sprawling two-story building built into the hillside. From the front, the lower level was completely hidden. But from the back, it opened wide, overlooking twenty-seven holes of golf.

It reminded me of how often I had been underestimated, how many times people looked through me or took one look and thought they knew the whole story, uninterested in the pages within. I was just like that clubhouse. My potential had always been buried beneath the surface, invisible to most unless they were willing to look.

I turned the corner into the parking lot two weeks later, returning as one of four finalists for the head professional position. My hand paused on the car door handle for a brief moment before I pushed it open. The worn soles of my polished dress shoes scuffed lightly against the pavement as I made a direct line toward the clubhouse.

As I veered around a parked car, my path shifted left about twenty yards toward a white Styrofoam cup and lid with a straw through it laying on the ground. I bent to pick it up, smiling as a memory surfaced: Sean Farren and the Trash Gods. I carried the cup toward the clubhouse, just like I had back then, only now I had done it so many times I often didn't even know I was doing it.

The day's agenda included over an hour of questions, followed by three golf lessons: one for the president of the club; Jody, the committee chair; and Mike Taylor. After lunch, we'd play a few holes, then head back to the executive room for a second round of questions before wrapping things up.

"Good morning," I said as I moved around the room, shaking hands as the high-pressure atmosphere of the executive room settled on my shoulders.

"Jason, why don't you sit here," Jody said, motioning toward the head of the table.

That's a good sign, I thought, pulling the chair back. During the first interview, I'd sat in the middle.

Nine pairs of eyes fixed on my every move. I took a sip of ice-cold water, letting it cool my throat as my gaze moved around the room, mapping the layout of the table. Finally, my eyes landed on Jody's.

"So, Jason, are you surprised we asked you back?" he said.

I quietly canvassed the room, my gaze meeting each person's eyes for a brief moment before returning to Jody's.

"No, sir, I'm not surprised," I said, pausing for just a second. "I've been preparing for this moment since the day I walked into Larry Kelley's office seven years ago and said, 'Larry, I want to be you. How do I become you?' Every decision I've made since that day has been with this moment in mind. I'm honored to be here, but I'm not surprised."

My mind was as still as my dad had taught me to keep it while walking the woods during deer season. I watched the committee members exchange glances around the table. It was in this moment that I first realized how many people had invested in me. I could feel their presence filling the room. All the potential my mentors saw, all the advice, the patience, the pushing: It had shaped the person sitting in that chair. Everyone in my life had played a part in preparing me for this.

I'd always wondered what that feeling of belonging would be like. I wasn't nervous like I had been the first time I met Bob. And somehow, my mother's posture had found its way into my spine. Confidence poured out of my body like liquid in a glass that was overfull as I thought back on my journey.

"Well, we are happy you are here," Jody said.

"Thank you," I replied. "Before we get started, I put this packet together for everyone," passing a stack of bound booklets down the table.

"What's this?" someone asked.

"This is what you get if you hire me. I have included everything from my teaching philosophy," looking at Mike, "to growing junior golf," while making eye contact with Jody. "I have included my administrative skills, and I have a goal of playing in a PGA Tour event one day. I have listed my team philosophy, my mentoring philosophy, and my merchandising beliefs. This is what you get if you hire me."

"Well, this is as good a place to start as any," Jody said. "Let's see what you have in here."

After lunch, as planned, we walked out to the range so I could give a few golf lessons. I had packed a suitcase with cameras, tripods, and a laptop loaded with the latest teaching software.

Mike was up first. "You ready?" he asked.

Oh, I was ready. I had been at the mercy of their questions all morning; now, they were stepping into my office.

Before the trip, I had called Billy to tell him I'd be giving Mike a lesson and asked if he had any advice.

"Mike's the best player you'll ever teach," he said. "He's won the Mississippi State Amateur ten times."

"Damn, that's impressive."

"Whatever you tell him," Billy warned, "make damn sure you're right. He'll know if you're full of shit."

I filmed a few of Mike's swings from different angles and loaded the footage onto the software. Billy wasn't lying. Mike's swing was the best I had ever seen.

After watching the clips at full speed, then slowing them down and analyzing the motion, I turned to him.

"What's your miss, Mike?"

"Low in the face," he said.

"I can see the tendency in your swing for that to happen," I said. "Watch your hands as they move to the top of your backswing. See how they shift slightly forward, toward the ball? Right there," I pointed to the computer screen. "They're coming off plane."

"I want them to stay on this path instead," I added, drawing a clean line on the screen to show the intended motion.

Mike grabbed his club and began rehearsing the adjustment. "This what you want?"

"Not quite. Your hands need to move back a couple more inches."

"Like this?"

"Yes. That's perfect. Just like that."

He ran through a few more rehearsals, then pulled a ball in front of him and took a swing. The sound of compression rattled the range before the ball flew through the air.

Mike turned around before it even landed and walked back toward me. I loaded the swing into the software and played it back at full speed.

"Slow it down?" he asked.

I nodded and ran it in slow motion, drawing a line on the screen again. His hands traced it nearly perfectly. He had made a three-inch adjustment in a single swing.

"That's great," Mike said, nodding as he studied the video. "I like it."

"All right, Jody, you're next," I said, stepping aside as he grabbed his 7-iron.

I watched him stripe eight or ten balls, each one flying straight at the target. They were solid, consistent shots, but after seeing Mike's swing, any comparison would've been unfair. Jody stood unusually far from the ball, his posture rounded, arms disconnected from his body. It didn't look like a single-digit handicap setup.

"So, Jody, what are you—about a fourteen handicap?" I asked.

"Hell no," he shot back. "I'm a four."

Oh, shit. Not good. A golfer's handicap is a badge of honor, and I'd just insulted one of the guys who held my future in his hands. First, the sleepy clubhouse fooled me. Now Jody's address position had done the same.

I smiled, trying to recover, gave a laugh, and said, "You must chip and putt great."

Throughout the lesson, I focused on posture. I moved him closer to the ball, straightened his spine, stood him taller, and reconnected his arms to his body. Then I pulled up the video. Side-by-side, his before and after swings told a clear story.

"Jody, which guy do you want to play against?" I asked, pointing to both images.

He laughed, pointing to the older swing. "This guy."

Before leaving the executive room that afternoon, I paused at the doorway, looked around the table, and said, "Thank you all for your time. I want this job, and I hope you'll give me the opportunity."

A small white envelope greeted me on my desk at the Country Club of Jackson on September 1, 2004. I tilted my head, sliding a pencil through the top crease to tear it open.

A Sleepy Clubhouse

My heart skipped when I saw the Oakmont logo at the top of the letterhead inside. The first letter I received in my new job was from Bob Ford.

I leaned back in my chair, eyes drifting to the ceiling as my lungs filled with air. I could see those dew-covered fairways again, hear the faint clink of clubs in the morning stillness. I replayed the entire Oakmont journey in my mind.

I made it, Bob. Thank you.

Each year on my anniversary at the club, I made it a point to call Jody and thank him. One year, he paused on the other end of the line and said, "You know what put you over the top?"

We wonder what separates us from the others when we're chosen out of a pool of candidates. Was it the guts to go to college at twenty-six? My GPA? Where I worked? Who I knew, or who knew me? Trying to remember all the choices and crossroads that led to that moment felt as impossible as counting stars in the sky.

"What?" I asked.

"I saw you pick that cup up and throw it away," Jody said.

"The one in the parking lot?" I asked, surprised.

"That's the one. I told the committee, 'If he's willing to pick up a cup when no one's watching, we need to hire him.'"

I laughed. "I might be the only guy who ever got a head professional job for picking up trash."

"You might be," he said. "Doesn't matter, you're here."

"Yes, I am."

I had earned my seat at that table, one of nine selected from over a hundred applications. Someone once told me, "Not everyone sees the little things you do, but eventually, the right ones do. So keep doing them." They were right.

33

HOMEWORK

I knew plenty of people who had seen a therapist, but knowing someone and being that someone were two very different things. It was easy to tell a friend, "Hey, I think seeing a therapist would be good for you." It was another thing entirely to take that advice myself. Courage felt different when it had to be lived rather than spoken.

My career was full steam ahead. A lot had happened in the few years since I arrived in Jackson, Mississippi, including falling in love and getting married. I was a couple of kids, a dog, and a white picket fence away from having nearly everything I could ask for. On the surface, life looked like it was unfolding exactly as planned.

But cracks have a way of forming quietly, where even you can't see them. The shift wasn't sudden, not really. It crept in slowly, disguised as fatigue, restlessness, maybe even ambition. And then one day, without warning, my heart started sprinting for no good reason. That was the moment everything

I'd been holding together so tightly started to erupt.

I would be sitting on the couch, standing in a golf lesson, or driving down the road when my heart would suddenly race so fast it felt like my chest might explode. Multiple doctor visits and a stress test later, I was told my heart was fine. While that should've been reassuring, I knew better. I wasn't fine. Something was wrong.

I had done everything right. I had sacrificed nearly everything to be standing where I was. By now, I should have been the towering redwood: rooted, distinguished, high in the sky with certainty. But inside, something felt off. I called out to my future self, looking for clarity or reassurance as I looked him in the eye in my mirror, but my voice only bounced through the hollowness inside me.

And yet, I was far from empty.

I felt like an overfilled subway car crowded with strangers, no one moving, yet everyone somehow heading somewhere fast. Every time that subway car accelerated, I tried to describe it. I tried to put words or emotions to the chaos, but nothing came. No name. No label. Just pressure, motion, and noise.

Days and weeks passed. Sometimes the subway car was almost nonexistent. Other times, it barreled forward out of nowhere, hijacking my body with a sudden jolt. I couldn't decide which was worse: the movement, or the knowing that at any moment, it could start moving again.

As quickly as I had fallen in love, gotten married, and started threading my personal life into the fabric of my career, I became miserable. I shut down at home. I took my unhappiness out on my team at work and on anyone who got too close.

The monsters I thought I'd left behind or buried deep inside had awakened.

Calling for my future self had summoned my past. Versions of my old self rose to the surface, each one expecting recognition and demanding my attention. They didn't care who I was trying to become. They wanted to be heard. They insisted that both my current and future self acknowledge their existence.

Anxiety and depression didn't knock. They arrived unannounced. The people around me noticed before I did. They saw the way I changed, how I withdrew. But I was too close to it to realize I was no longer the same. Then came the full-force panic attacks that ripped through my body like lightning bolts on a cloudless day.

There was a reason I couldn't describe what I was feeling: There wasn't a single emotion to name. They were all there, tangled and crashing into one another. It felt like every emotion I'd ever experienced—joy, rage, shame, love, fear, pride, and hope—had been poured into a blender. It reminded me of the "graveyard" sodas I used to make as a kid, standing at the fountain machine, pushing every button in the row. The result was a twenty-four-ounce cup of syrupy confusion that didn't taste like anything in particular and definitely didn't taste good.

That was what lived in me now. A chaotic mix of everything I hadn't dealt with, foaming to the surface and spilling over the rim.

"The best way I can help you is if you're honest," Zoe said, handing me a pencil and the dreaded personality test.

I came back a week later. After that session, she said, "I want you to see a psychiatrist colleague of mine."

"A psychiatrist?" I asked. "What for?"

"I think you suffer from anxiety and depression. A psychiatrist can prescribe medication to help you."

"I don't know," I said, shifting in my seat. "I'm not a fan of meds."

"Will you at least talk with her?"

"If you think I need to go, I'll go . . . but I don't know about the meds."

I saw Zoe's colleague twice the following week and walked out with a prescription for something I couldn't spell or pronounce.

"This is a bad idea," I said, sitting across from Zoe a few days later. "I don't like this. I'm screwed up, but meds aren't gonna fix it."

"What are you afraid of?" she asked.

"I'm screwed up the same way a golf swing is when someone asks me to fix it. A slice in golf is a symptom. If I don't find the root problem, nothing changes. If I fix the real problem, the symptoms go away."

Zoe nodded. "They might," she said.

"Meds are gonna make the symptoms go away. Not the problem. So how will I know if I'm actually getting better?" I paused. "Will you help me figure out what the problem is?"

"Of course," Zoe said gently. "The medication is there to help you along the way."

"Okay," I said, nodding slowly. "Tell ya what, I'll take the meds if I need them. But let's try it without first."

A year and a half later, on a Tuesday, I walked in and sat in my usual middle cushion seat on the couch across from Zoe.

"How'd the homework go?" Zoe said.

"It was okay," I said.

"Was it hard to make a list of everything you would change about your life if you could?

"Nah, not really. Well. I mean. I thought about it all weekend."

"Did you bring it?"

"Yeah," I said, leaning to the side and pulling a folded sheet of paper out of my back pocket.

I watched Zoe place the sheet of paper on her notebook that rested on her lap, my life contained between the folds. A calmness had filled me as I walked into her office that morning like a rainbow forming on the horizon. The storm had ended high in the atmosphere, and it would be several minutes before the last raindrop landed between us.

Zoe's eyes dropped, and the crinkling of the paper filled the room as she worked to unfold my list.

Zoe looked up and said, "Jason. There's nothing on here."

I nodded.

Zoe sat silent.

"I know. Wouldn't change anything," I said.

"You wouldn't change anything? Nothing at all?" she asked.

Shaking my head, I said, "Nope. If I change anything, even one little thing, my life is different. I'm different. I like who I am."

Zoe sat quiet, patient as always, knowing I wasn't done.

"Don't get me wrong. I mean, I wish George was still alive. His death beat me up. I wish Brian never sold Speedwell. I have never felt so lost in my whole life. I wish Kathleen and I had never broken up. My heart was broken for such a long time. I wish my mom was like she was when I was a kid. I hate that Dad moved so far away. I hate that I'm divorced like my parents."

I sat there in front of Zoe, hearing the words for the first time, shared with someone other than the guy in the mirror, and nothing had ever felt that true.

"It haunts me that I've hurt some people, people I care about. But I have forgiven myself for the mistakes I've made, and I had made a lot of them. I wish I hadn't made those decisions, just like I wish the bad things hadn't happened. But I can't change the fact I made 'em, and I can't control what those people think of me. All I can do is hope they will forgive me someday. I wish all the bad things didn't happen in my life. But they did. And I survived them. All of them. They made me who I am, and I like who I am."

Those words sat comfortably in the air and in me. It was as if the air became lighter somehow, and I was able to breathe through my skin.

I looked at Zoe. Her body looked as comfortable as mine felt. I said, "When I thought about changing the bad, I asked myself if I would want to change the good, and the answer was . . . no way. Life has both good and bad. One can't exist without the other."

I paused, then continued. "The bad fucking sucks and the good is fucking amazing. I survived. I wouldn't change anything."

"Good for you," Zoe said, smiling.

I explained to Zoe that Dad once told me, "Everything in life falls into three buckets. Something can either be proven to be true or false. If you can't put that something into either of those two buckets, then it goes into the third bucket, which is the bucket of faith. And you have to rely on your faith to find your answer."

At the time, he was referring to religious faith. But as I got older, I realized the faith bucket wasn't just about God or heaven or things unseen—it was about people, too. It was about believing in someone when there wasn't enough data to guarantee they'd come through. And it was about believing in yourself when nothing in the world could prove you were ready except your willingness to try.

That third bucket for me is bigger than the other two, much bigger. Decisions I couldn't explain. Gut feelings I couldn't defend. Choices I made when logic and certainty were nowhere in sight. I had leaned into that bucket more times than I could count. Every time I packed up and moved, every time I said yes to something that scared me, every time I got back up after being knocked flat.

The truth was, the faith bucket wasn't the last resort. It was the one that carried the most important things.

"Zoe, does it make me selfish? Am I selfish for not wanting to change anything because I like who I am?"

"No, it doesn't. Not at all."

"Okay, good. Someone told me once I was selfish, and that really hurt."

"I've carried that for a long time," I continued. "Tried to outrun it, disprove it, bury it. But I think I finally understand, wanting something for myself doesn't make me selfish. It makes me human."

I sat there on the couch looking around Zoe's office and I felt oddly empty and full. I looked at Zoe, patiently waiting and said, "I don't think I need to see you anymore, do I?"

Zoe smiled softly. I had come full circle. I was whole enough to walk forward without apology. I had walked through years of doubt, pain, heartbreak, ambition, and expectation. And standing on the other side, I liked who I had become. Not despite it all, but because of it. That moment didn't feel like an end. It felt like a beginning.

"No, I don't think you do," Zoe said, smiling.

34

ANCHORS AWEIGH

A few months passed. The bermudagrass, once dormant and brown, had awakened from hibernation. The scent of clove hung in the warm breeze, signaling the azaleas were in bloom. Spring had arrived in Mississippi, and with it came a new golf season. The cabin fever that had gripped the Country Club of Jackson all winter had finally broken.

    The sunlight hit my face that morning. It was odd how the warmth felt different after saying goodbye to Zoe for the last time. The sun seemed to penetrate my skin now as I stood outside the pro shop watching my members knock the winter rust off their golf swings on the range. The coolness of the aluminum railing shot through my arms, and I thought about that young man who signed his life away at the hope of a ticket to the promised land by borrowing tens of thousands of dollars. For years, my ship of debt rocked like a fishing bobber in the water, double anchored by government-funded loans at the stern and a loan funded by my mom at the bow, and more than a decade of monthly payments were shackled to my ankles.

At the time I signed the papers, the hope for a better life outweighed the stress of years under financial burden. Borrowing money from the government, a faceless and emotionless institution, carried one kind of anxiety. But owing money to a parent was something else entirely. That kind of debt came with emotional strings attached that I had been unprepared for, a constant fear of disappointing someone you love.

It affected everything: what I ate, what I drove, where I lived. Every dollar I spent felt like a dollar I wasn't using to repay my mom, adding to the invisible weight I carried with me every day.

The last payment to my mom had cleared my bank a few years earlier, and with it, the stern of my ship of debt broke free. I remembered feeling my spine decompress, as if I'd taken off a hundred-pound backpack. I was still years away from paying off my government loans, but one anchor had finally lifted from the ocean floor. Only my ship didn't move as I had hoped, still connected by weights I couldn't yet see. That was until the day I walked out of Zoe's office for the last time. That quiet call of "anchor's aweigh" marked freedom. It was time to help someone else catch their own wind.

I scrolled through my phone until I landed on Paul Wheeler's name. Paul had been a lifelong friend, and now, as the athletic director at Lyndon Institute, my high school back home, he was exactly who I needed to talk to.

"Golf's been good to me, and I want to give back," I told Paul.

"Wow, that is great to hear," he said.

"I wanna do a scholarship for one of the kids on the golf team," I said.

"That'd be wonderful. What are you trying to accomplish?"

"I remember what it was like. College is expensive," I said, "I just want to help."

"This is amazing, Jason. Thank you."

"Yeah, you're welcome," I said, already hearing a student's name being called in my mind as the first recipient of the Jason Prendergast Award for Excellence in Golf. I pictured them walking across the auditorium stage on Senior Night, a proud smile on their face as they were recognized.

Paul paused for a moment before adding, "The downside to a scholarship is that it only helps one student. Not everyone goes to college."

I began pacing the veranda outside the pro shop. "Yeah. You're right. Hadn't thought about that. Just wanna make a difference," I said.

But the truth was, Paul wasn't exactly right. I wasn't just helping the one student who would be awarded the scholarship.

I also heard my own name in that auditorium on Senior Night. I saw myself sitting in the crowded room watching as the graduating senior walked among the clapping hands and smiling faces.

Someone else was benefiting too: me. I thought back to Zoe and our discussion about selfishness. I had told her how, on bad days, I would walk out to the range and find someone hitting balls. I'd offer to help them with their swing, free of charge.

Zoe had asked me why I did that.

"Because it makes me feel good," I said.

Then I asked her, "Does that make me selfish, for seeking joy in that?"

She looked at me and asked, "Were you helpful to those members you gave lessons to?"

"Yes," I told her.

"Then it's not selfish," she said.

Only this felt more like recognition for myself than for anyone else, and yet that wasn't why I had called Paul. I genuinely wanted to help someone like me with a dream in their heart and fear in their chest.

"I have an idea," Paul said. "What if you help sponsor the golf team instead?"

"Sponsor the team?" I asked.

"Yeah. Take the money you were going to use for the scholarship and use it to buy things the team needs. This way, you impact everyone, not just one student."

"I love it. Let's do it," I said.

What had begun as a potential scholarship evolved into a team sponsorship. Paul told me that Mr. Legge, an alum and early supporter, was already providing some funding for the team, but they still needed more to fully meet the program's need. I offered to pitch in, so long as Mr. Legge didn't mind sharing the honor.

"Who's coaching the team these days?" I asked.

"Fred Miller," Paul said. "He's been coaching for a while. Great with the kids."

"What about a golf school?" I said. "What if I fly up and teach a school for the kids? You think Fred would mind?"

"That would be amazing. Fred would love to have you do that, and the kids would too."

"If I'm going to help, I have a request," I said. "Everyone makes the team. This is about growing the game and changing lives. They don't all have to play in tournaments, but if someone wants to be part of the team, they're in. Can we make that happen?"

"Yeah," Paul said, "we can make that happen." I heard the smile in his voice. It was a shared understanding that this was bigger than the game of golf. It was about building a community, providing an opportunity, and creating space for someone to feel seen and believed in, just like I once needed.

The diner never felt the same after George passed. By 2011, twenty years had gone by, though the building hadn't changed much. Time had moved faster for me than it had for that little corner of town. The floor still creaked in the same places, the stools still wobbled, and the windows still fogged from the warmth inside. Some of the faces were new, but many were the same regulars who had once nodded to me as I slid into the seat next to George for breakfast.

"You still like coffee?" one of the servers asked.

Nodding with a smile, I said, "Please."

A calm settled over me as the warmth from the cup seeped into my hands. The smell of roasted beans tickled my nose and stirred memories I hadn't tasted in years. In that moment, I wasn't a head golf professional from a prestigious club. In that moment, I was just a kid back home, sitting in a booth where a dream had taken root. It was good to be back.

"How long you in town for?" she asked, sliding me a menu.

"Just a few days. Doing a golf school for the LI golf team."

"I heard," she said, her face lighting up. "My son's on the

team. He's so excited. Thank you for coming back home to help."

The pride hit me like the rising steam from my coffee. The feeling I had anticipated with a scholarship surged through me in front of one person, not hundreds. I was giving back to the place where it had all started.

The golf school became an annual tradition, quickly growing into one of my favorite weeks of the year. On the last day of school, a year ago, one of the boys looked up from cleaning his clubs and said, "Are you gonna be at the tournament tomorrow?"

"I don't know," I said, glancing at Fred. "Where is it?"

"It's here," Fred said.

"It'd be so cool if you were here," another boy added, his voice excited and hopeful.

I looked around at the group, realizing my flight was already booked, and I was set to leave in the morning.

"Yeah," I said, smiling. "I'll be here. Don't want you to be nervous, though. I'll meet you at the scoreboard after."

My rental car was parked at St. Johnsbury Country Club the following afternoon, not far from where my old Jeep once sat before I walked into my pro's office all those years ago and said, "Larry, I want to be you. How do I be you?" Now, more than a decade later, one of the kids from the team came sprinting across the putting green and into the parking lot, yelling, "I just had a career round!"

"Awesome," I said, meeting his raised hand with a high five. "How are we doing?"

"We're winning, but three guys are still playing," he said.

As we walked toward the scoreboard, he rattled off every great shot he'd hit that afternoon, thanking me over and over for helping him. We won the tournament that day, the first event of the season. A few kids had career rounds, and I heard more stories about great holes played than I could count. They had worked so hard over the past three days, and it filled me with a kind of pride I hadn't expected.

Until that afternoon, I believed I was simply supplying shirts, golf balls, bags, and offering a few days of instruction. I knew the kids appreciated it, but I had no idea how deeply my presence and support would resonate. In trying to help shape these kids' futures, I hadn't realized they were reshaping mine.

So many things had to happen years ago to put me in this position. One of those things was Mr. Legge's early sponsorship of the team. In his honor, I made sure that as long as I was involved, his initials, RGL, would be embroidered on the team bags and uniforms. I used to want to hear my name announced on Senior Night because I wanted people to know I was helping. But I came to understand that as nice as it is to hear your name over the PA, it's nothing compared to standing beside someone else and calling their name.

I didn't need recognition. I just needed to show up and care about the kids, my high school, my hometown, and the game of golf. I remembered what George Nichols told me years ago at the diner, talking about Charlie, the man who bought five dollars of gas every day: "You just gotta care, Jason."

George was right, only he never told me how good it felt.

The game of golf had been the vehicle for so much joy in my life. Little did I know it was about to light the path back to the classroom and to a life I wanted decades ago.

35

CRAYOLA AND ELMER'S GLUE

A few withering piles of melting snow and the scars left by Old Man Winter in 2014 were all that remained after several dark and cold months in Vermont. As I drove through the front door of my hometown, exit 23, I felt my heart lighten, welcomed by the warmth of home once again.

Yes, I had come back to run the golf school, but that wasn't the only reason I returned. There was something deeper pulling me north. Coming home hadn't just been about teaching golf; it also reminded me of who I was before the dream ever took hold. I came back to remember and to reconnect because this place still knew me and all the parts I had forgotten that no one in my new life had ever known.

I always looked forward to visiting Ma when I came home, and I never made a trip to Vermont without spending time with Kathleen and her daughter, Izzy.

Years ago, I had come to terms with the fact that Kathleen and I would never be together. It took a long time, but eventually,

I had set my heart free to move on. Still, I remained incredibly grateful to have both of them in my life. Izzy was growing up fast, almost fifteen now, and the little girl who once hid behind Kathleen's legs before warming up to me no longer existed. She didn't sprint across the living room clutching her new favorite book, eager for me to read it while she sat on my lap. Instead, she smiled and waved at me, her hand flashing through the air when I arrived. I watched her grow up in front of my eyes, one visit at a time, and it made me think about how much this place had meant to me and my life. Every time I visited, it felt like just yesterday that I had been cuddling with her mom in that same house, when Kathleen and I weren't much older than Izzy was now. I remembered standing at the kitchen counter teaching Izzy how to shuffle cards with her tiny hands when she was eight or nine, the same counter where Ma, George, and I had once shared dinner before the last round of golf I ever played with him.

So many memories had been created inside those four walls. That house held a cache of joy and tragedy, of hope and despair. And somehow, in the quiet of those moments, I felt the weight and beauty of it all. Spirits, connected by a common thread and sewn together by the same seamstress.

Years ago, the three of us laughed on the deck when Izzy said, "Ugh, this is so hard!" as I taught her how to juggle. I remembered on another visit, Izzy grabbed my hand, saying, "Come on, Jason. Come see my room," as she led me up the same stairs George used to walk down before waking me up on the couch at 5:00 a.m. On one visit, I stood there watching Izzy play the piano, and it felt like a time capsule cracked open.

Crayola and Elmer's Glue

This was Kathleen's old bedroom, the place where she and I had once spent hours talking, dreaming, and falling in love in the way only young hearts can. Now it belonged to her daughter, Izzy, and her dreams.

The moment stirred the times when I thought rooms like this would always hold my future. But standing there, I didn't feel sadness about what never came to be. I felt blessed that life had allowed me to remain part of theirs, even in a different way than I once imagined.

In Izzy's music, I didn't just hear her hope. I heard my own healing. I no longer looked at that younger version of myself with regret or longing. I saw him clearly and kindly, as someone who was learning. Someone who didn't yet know that love could change forms and still remain real. Someone who would lose things, yes, but gain even more. I no longer needed that past to be different. I only wanted to be present for what remained and what would become.

Kathleen had been teaching middle school math and asked me to speak to her students while I was home for my annual golf school. She was inviting people from different careers to talk about how they used math in their daily lives, and she wanted me to be one of the speakers. So, of course, I said yes.

As I stepped inside the school, the scent of Crayola crayons and Elmer's glue lingered in the air, drifting from the autographed masterpieces lining the hallways. Each piece of artwork, proudly colored just outside the lines, transported me back to my own childhood.

My mother used to tell the story of the night before my first day of kindergarten. She had tucked me into bed like usual, but the next morning she found me sound asleep on top of the covers, my arms crossed on my chest and fully dressed in the outfit we had picked out for the big day. She would always laugh and say, "You looked like you were in a casket."

Kathleen's smile lit the room as I walked in. "Hey, ya made it," she said. "The kids are excited."

The bell rang, and the halls came alive with movement. "Quiet down and take your seats," Kathleen instructed as a few stragglers hurried in. "Everyone, I'd like you to meet a good friend of mine, Jason Prendergast. He's a golf professional in Mississippi, and he's here to talk about how he uses math every day."

My nerdiness danced with Kathleen's as we discussed selling shirts and calculating profit by working the math on the whiteboard. We discussed the basic physics of a golf ball flying through the air, and how one ball would go higher if it spun more than another, or how each club made the ball go a different distance.

The bell rang, and the shuffling of little feet began once again. One of the young girls walked up to me on her way out and said, "Are you really a golf pro?"

"I am," I said, smiling back at her, knowing she was Kathleen's niece, daughter of her brother, Brian.

"That's sooo cooool. Can I have your autograph?"

"Sure," I chuckled to myself.

"Is Brian your dad?" I asked.

"Yeah," she said in a startled tone.

"Tell him I said hi." I handed her the golf ball I just signed.

"You know my dad?" she said with her eyes wide open.

Crayola and Elmer's Glue

I wanted to tell her how her dad and I were best friends before she was born and how her Aunt Kathleen and I used to date in high school, but instead, I said, "I do," and smiled.

"That's sooooo cool," she said again, then ran out of the room.

I hung out with Kathleen for the rest of the day, watching her come alive in the classroom, fully absorbed in math and the energy of eager young minds. Between classes, we caught up on old times, laughing about memories, sharing updates about Izzy, and talking about how excited Ma was for her upcoming cruise to Alaska.

Teaching math was clearly Kathleen's calling. Like her brother, Brian, she had sold her share of the family business to pursue what truly mattered to her. Life hadn't been easy for her in recent years between the sale of Speedwell and her divorce, but as I watched her work with her students, she looked happier than I had seen her in a long time.

The golf school ended a few days after my visit to Kathleen's classroom. I was in the parking lot at St. Johnsbury Country Club, stuffing my golf clubs into the travel bag. My flight was in a few hours, and I was about to head to the airport when my phone rang.

"You left town yet?" Kathleen asked.

"Nope. Just finished golf school. 'Bout to head out. What's up?"

There was a pause on the other end, just long enough to notice. "I need to talk to you before you leave."

"You okay?"

"Yeah . . ." she said, her voice suddenly small. Then silence.

It stretched just long enough to start meaning something. "I think . . . I think I love you," she said.

"What?" My whole body locked into place.

"I think I love you. I . . . I don't know. I need to talk to you," she said.

"Seriously?" I said. "I'm leaving in like five minutes. I'm canceling my flight. Where are you?"

"I'm at school. I can't talk right now. I'm sorry. I'll call you tomorrow . . . I'm sorry. I've gotta go."

And just like that, the line went dead, leaving me standing in the parking lot, a plane ticket in my pocket and a heart suddenly louder than my thoughts.

What just happened? Are you kidding me? I paced the length of the car, running a hand through my hair. *Seriously?* I looked at my golf bag, half-zipped in the travel case, then back at my phone. *What the hell just happened?*

I lifted my head and stared across the hood of the car toward the hill on the sixth hole, where George told me he had indigestion the day before his heart attack.

Come on. Answer the phone already.

"Hey, Jas, what's up?" Uncle Tom said.

"Kathleen just told me she thinks she loves me. What am I supposed to do with this?"

"Wow," Uncle Tom gasped. "Where are you?"

"The parking lot at St. Johnsbury Country Club. My flight leaves in a few hours. Wha—what am I supposed to do with this?"

"Listen to me. Get in your car and go to the airport. You hear me?"

"Yeah," my voice trembled.

"Get in your car. Go to the airport and get your ass on that plane. You don't know what this means."

"I know, but . . ."

"No buts. Get your ass back to Mississippi. Don't you call her. Think long and hard about everything you've accomplished."

"I don't know, Uncle Tom."

"If she loves you, she'll call. Get your ass on that plane and call me when you land."

Nearly two decades earlier, I had driven out of this same parking lot with a plan to chase the crazy dream of becoming a golf professional. Back then, my tank was full of hope and ambition. Now, I sat in that same parking lot, paralyzed by uncertainty, struggling to leave.

As I approached the interstate, my car slowed, my hand hovering over the blinker lever. The hell with him. I didn't care what he said. I was staying. I mean, I had to stay, right?

"Fuck me," I muttered, leaning my head back and slamming my eyes shut against the car's roof. A million thoughts collided in my mind. Each memory from my past—Kathleen, Izzy, George, Ma, Brian, the diner, the golf course—binding with an emotion like a snowball rolling downhill, getting bigger and bigger.

Uncle Tom was right.

"You've got to be kidding me," I muttered, yanking the blinker lever down, *click, click, click*. My eyes locked on Speedwell's roof in the distance, that weathered silhouette of my past. I couldn't believe I was doing this. My hands turned the wheel, almost on their own.

The entrance ramp to Interstate 91 stretched out before me like a dare. My gaze shifted from Speedwell to the road ahead, that long gray ribbon leading me out of town, away from my roots, and away from what might have been nearly twenty years ago and what might be now.

Each mile stretched like taffy, dragging time and memory along with it. I could almost see it: my life before Kathleen, my life loving her, and my life after letting her go, all barreling toward each other like cars in a slow-motion collision. And I wasn't sure which version of me would walk away from the wreckage.

The ringing of my phone released my foot from the gas pedal. My head shook instinctively from side to side as my eyes blinked rapidly, trying to snap myself back to focus.

"On the road yet?" Uncle Tom asked, his tone sharp and unmistakably stern.

"Yeah," I said, exhaling. "On the interstate."

"Good."

"What am I supposed to do with this?" I asked

"I know, Jas, I know," he said more gently now. "She sees who you've become. What you've accomplished."

"I guess . . ." I muttered.

"Deep down, she's probably always loved you," he said. "You've worked too damn hard to come back now. There's nothing in Vermont for you. What are you gonna do, pump gas again? Milk cows? Go back to fixing heating systems?"

His words hung in the air like humidity. Part truth, part protection. I wanted to scream. I wanted to turn around. I wanted to do anything but drive toward the airport.

Two long days later, just like Uncle Tom had said she would, Kathleen called.

"I love you," she said, her voice low and certain. "I just don't know if I love you like a brother or not."

"Does Ma know? Have you told her?" I asked, my heart pounding in my chest.

"No," she said quickly. "I haven't told anyone. You can't say anything until we figure this out."

I sat in silence for a long time after hanging up, my thoughts winded, but none of them found a place to rest. What did she mean? "I love you . . . I just don't know if I love you like a brother or not." That wasn't nothing. But it wasn't clarity, either. It was as if she'd cracked open a door that had been bolted shut for years, just enough to let in the light, but not enough to walk through.

After everything we'd been through, after all the years, why now? I leaned my head back against the wall, staring at the back of my eyelids as if they held answers in the dark my eyes couldn't see in the light. I thought about my time with Zoe and pictured her sitting across from me, asking questions that probed me to dig deeper than I wanted or realized I could.

Zoe would remind me that I'd grown over the years, that I wasn't the same teenage boy who once loved Kathleen. Then she'd ask if I believed Kathleen had grown too. I'd nod and say yes, we've both grown, but I'd also remind her that some things don't change. At our core, we're the same people raised by the same hands, shaped by the same small town, the same hearts. I loved who she was deep down, and I loved who she had become as an adult, as a mother.

Then I would remind Zoe that I wouldn't change anything. I would tell her I had learned that the only way to experience life on a deep level was to risk losing it. And while it would have hurt to find out that Kathleen only loved me like a brother, I knew I wasn't going to lose her. That risk didn't outweigh the joy of knowing there was a chance we might spend the rest of our lives together.

36

A SECRET CODE

The picture I once drew on a puzzle box told the story of my younger self and the image I believed all the pieces were meant to form. Back then, every day was about fitting those pieces together with my ambition and imagination. My first puzzle ran out of pieces at twenty-six when Brian sold Speedwell. Now, at forty-two, I found myself staring at a different puzzle that I had been putting together for the last seventeen years.

I realized that the philosophy of reverse engineering my career didn't work when it came to matters of the heart. I wasn't trying to build this part of my life anymore. I had decided to simply live it. I no longer needed to have every piece in place before I could breathe, and I let my personal life happen. In that release, I had learned to accept that some pieces might never fit the way I thought they would, and the ones I never saw coming slid perfectly into place when I wasn't even looking.

The past held ambition, hunger, and design. The present held presence, openness, and trust. I had once thought success in my personal life meant shaping life into what I wanted. Now I understood the strength of allowing life to shape me.

Kathleen and I had spent the past several months discussing what a future together might look like. Almost two thousand miles, two careers, two divorces, Kathleen's daughter, and a shared history all stood between us. None of it was simple. It wouldn't be easy, if it could work at all.

One morning, about a week before Christmas in 2013, Ma's name lit up my phone. It was just after eight. She and Don, the man she'd built a life with after George passed away, had moved down to Florida a few years earlier. Her voice always brought me comfort, but she never called this early.

Before she could say a word, I answered, "Good morning, Ma."

"Jason, this is Don. I didn't have your number. Marilee's had a heart attack."

"Oh shit. Is she okay?"

"I don't know. She didn't wake up this morning."

"I'm gonna take the first flight out. Have you called Brian and Kathleen?"

"I did, but they didn't answer."

"Okay, I'll call them right now."

My head fell into my hands as I struggled to breathe. *No way, I can't believe I have to do this again. Come on, answer the damn phone, Kathleen. Damn it.* I hung up as I heard her voicemail. *You've gotta be kidding me.* I searched the Internet for the Lyndon Town School phone number.

"This is Jason Prendergast. Transfer me to Kathleen Nichols' room. It's a family emergency."

A Secret Code

"Hello?" Kathleen said, as if this was the first time the phone in her classroom had rung.

"Kathleen, it's Jason."

"Why . . . why are you calling me at school?"

"Your mom had a heart attack. She's on the way to the hospital."

"Are you serious?" Her voice was full of shock.

"Don just called me. Call Brian."

"You have to stop calling me," she said through her tears.

"I know. I know. I'm sorry."

"Is she okay? Is she gonna be okay?"

"I don't know. Call Brian."

"Okay," she said, crying. "What do I tell Izzy?"

"Tell her Ma is sick and in the hospital. I am going to take the first flight out. I'll call you later. Don't forget to call Brian."

My head fell into my hands as I struggled to breathe. Grief had loosened its grip from the last time, when Kathleen's father passed away, and now that fear was back, and it was suffocating. The puzzle of my life that I had spent decades carefully piecing together suddenly shuffled like the box was being shaken with the remaining pieces inside. My heart that had recently been injected with excitement was now oozing fear of the worst kind. Kathleen needed Jason at that moment. She needed the Jason who was there for her when her dad died. She needed the Jason that Ma saw as her son.

I arrived in Florida later that afternoon, and Ma's petite body looked frail on the hospital bed. Aunt Rachel had flown in with Kathleen and Izzy on the earliest flight they could find the following day, and Ma and Don's three-bedroom retirement home suddenly held more suitcases and people than it did beds.

Throughout the day, I kept watch over Kathleen. I would hand her a granola bar, slide a plate of food in front of her, or twist the cap off a protein drink. I needed her to eat. Izzy needed her to eat.

When the doctor walked into the waiting room, Kathleen grabbed my hand.

"Marilee isn't going to make it," he said softly. "Blood clots have filled her lungs."

I watched the last bit of hope drain from Kathleen's eyes just before she collapsed into me.

"Momma, are you okay?" Izzy whimpered as she hugged her.

"I'm okay, Iz," Kathleen whispered, pulling her daughter close. I wrapped my arms around them both, holding everything I could in place while the center of our world was slipping away.

Over the next two days, Aunt Rachel took charge as we arranged for Ma to be moved into hospice, where she would spend her final days. Ma's new room looked nothing like my old one in the Airstream, but two things were present in both places: love and family.

Kathleen pulled me aside after we got Ma settled into hospice a few days later. Her eyes were tired and red.

"I can't believe Izzy is losing her Grammy over Christmas," she said quietly. "Christmas is supposed to be a fun time with family."

I hadn't given much thought to Christmas since arriving in Florida. My focus had been on Ma and holding everyone else together. But Kathleen was right. Izzy was just a kid, barely a teenager, and her world was being turned upside down during a season meant for joy and giving.

Houses decorated with Christmas joy cast warm glows across the sidewalks, a stark contrast to the life we were living. Izzy and I walked slowly through the neighborhood that next night as I watched her process everything. Her small hand swung gently beside mine before I reached over and put my arm around her.

"You doing okay, kiddo?" I asked, keeping my voice soft.

"Yeah . . . I'm sad," she said, barely above a whisper.

"I know, sweetheart. Me too," I said, pulling her closer.

I could feel how fragile she was in that moment, and I knew that kind of sadness. I'd lived it before.

"You know what we should do?" I said.

"What?" she asked, looking up at me from behind the grief.

"I think we should surprise everyone with a Christmas."

"You do?" she asked

"I do. I think your mom, Aunt Rachel, and everyone would love it."

"Do you think Grammy would love it?" she asked,

I smiled and looked at her. "Grammy would love it too, sweetheart. Christmas is in a few days. You think we have enough time?"

"Yeah. But . . . how are we gonna get presents?"

"Tomorrow, I'll tell everyone I need to run to the store and ask if you want to go with me. We can go Christmas shopping then."

"Oh yeah, that would work. Can we buy wrapping paper too?"

"Of course."

"Ohhh, and stockings. Can we get stockings for everyone?"

"That's a great idea."

We walked a little further before Izzy stopped, planted her feet, and turned to face me with a sudden burst of excitement.

"You know what we need?"

"What's that, sweetheart?"

"We need a secret code. Ya know, for when we go shopping."

A laugh broke from my chest. "Ohhh, I love it."

"I know . . . what if we do this?" she said, lifting her shoulder to her ear and rubbing them together in a silly gesture. "This could be the code."

"That's perfect. I love it."

In that small moment, between grief and glittering lights, Izzy reminded me that even in the middle of loss, love could still surprise us. Maybe Christmas wasn't canceled after all— maybe it was about to be saved by a kid with a secret code and a whole lot of heart.

The glow from the hallway stretched faintly into the room as Kathleen crept out of the bedroom that night.

"She asleep?" I whispered.

"Almost," she said.

There was exhaustion and sadness in her tone.

"Thank you," she said.

"For what?"

"For everything. For being here. For taking care of me and Izzy. For being here for Mom."

I turned to look at her.

"Of course. There's nowhere else I would be. I'm here for

you. Always."

She didn't say anything, and her shoulder pressed against mine. Izzy and I exchanged secret smiles over the next three days, flashing our code whenever one of us wanted to slip away.

That year, our shopping adventures took us to a handful of random stores and, of course, Izzy's favorite place: the bookstore. We found stockings for everyone and carefully picked out little treasures to tuck inside them. Each time we returned to Ma's house, we spread everything across the living room floor like kids at a sleepover, proudly surveying our growing stash of stocking stuffers.

Izzy's face lit up like the decorated yards we had walked past just nights before. She poured her heart into every gift, no matter how small. To her, the wrapping paper wasn't just to hide what was inside but a way to keep her love attached to the gift.

All the stockings were identical: the classic red and white felt. To make them more personal, Izzy and I crafted homemade ornaments out of manila folders, cutting them into trees, stars, wreaths, and snowmen and coloring them with markers.

"Who do you think this one should be for?" I asked, holding up a manila star just as the front door creaked open.

Izzy's head whipped toward the sound, her eyes wide as the wreath she had just colored. "Who's here?" she whispered in fear.

"Don't know," I said.

Before I could get up, Ma's best friend, Gail, stood over us. "What are you two doing?" she said, smiling.

"Wrapping presents," I said, looking at Izzy frozen on the floor.

"It's a secret," Izzy said. "Don't tell anyone."

"What a great idea," Gail said and smiled. That smile seeped into Izzy, feeding her desire to make this Christmas happen.

Stuffed with love and topped with a perfectly chosen ornament, the stockings lay snuggled together in the trunk of my car on Christmas Eve. After everything was ready, I kissed Izzy on the forehead as I tucked her into bed.

"Don't forget to wake me up," she said.

"I won't. I promise," I said, contorting my face into a wink that made her giggle.

The smell of coffee drifted through the house the next morning. One by one, everyone emerged from their rooms, sleep still lingering in their eyes, murmuring, "Merry Christmas."

"I'm going to see Ma," I said, standing up and stretching. "See y'all over there."

"Can I go with you?" Izzy asked.

"Sure, you ready?"

"Yup. I'm going with Jason, Momma," she said, giving Kathleen a tight hug.

"I couldn't sleep last night," Izzy said as we buckled into the car. "I was too excited."

"I know, right?" I said, matching her grin.

Izzy and I had planned every detail of this morning like a secret mission. We would get there early, put a Christmas channel on the TV in the waiting room, and arrange the stockings beneath the little tree that someone had already set up. It wasn't much, but it was more than we'd had a few days ago, and it felt magical.

There she was, still in her pajamas and a Santa hat, kneeling in front of the tree, arranging the stockings just right while soft Christmas music played from the television. She looked like a tiny elf making everything perfect.

"I bought this for you," she said, turning around and handing me a green hat with a tall wire spring and a pompom bouncing at the top.

I laughed; it was the dumbest Christmas hat I'd ever seen. *There's no way I'm putting this on*, I thought.

"Isn't it cute?" Izzy said.

I stared down at the ridiculous Grinch-like thing in my hands, then back at her hopeful face.

"I love it," I said, pulling it over my head. "I love it."

"It's soooo cute. I love it too," she said, beaming.

"Is it time? Are we ready?" I asked.

She nodded, her smile nearly as big as the tree. "We're ready."

"Okay," I said "Let's go get everyone."

As we walked down the long hallway toward Ma's room in hospice, Izzy kept glancing back at me, her face lit with the kind of joy only Christmas could bring. Just before we reached the door, she stopped, turned around, and wrapped her arms around me.

"Thank you," she whispered.

"You're welcome," I said, hugging her back as I closed my eyes, holding the moment still for just a second longer. "Thank you, too."

"Come on, Momma," Izzy said, grabbing Kathleen's hand with a spark in her eyes. "We have a surprise for you."

"A surprise?" Kathleen asked.

"Yup, a surprise for everyone. Come on," Izzy said, her energy contagious as she led us back down the hallway and into the waiting room.

"Merry Christmas!" she announced, spreading her arms wide as if she were a magician.

The stockings we had carefully prepared lay around the little tree. Holiday music floated from the TV, and the scent of cinnamon from a small candle someone had placed in the corner filled the room. For a few moments, amid the struggle of watching Grammy die, Izzy was just a kid again. The magic of Christmas lived in her voice and in her spirit.

Christmas was as normal as it could be. Even for just a short while, it gave us all a moment to breathe, to feel something other than sorrow. The joy I saw in Izzy that morning was unlike anything I'd ever seen. She didn't care about unwrapping presents; she just wanted to watch her magic touch the people she loved.

A few mornings later, I woke up already smiling. I could hear movement in the kitchen, and sure enough, Kathleen was making coffee.

"I just had an amazing dream about Ma," I said as I walked in.

"Yeah?" she said.

"She was in a wheelchair, being pushed by someone. They stopped. Ma stood up and walked out of sight."

"Wow," Kathleen said.

"It was so real,"

"I'm going to see Mom," Kathleen said, setting her coffee down.

"Want me to come with you?" I asked.

"No, it's okay," she said, giving a faint smile. "Will you bring Izzy when she gets up?"

"Of course."

A couple of hours later, Izzy and I arrived at the hospice. We hadn't been there long when Kathleen walked into the waiting room, her eyes already locking on to mine. I stood up instinctively and reached my arms out.

"She's gone," Kathleen said as she folded into me.

"I'm so sorry," I whispered.

"It's okay."

"Are you okay, Momma?" Izzy asked, hugging her mother's waist.

"I'm okay, Iz."

Kathleen wiped her eyes, then smiled through the sadness. "It was amazing," she said. "I was holding Mom's hand and talking to her. I looked at Gail and said, 'I think she's gone.'" Her voice cracked. "And she was. Just like that. Like she just slipped away."

What flashed through my mind in the days that followed were all the people I'd lost, the chapters I thought were finished, and the truth I didn't want to face: Maybe we don't get to finish our puzzles. Maybe we just learn to love the unfinished imperfect image as it is.

"I want you to do Mom's eulogy," Kathleen told me. "Can you do that for me?"

"Does Brian want me to do it?"

"Yes, I talked to him. We both want you to."

"Okay. Of course I will."

"I don't know what happened between you and my brother years ago, but you need to talk to him," said Kathleen, referring to an incident that had taken place between Brian and me when he had sold Speedwell.

"I know . . . I know. I'll talk to him."

I sat on a bench overlooking a little pond in Ma and Don's neighborhood, watching ducks glide across the water as I searched my soul for the right words to capture who Ma was. My pen hovered over the notepad, but the words felt unworthy of the ink. Hours passed. The pages remained blank while memories poured through me faster than I could process them. How was I ever going to write this eulogy? There was just too much to say—too much love, too much history, too much of her in me.

Later, as I waited in the Orlando airport parking lot for our friend Christina to arrive from Spain, I thought about Zoe. It was as if Zoe was talking to me from her chair, with her feet resting on the stool. I realized the eulogy was my bridge between grief and gratitude. Between what's gone and what remains. I gathered myself, opened the voice recorder on my phone, and simply started talking to Ma as if she were sitting next to me in the passenger seat.

The moment I spoke her name aloud, tears streamed down my face. And then, in counting the years on my fingers, I realized I had only known George for four years. Four. How was that even possible? It felt like a lifetime. I swore he had been in my life longer. I was barely a year older than Izzy when George came into my life. And now, Ma and George were both gone.

In retrospect, Ma's eulogy wasn't about finding the perfect words. It was about being a living sentence of everything she stood for. Compassion. Humor. Loyalty. Strength. Love. Belief. That eulogy wasn't just a goodbye. It was a way to share her story. A way for me to tell Ma, "We carry you forward." It was a way of saying to the world that love like hers, the kind that is given, doesn't end. It finds its way into others.

37
THE RING POP

Conscious of every heartbeat, I drove through Lyndonville on Wednesday, April 30, four months after Ma passed away. I was back for two reasons: my high school's annual golf school and, more importantly, for a kiss.

The first kiss. For the second time.

A kiss I hoped would lead to the life I had let go of years ago.

Kathleen and I had once been young and reckless together, tripping through high school hallways and sneaking moments between the cracks of small-town life. And now, here I was, older, broken and rebuilt, hoping that a single kiss could unravel time.

Was this actually happening?

I wished Ma and George were here. I wondered what they would be saying to me—and to Kathleen. Would they be excited, hopeful? Or would they be afraid of the power this kiss might carry? What if Kathleen felt like she was kissing her brother?

The Ring Pop

I sat in the driveway staring at the house that held more of my history than any other place on earth. Were Kathleen and Izzy part of a new puzzle? Or were they the pieces still in the box?

"Hey, you made it," Kathleen said as I walked into the kitchen.

"I did. You ready to go?"

"Yup, all ready. We need to be back by 3:30 when Izzy gets out of school."

The thirty-minute drive out of town brought us to Littleton, New Hampshire, for a lunch date, our first one in over two decades.

Walking through town, I'd look at her and think, *Is she gonna kiss me already? When is this happening?* We wandered in and out of stores along the strip, pretending to browse while trying not to trip over the tension.

"Hey, let's go up there," I said, pointing up a hill to what looked like a small park.

Minutes later, we sat on a bench overlooking the town below. *What am I, fifteen again? What if it's not good?* My thoughts wouldn't stop. *Just kiss her already.*

I turned toward her, stiff at first, then softer as our eyes met. My body finally surrendered to the moment. I leaned in, and our lips met. Her kiss was familiar and yet brand-new. When we pulled apart, my eyes opened slowly, reluctant for it to be over.

"Well . . . that wasn't bad," she said, with a playful smile.

"No, it wasn't," I said, cupping her face in my hands. I tilted her head and kissed her again, longer this time.

"Phew . . . I was a little worried," she said as we came up for air.

We stood, hand in hand, and began walking back down the hill. I said, "I am not going to ask you to marry me, ya know."

"You're not?" she asked, surprised.

"Nope. Not a chance. You're gonna have to ask me first."

"Are you serious?" she said, laughing.

"Yup. On one knee. A ring. The whole nine yards."

"Seriously? A ring?"

"Oh, hell yeah."

"A Ring Pop, maybe," she teased.

"Watermelon's my favorite," I said, giving her hand a squeeze.

Blending our lives wouldn't be easy, but not much in life ever was. Kathleen told me I had worked hard in my career, and she didn't want me to throw it all away by moving back home. As much as I wanted them both to be with me in Mississippi, I couldn't ask them to move. There was no way I could ask a teenage girl to leave her friends, her school, her home, and most of all, her father.

My dad was one of the most important people in my life, and it shattered me the day he left. That kind of absence leaves a mark that never fully heals. I couldn't be the reason Izzy felt that same void. I couldn't ask her to trade one life for another just so I could have the life I wanted.

Choosing not to ask them to come wasn't the same as not wanting them there. It was love, twisted in sacrifice. Emotionally, it meant accepting that love doesn't always unfold the way we dream it will.

If they wanted to come, the door was open. But I wouldn't be the one to pull them through it. We had planned for Kathleen to

The Ring Pop

move to Mississippi once Izzy graduated from high school and went off to college. For four years, our perfectly imperfect life would have our blended family separated by fifteen hundred miles. I flew home once a month for a few days, doing my best to be present for as many important moments in Izzy's life as I could.

The box that holds the pieces of your life is blank for a reason: Only you can imagine the picture. Its emptiness isn't a void; it's an invitation. A call to dream.

38

PEANUT

Dust billowed in the rearview mirror, and a bitter, metallic taste filled my mouth as my rental car bounced down the dirt road that led to Brian's farm. The clock on the dash read 10:06 a.m., though time felt irrelevant.

I used to ask Ma about Brian and his girls every time we spoke on the phone, my words filled with sincerity and regret. But I hadn't laid eyes on him or heard his voice since the day I left for Mississippi, nearly two decades ago. In the days following Ma's passing, Kathleen firmly said, "I don't know what happened between you and my brother years ago, but you need to talk to him."

She was right. I knew it the moment she said it, and I hated that she had to be the one to say it. I had been home more times than I could count over the years. Weddings, holidays, deer season, and golf. Each time, I found a reason not to reach out. Each time, I drove right past the farm, my heart lodged in my throat. I'd always told myself it wasn't the right time. That

Peanut

he probably didn't want to see me anyway. But the truth was, I was scared shitless to face the look in his eyes, afraid of the words I'd have to find, afraid of what he would say to me after all these years.

Guilt had been alive in every shadow I cast. It was the kind of guilt that whispered when you least expected it. In the middle of the night or watching two brothers play golf. I had lost my best friend. Not to time or distance, but to a decision I made in a moment of weakness when I didn't do the right thing. An act I couldn't undo.

Twenty years ago, emotions overwhelmed me like a flash flood, leading me to make a decision in the midst of that chaos—a bad decision. How do you explain something like that? Something that still burns, even after twenty years? How do you explain something you still don't fully understand yourself? Doing the right thing is always the right thing to do even if it is the hardest choice. And I hadn't done that, not when it counted before I left town.

My mind relived the day as I sat in the car parked on the dirt road. I had relived this day so many times, and instead of becoming numb to the emotions of disappointment, shame and guilt burned deeper every time. Brian had recently told me he sold Speedwell. I had to finish a heating system installation job before the sale. Upon leaving, the owner handed me a check and thanked me for all the hard work. I looked at the check, and there it was: *Pay to the order of Jason Prendergast.*

I had packed my Jeep and stopped at Brian's house on my way out of town. After I said goodbye, he said, "You got that check?"

I pulled my wallet out and handed him a wad of folded hundred-dollar bills and said, "It's all there."

Brian's stare burned through my eyes and into my soul. "I'm so sorry," I said.

Brian stood still, staring me down. He turned and walked away.

Fuck me. What have I done?

I remembered the look on Brian's face as if it were yesterday. His eyes were cold, like a door I no longer had the key to. Would I see that same look again today?

For two decades, I had been telling myself that the scared kid who made that choice wasn't me. In my mind, I had gone back to that moment more times than I could count. I had wrapped my arms around that younger version of myself, told him it was a mistake, and told him I forgave him. But forgiving myself had never felt complete, not really—not without facing Brian.

It was time for that skeleton to cast its last shadow on my life.

I held my breath as I approached the driveway, pressed the accelerator, and drove past the farm without slowing down. I continued down the dirt road, around the corner, and up the hill before finally pulling over to the side.

How could I explain what I had been thinking twenty years ago? The truth was, I had been mad at him for selling Speedwell. That place had meant something to both of us. It was my connection to George, my identity, my everything. At the same time, I was filled with excitement about starting school, but underneath it all was a fear of failing, of not being enough in every way imaginable. In that moment of weakness, holding that check, I had justified all the nights and weekends I'd put in. I had convinced myself I deserved it.

But I didn't. Not like that.

I wished that check had never had my name on it. Even now, two decades later, I could still feel that sickening knot in my stomach, shame mixed with regret that never dissolved.

I took a deep breath, turned the car around, and drove back down the hill. The tires crunched as I pulled into the driveway, a familiar landscape of my past, of the person I had been and in many ways still was now. I wondered if he was inside, maybe already watching me from behind a window.

As I opened the door, heart pounding, Brian walked around the corner of the barn without warning. It was him. And it was now.

"Brian," I said as I stepped toward him, extending my hand.

"How's it going?" he replied, shaking mine firmly.

"Good," I said with a nod. "You?"

"Good," Brian nodded back.

"I'm so sorry about your mom."

"Yeah, sucks," he said in a low voice. "She was your mom, too. Thanks for being there."

"Of course," I replied, pausing to take a deep breath as words pressed against the back of my throat.

"Look, I'm sorry," I said, shaking my head. "I was broke . . . mad . . . scared. I was young, but that's no excuse. It's haunted me since the day I left . . . I'm so sorry."

"It was a long time ago," he said quietly. "We were both young."

Then he looked me in the eye, the way my dad had taught

me as a young boy, and extended his hand. "What do you say . . . water under the bridge?"

The tightness in my chest finally gave way, and I exhaled two decades of guilt I had carried like a second skin. In that moment, I wasn't standing next to Kathleen's brother. I was posted up outside the farm with my older brother and best friend from a previous life.

Locking hands and nodding, I said, "Water under the bridge."

We talked for a while, slipping back into conversation like no time had passed. Brian told me about his kids, how fast they were growing, what they were into, and I shared stories about life in Mississippi, the ups and downs of farming, and what it was like working as a golf professional. Eventually, the conversation turned to Ma.

"I saw the video," Brian said. "Good job on Mom's eulogy."

"Yeah, thanks. It was hard to write."

"Bet it was," he said with a slow nod, his voice trailing off into the silence that followed.

As we walked past the old farm truck, Brian reached into the cab and pulled out a couple of beers and tossed me a Coors Light.

"I can't believe your dad used to drink warm beer," I said.

Brian laughed and shook his head. "Yeah, he sure did."

"I miss him," I said.

"Yeah, I miss him too."

We stood there for a moment, two brothers in everything but blood, the past still lingering but no longer pulling us under. Just two men sharing a beer and the weight of everything time hadn't managed to erase.

Peanut

I thought about Zoe as I left the farm later that day. I had never told her about this mistake and how it had suffocated so much of who I saw when I looked at myself. I'd intentionally never told her about how Brian and I grew apart. Hell, I'd never told anyone. I was too ashamed. Too afraid to hear the story out loud for the first time. But now, as my car bounced across the washboarded dirt road, I could hear her telling me that guilt's a funny thing. It pretends to be noble, like it's holding you accountable, but after a while, it becomes a kind of self-punishment. And that can keep you stuck.

I felt a soft smile on my face, the kind I saw so often on Zoe's as I drove away from the farm. I had stopped seeing her years ago, but her voice often visited me. That day, she said, "You know, Jason, people talk a lot about accountability like it has to be loud or dramatic. But sometimes, accountability shows up in remorse. A handshake. A beer. And a decision to stop letting one bad moment define your life."

Later that year, in February, the day had finally come. I had been hiding her engagement ring since I arrived in Vermont, waiting for the perfect moment. I knew we'd get married; it was never a question following our first kiss after decades. But a few months earlier, she'd caught me completely off guard when she got down on one knee, held up a Ring Pop, and said, "Will you marry me?"

"Only if it's watermelon," I had said, smiling as my heart nearly burst.

Now it was my turn.

Izzy was out having dinner with her dad, and Kathleen and I had made plans to snowshoe from our condo down the mountain to the ski lodge for dinner. It was going to be perfect. My plan was simple: Once we reached the bottom of the slope, I'd ask her to sit for a minute and look at the stars with me. Burke Mountain had become our place.

The crisp mountain air dried my throat as we moved through the trees, the snow falling gently around us, glittering in the light of our headlamps. My heart raced, only this time it was running toward something and not away. As we reached the edge of the woods, I stopped and said, "Hey, let's walk up the trail a little and sit under the lift for a few minutes before dinner."

"Nah, I'm hungry. Let's just go eat," she said, barely breaking stride.

"Come on, baby, it's so pretty out," I tried again.

"Nope," she said, tugging my hand as she marched toward the lodge. "A glass of wine is calling my name."

Are you kidding me? Getting Kathleen alone in a romantic setting wasn't easy, especially since I was only in Vermont once a month. And now, after all this anticipation, she hit me with, "A glass of wine is calling my name." *Seriously?* Asking her to marry me was calling my name right now.

"Okay, let's do it after we eat," I said.

After dinner, we strapped on our snowshoes and started climbing back up the mountain. "Hey, let's sit under the stars," I said, hoping she'd finally go along with it.

"Nah, let's just go home," she replied, already blazing ahead through the freshly fallen snow.

Seriously? This was my one shot. I stopped halfway up the trail and dropped to one knee, watching her walk ahead of me, completely unaware. She had gone a little way before realizing I wasn't right behind her. She turned around.

"What are you doing?" she called, walking back toward me. "Are you okay?"

"I'm okay. Just come here," I said.

Reaching into my pocket, I pulled out the ring box. Flipped it open, and said, "I have loved you my whole life. Will you marry me?"

Her eyes widened. "Oh my god. I thought you were sick or something." She hugged me. "Yes, I will marry you. I wondered when you were gonna ask me. Took ya long enough."

"I've been trying to ask ya all damn night," I said, shaking my head.

"Ooohh, that's why you wanted to sit under the stars. Aww . . . that's so romantic."

"You're killing me," I said.

The days that followed were as full as they had ever been. As I reflected on my life and the person I had become, my mind flashed through all the versions of myself I had been. It was rare to go through life without a nickname. Parents often spent hours considering and debating what name best suited their newborn. They searched for meaning and tradition. But nicknames? Those came quickly and could stick with you for a lifetime.

Izzy had a few nicknames already, but like her DNA, none of them were mine. I loved her with all my heart and wanted something that was ours. She already had a dad; she didn't need another one. She would tell me I was her Jason, and I always called her Izzy. But I wanted something more. I wanted a name that connected the two of us.

For months, I searched for the right nickname. I'd try out a few in my head, but none ever felt right. Too silly, too forced, too impersonal. A nickname wasn't just a name. It was a kind of unspoken promise that said, "I see you, and you matter to me in this world."

One night, Izzy looked up at me from the couch as I walked by. Her long brown hair fell back across the cushion. She smiled, just for a second, and I leaned over, kissed her forehead and said, "Good night, Peanut."

"Peanut?" she asked, her eyebrows lifting as she tilted her head.

"Yeah," I said, smiling. "You're cute, like a little peanut."

My heart swelled as I walked up the stairs that night. It was our family tree: mine, Kathleen's, and Peanut's.

Lying in bed, watching the ceiling fan swirl above me, I could hear Zoe's voice in my head: "So, how did it go seeing Brian again?"

I imagined telling her the truth. That it felt like something finally let go. That I'd been carrying that pain for so long, and when Brian said, "We were both young," it was like he reached back through time and handed me permission to stop punishing myself.

She'd nod, gently. "Did it feel like forgiveness?"

"Yeah," I'd say. It did. For him. And for me too.

I used to think growth was about charging forward. But now I know, sometimes it's about turning around and going back to face the things we ran from.

My thoughts drifted to Peanut. God, I loved that kid. Not just because she was Kathleen's daughter. I loved her like she was my own. But that was always the line I was afraid to cross. She had a dad. And I wasn't trying to replace him. I wanted a role in her life that didn't feel borrowed.

Zoe would ask, "What kind of role?"

I'd tell her. I wanted to be the kind of father my dad had been. Not perfect, but safe and present. The kind of man who showed up even when he didn't have the right words. The kind of man who stood in the doorway and waited, letting you know he wasn't going anywhere. The kind of man like my dad who believed in me more than anyone on earth and had a way of making me believe in myself in a way nobody else ever could. I wanted to be like George, too. The way he made space for me without asking me to be anyone other than who I was. Ma and George taught me how to love a kid who wasn't yours and how to love them like they were your own.

That's what I wanted to give Peanut. That's why the nickname "Peanut" mattered. It sounded small, maybe even silly, but it wasn't. It was my way of saying, "You're my daughter too. I am here for you. Always."

My eyes wandered up the hillside on October 3, 2015. The autumn light softened everything it touched, including the hundreds of headstones. As I stood there, my gaze moved through the remnants of dreams that had come true and dreams that had shattered long ago.

The sky above was a brilliant blue, scattered with cotton-white clouds drifting slow and steady with nowhere to be. Just beneath them, two maple trees stood, their leaves igniting in fall foliage. They marked the place of Ma and George's spot. The wind moved through the branches and, for a moment, I let myself imagine it was their way of saying good morning.

Reaching the trees, I squatted in their shade, placing my hands on the cool granite stone. The wind rustled through the turning leaves above, and I looked up into the sky.

"Hey Ma. Hey George. How are ya?" I said. "I miss you guys."

I ran my fingers along the engraved names and dates, the stone firm beneath my touch. "The last time I was here, I asked permission to marry your daughter. You never answered me, so I'm not sure what that means," I said, glancing out over the valley. "I'm going with yes," I added, with a laugh that pushed tears from my eyes.

"Well . . . today's the day. I didn't think today would ever happen . . . God, I wish you were here." I wiped my eyes dry with the back of my hand. "I hope I've made you proud."

I paused, letting my breath settle.

"I love Kathleen and Peanut with all my heart. Don't worry about them. I'm gonna take care of them both for you. I promise."

My voice broke for a moment. "I love Peanut the way you loved me. Thank you . . . for teaching me how to do that."

I sat in silence for a minute, just breathing, as I looked out over the town. I glanced up and smiled. "What? No ducks this time?"

The breeze picked up and I imagined George grinning, eyes squinting in that way he always did when he laughed.

"George," I said, "my dad's going to walk Kathleen down the aisle today. I hope that's okay. Try not to let me pass out, alright?"

A lump caught in my throat.

"God, I miss you guys."

I kissed my fingers and pressed them to the top of the stone, holding them there for a moment. "Thank you," I whispered, looking skyward once more before closing my eyes.

As I walked slowly down the hill, I paused at the bottom. Turning around, I whispered, "I love you guys. See you at the wedding."

I stood on a ski trail halfway up Burke Mountain later that afternoon, exactly 10,229 days after I had first asked Kathleen to go out with me on October 1, 1987. A whole lifetime had passed between those two moments. Joy, heartbreak, growth, mistakes, second chances—twenty-eight years of living packed between then and now.

Mother Nature's fall canvas stretched around us in every direction. The fall colors shimmered in the late afternoon sun, but today, even Mother Nature took a back seat. All eyes, including mine, were on Kathleen as she made her way down the slope in a navy dress, arm in arm with my dad.

The ski trail, just weeks away from its first dusting of snow, had never looked more beautiful. A dream I had long ago tucked away with the rest of my teenage hopes was unfolding before me, finally and impossibly coming true. Back in the nineties, I thought this moment might happen. I let it go, convinced it never would. And yet, here it was.

My heart tugged in two directions, pulling Kathleen toward me while at the same time wishing she would slow down.

When they reached me, I extended my hand toward hers, and Dad looked me straight in the eye.

"I love ya, son," he said, his voice thick with emotion.

"I love ya too, Dad."

There we stood, Jason and Kathleen, on a mountainside surrounded by the blazing colors of fall, with our closest friends, family, and the quiet presence of spirits we both felt in our souls.

I scanned the faces gathered around us and found Brian. He met my eyes and gave me a simple, steady nod. It said more than words ever could.

Then I looked for her: Peanut. There she was, nestled beneath Dad's arm, his hand resting over her shoulder in that protective, familiar way I remembered from my own childhood. That one-handed hug that said, "I've got you."

My eyes softened as I looked into hers.

"I. Love. You. Peanut," I whispered, the words carrying across through the mountain air.

"I. Love. You. Too."

39

FOOTHILLS OF GREATNESS

The years that followed the wedding moved both slowly and all at once. Life had a way of filling up with short visits back to my family in Vermont, hikes, dinners around the table, and laughter filling our condo. The kind of days that felt ordinary in the moment, but later, you'd realize they were the foundation of everything.

Peanut settled into high school, bringing with her the same mix of curiosity and independence that had always made her feel like an old soul in a young body. It was as if Kathleen's mom lived inside her. Then came the day she fell in love with the idea of spending her junior year of high school studying abroad in the Canary Islands.

She went to live with Christina's family, the same Christina I had waited for in Orlando when I wrote Ma's eulogy. The same Christina who'd spent her senior year with us in Lyndonville as an exchange student, an exchange of daughters, in a way. Peanut thrived abroad in a Spanish-speaking school with only a year of Spanish under her belt. I thought about my Spanish class, the very class that brought her mom and I together for the first time. I smiled and then shook my head. There was no way I would have survived a Spanish-speaking school after that one year of Spanish. We missed her voice in the hallway and the way she flopped on the couch after school, but we knew this was part of letting go. Letting her chase her own horizon.

When she came back for her senior year, she wasn't quite the same. She was more confident. Unlike me at eighteen, shedding a skin that was too tight, Peanut grew into herself the way a conch adds to its shell. It was as if Spain had her standing on the edge of a map, and she realized she could go wherever she wanted.

The Country Club of Jackson began hosting the PGA Tour's Sanderson Farms Championship in 2014, and from that very first year, my lifelong quest for greatness brought me to the heart of it as I walked the fairways alongside the best players in the world.

And I wasn't just walking as a golf professional. I was representing the Country Club of Jackson membership, the PGA of America, my peers, my mentors, my family, myself—and the dream I had been carrying since I left Vermont at twenty-six years old.

Every step I took, every conversation I had, every interaction with the team, spectators, sponsors, and players had meaning. I remembered my time watching George at Speedwell, Mr. Bryan at Old Waverly, and Bob Ford at Oakmont, and I realized they had prepared me for this stage.

I was no longer just following in footsteps: I was leaving

them. The same way I had felt those imprints deep in my body when I stood at Oakmont years ago, trying to absorb what greatness looked and felt like. Now I was the one, managing moments I never dreamed would happen, standing where others might one day look to for inspiration.

And every fall, our home filled with family and friends flying in from across the country to volunteer, support, and be part of something greater than themselves. It became a tradition, a gathering rooted in love and purpose.

I often found myself standing still in the merchandise tent or before daylight as I helped Stanley Reedy, superintendent and my best friend, prepare the course, or on our back porch with a drink in hand as the house filled with family and friends. I'd think about the long road that brought me here. The wins, the losses, the risks I took, and the people who helped shape every chapter. I would often find myself struggling to breathe as the reality unfolded.

But it also lit a deep sense of responsibility. I wasn't just living a dream; I was delivering on the promise my younger self had made. The one who believed he could build something meaningful. The one who didn't quit.

And now, the future version of that young man carried the weight of that legacy forward with pride and purpose.

I was dream driven, focused, and fully committed to making an impact in the game I loved and in the lives of those around me. Between 2009 and 2019, I had been honored with the Gulf States PGA Merchandiser of the Year award for private clubs four times. In 2018 and 2019, I was named a national finalist, becoming the most decorated merchandiser for private clubs in Mississippi history and shared the title of the most wins in the history of the Gulf States Section with David Marchand, a fellow PGA professional in Louisiana.

But those accolades weren't mine alone. Four different teams I had the privilege of leading were recognized during that time, and two of them advanced to the national stage. I carried a deep sense of pride in what we had accomplished together.

Every recognition fueled the next. Every award made me want to work harder and to keep raising the bar for the people who trusted me to lead. I was always looking forward, always reaching for more.

A couple of years into hosting the tournament, Kathleen and I were cleaning up after tournament week when she looked at me and said, "I think your mom would love to come."

I paused, caught off guard. I hadn't talked to my mom much in years.

Kathleen looked at me and said softly, "I don't have either of my parents. I'd give anything to have them still alive. You have both of yours . . . and you don't talk to your mom."

Her words landed hard. It wasn't judgment; it was truth. I didn't see disappointment in her face. Instead, I saw sadness. Sadness for me. Sadness for my mom.

It sat with me for several days. I had been so focused on chasing my dream that I hadn't realized what I was still running from.

I soon found myself sitting alone in my truck, parked on a dirt road in Mississippi. I stared at my phone for a while before finally dialing my mom's number.

When she answered, I told her I was sorry for all the things I had done as a kid, for the times I put her in impossible situations. I told her I hadn't realized back then that she was hurting too. I had been too young, too angry, too blinded by my own pain to see hers, and I was sorry.

I told her we didn't need to go through the past. We didn't need to unbox old memories or try to untangle everything that had happened. I let her know I didn't need an apology or explanations. I just wanted one thing: for her to be in my life.

I told her those years were hard on all of us, and we didn't need to relive them. There was a long pause on the other end of the line, and then I heard her start to cry, which made my own tears fall. "I would like that very much," she said.

"Would you like to come to the PGA Tour event? Kathleen and I would love to have you be a part of it, and I'd really like you to see the person I've grown into."

She came to the next tournament and she never missed another after that.

Brian had taught me how to have that conversation. Not with words, but with grace. When he forgave me, when he looked me in the eye and chose to move forward instead of dragging me back through the wreckage of our past, he gave me a map for my own healing. He showed me what real forgiveness looks like.

I told my mom I forgave her—for all the things I had carried against her for so long. And in saying it, I realized something deeper: She hadn't done anything to me on purpose. Like me, she had been trying to survive, to hold herself together in a world that didn't give out instructions for broken hearts.

That moment on the phone wasn't about fixing the past. It was about opening the door to something new. And I felt like we both walked through it together, mother and son.

Shortly after the 2019 season wrapped, I was approached by a recruiter representing one of the most prestigious clubs in the South. It was the kind of opportunity professionals in my field dreamed about: a big name, a big budget, a national profile, and a membership saturated with society's elite. I interviewed, asked for a follow-up meeting to answer some hanging questions, and found myself invited to a final on-site interview as the lead candidate.

I called Bob Ford at Oakmont during the process, as I had done several times in my career, seeking his advice.

"Hey Bob. How do you know when you've made it?"

"What do you mean, Jas?" he said.

I took a deep breath and said, "I have been chasing greatness ever since I met you. How do you know when you've made it?"

I had hoped he would tell me I had made it or I was really close and that this job was the ticket to the promised land I had been chasing for so long. I was even okay with him telling me I had a ways to go, but I was on the right track. Anything, as long as there was validation for the worthiness of the dream.

"What does greatness look like to you?" Bob asked.

I paused and said, "It's all of it. Great at all the hats we wear, but what I noticed more than anything during my time with you was the impact you had on the game and the people around you."

In my mind, I could see Bob nodding and a little smile on

his face. Then he said, "Well, Jas, there isn't a list—a top 100 list of golf professionals."

"I know," I said, "I've been chasing this intangible idea of greatness for two decades, and I know my dream might never come true. But I'm gonna chase it anyway."

"You're doing the right thing, Jas. Keep working hard."

The morning after I was invited to the property for a final interview, I woke up to have coffee with Kathleen, and she said, "How'd you sleep?"

"Good, actually."

Kathleen nodded and smiled.

I nodded back and said, "I am pulling my name. I'm cancelling my trip."

"Really? What changed?"

"I don't know. Something isn't sitting right. It's hard to explain," I said.

"Are you okay?" she asked.

"Yeah, I am good. Really good, actually. I can't believe I am walking away from potentially earning more money in a few years than most people make in a lifetime."

I sat with that a moment, thinking back to the days when I had so little money I was using saved change to buy gas or food. "I thought it was on the path to my cheese," I said. "But it's not. I can't believe I am walking away, but I am."

Kathleen looked at me and smiled, her face emitting pride and happiness.

I called Bob that afternoon and said, "Bob, I have pulled my name. I'm not interviewing."

"What happened?"

"It wasn't perfect enough, I guess. It's hard to explain," I said. "It wasn't right for me."

"Good for you, Jas."

We chatted for a few minutes, and I was about to hang up when he said, "Hey Jas," he paused. "You've made it."

"I've made it?" I repeated as my entire body flooded with emotion of pride and the kind of disbelief you have when a dream comes true.

"You've made . . . " He paused, and what he would say next would shape the rest of my life. Bob had a way of telling you just enough while leaving a gap for you to fill in yourself.

He said, "You've made it . . . now it's time to get to work."

I sat there in disbelief after hanging up the phone. Arguably the greatest golf professional of all time had just told me I'd made it. My eyes welled with tears as my mind drifted back to that lost twenty-six-year-old sitting alone in a diner, the one whose life had been shattered into a million unrecognizable pieces.

Bob's words stayed with me for weeks. I kept turning them over in my mind, trying to finish the conversation he started. What did he mean by, "It's time to get to work"? I thought I'd been working. I thought that's what I had been doing all along.

Then I picked up *Greatness* by David L. Cook, a sports psychologist and mental training coach for elite athletes, and everything made sense.

In the book, Dr. Cook wrote, "Greatness is open to all but only pursued by a few. It is the space beyond success where calling and legacy meet and a noble heart is required."

That line hit me hard.

Foothills of Greatness

I realized the greatness I had been chasing, changing and impacting lives through the game of golf, was true and pure. The problem was, I had been measuring it through the lens of success: titles, awards, and recognition. I had been chasing the right thing, just using the wrong measuring stick.

I finally understood what Bob had meant.

I had reached the summit, but not the summit of greatness. I was at the summit of success. And from that vantage point, I realized I was now standing at the foothills of greatness.

As I reverse engineered the path ahead of me, it became clear: The journey was no longer about my own ascent. It was about the depth of impact I had on those around me, helping others climb *their* mountains.

George Nichols taught me about the power of relationships at Speedwell. I took great pride in my ability to foster relationships and show people they mattered to me. I had always taken pride in developing those around me, but I'd done it while climbing my own mountain. Now, I understood something deeper. Their ascent would become the very steps that carried me up this final mountain.

The truth was, to climb it, I would need to immerse myself fully in the journeys of others. And that kind of impact would require me to dive deeper within myself.

And with that clarity, I did what Bob Ford advised: I laced up for the greatest journey of my life.

Let's start climbing.

Dream Big

and Be

Dream Driven

ACKNOWLEDGMENTS

No one climbs alone. A memoir may carry a single name on its cover, but the story belongs to the many people who shaped the journey. This book is as much yours as it is mine. Thank you for believing in me.

To Mom and Dad, the roots of who I am, I will forever be grateful that you are the ones who raised me. My legacy is rooted in your influence. You provided me with a canvas for others to paint on.

To my brothers, Garett and Patrick, and my sister, Margaret: I am proud of what you have accomplished, proud to be your brother, and I hope you inspire your children to be Dream Driven.

To the Nichols family, thank you for adopting me into your family. I owe so much of who I have become and the lives I have touched to your love, guidance, and belief in me. George, you taught me more about relationships and business than any classroom ever could. Ma, you showed me how to love Peanut a child I didn't give birth to, with a heart wide enough to make her my own. And Brian, you taught me so much, but most importantly, you showed me how to forgive, maybe the most powerful lesson I have ever learned.

To my Uncle Tom: When times grew dark, you were the one I could always go to. Your presence gave me strength, and though you are no longer here, the memory of your steadying hand remains with me on every climb. Your guidance still reminds me that even the stem is enough.

To Kathleen, you appear again here because a single line in a dedication could never hold the depth of my love and gratitude. Your patience, encouragement, and belief gave me the courage to write honestly. You sat beside me on the roller coast through doubt, reminded me of who I am, and steadied me when I lost my footing. I cannot imagine life without you.

To Peanut, your life is woven into this story in ways words can barely capture. You remind me every day of joy, courage, and possibility. Watching you grow has been one of my greatest privileges, and this book would not exist without you in my life. The lessons I tried to teach you about facing your fears became lessons I needed to learn myself and produced the first words of this memoir.

To the mentors who changed my life:

- To Larry Kelley, who answered the question that started it all. None of my life as a golf professional would have happened without your guidance. Thank you for not hiring me.

- To Bob Ford, whose example at Oakmont taught me that true greatness is measured not in trophies, but in people. Thank you for always returning my calls and answering so

Acknowledgments

many of my questions only 80 percent of the way, forcing me to discover on my own what you hoped I would. Thank you for taking a chance on me.

- To the many mentors who guided me through this journey, some named here, many not, thank you for your wisdom, patience, and belief. Your influence lives in these pages.

- To those who opened doors at critical moments, from Mike Taylor finding me at Quail Valley Golf Club to Jody Varner leading the search committee that brought me to the Country Club of Jackson, thank you for believing in me and giving me the chance to serve at the highest level.

To the PGA of America and my fellow professionals, thank you for your dedication to growing the game, which has given me a life I never knew existed. I can't imagine my life without golf or your influence.

To Stanley Reedy, you helped shape me into the PGA professional I am today. The depth of our relationship, golf professional and superintendent, is rare, and I am honored to call your family mine.

To my colleagues and the teams I've had the privilege to lead—assistants, interns, and staff members—you gave me purpose beyond myself. Watching you grow has been the most rewarding part of my career.

To the members of every club I have served, thank you for trusting me with your traditions, your families, and your game. Your confidence has allowed me to live out my calling.

To my friends, near and far, who walked with me through hayfields and fairways, triumphs and losses: You reminded me to laugh when I was too serious and to keep going when I wanted to stop.

To Paul Wheeler, Lyndon Institute, and everyone involved in growing the game of golf in my hometown of Lyndonville, Vermont: The Golf Learning Center is a dream realized. That project stands as proof that small seeds of vision can grow when planted in the right soil.

To Zoe, thank you for walking with me through the hardest truths and for giving me the courage to face myself with honesty.

To all of you who encouraged me to tell my story, you know who you are. You kept me writing and blew on the coals when my fire smoldered. Thank you for your belief in me and for the support you offered when I reached out.

And finally, to you, the reader. Thank you for carrying these pages with me. My hope is that you'll see pieces of your own journey here. May you carry your Clover, sometimes all four leaves, sometimes only the stem, and remember that even when dreams feel intangible or out of reach, the climb is still worth it.

Together, we climb.

Dream Big and Be Dream Driven.

ABOUT JASON PRENDERGAST, PGA

Jason Prendergast, PGA, is a nationally recognized, award-winning golf professional, author, and mentor whose life's work centers on chasing greatness, defined not by titles earned or recognition received, but by the depth of his impact on others.

From milking cows and throwing hay in Vermont to the golf operation teams at some of America's most storied clubs, Jason's journey has been one of resilience, mentorship, and relentless pursuit of purpose. Over more than two decades in the game, he has served as host PGA professional for the PGA Tour's Sanderson Farms Championship and founded the Lyndon Institute Golf Center, an indoor golf simulator learning facility built to grow the game in his hometown and led with his "relationship first" philosophy shaped by legendary mentors.

A graduate of the Mississippi State University Professional Golf Management Program, Jason has continued his education through the PGA of America and the Golf Business Network, completing leadership and business development programs that strengthened his passion for mentoring the next generation of professionals.

Through his memoir, *Dream Driven,* and the Stem to Summit Platform, Jason invites others to dream big, live with conviction, and carry their own clover of Hope, Belief, Connection, Impact, and Resilience.

He lives with his wife, Kathleen, and their mini goldendoodle, Willough, named after one of their favorite places in Vermont, the Willoughby Gap.

www.ingramcontent.com/pod-product-compliance
Lightning Source LLC
LaVergne TN
LVHW030312070526
838199LV00069B/6463